The Seventh Generation

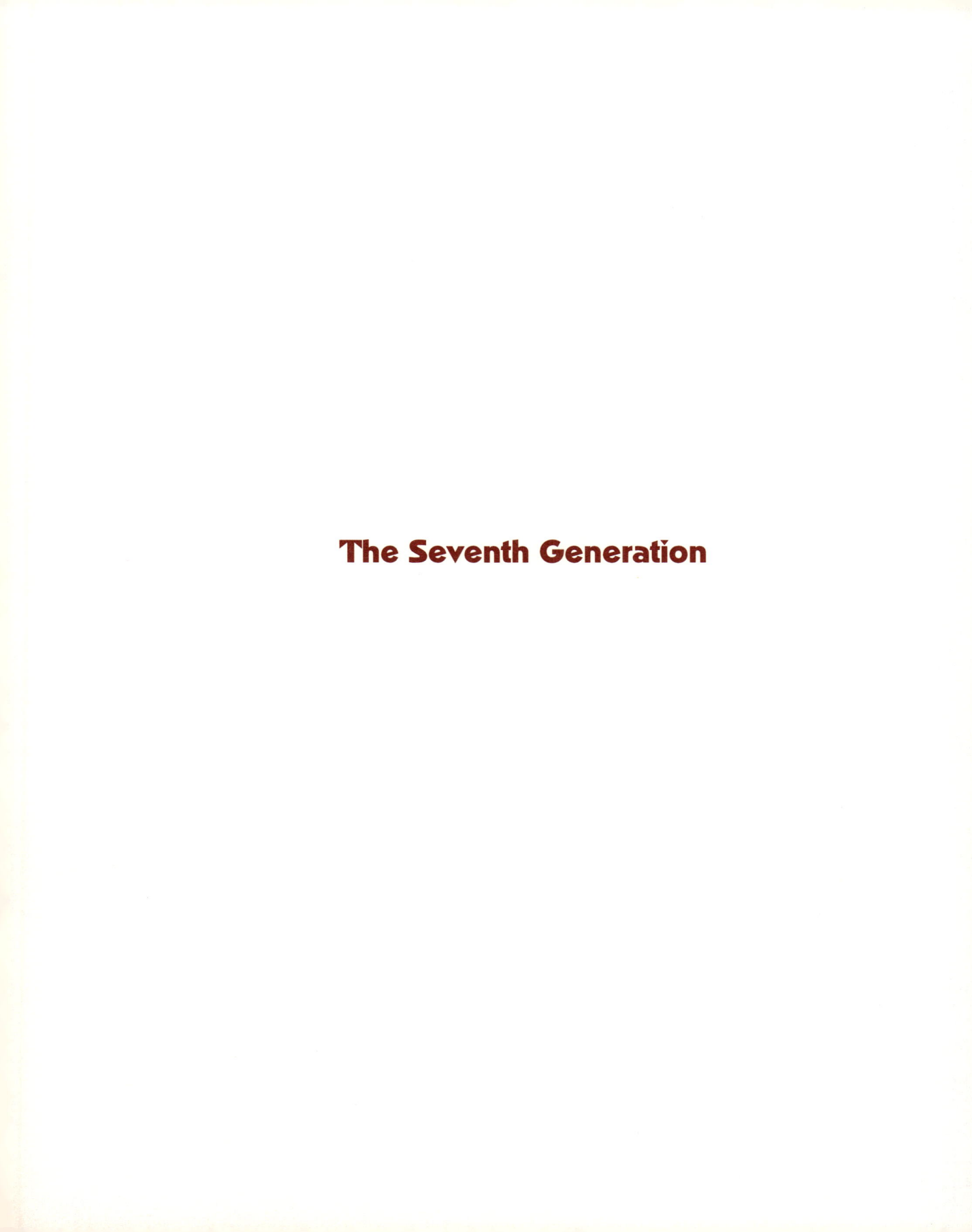

About the Authors

Amy Bergstrom, a member of the Red Lake Nation (Anishinaabeg) is director of the American Indian Teacher Corps Program at Fond du Lac Tribal & Community College and a faculty member in the Department of Education at the University of Minnesota at Duluth. She completed her bachelor's degree from the University of Minnesota at Duluth and her master's in education from Harvard University.

Linda Miller Cleary is a professor in the English Department at the University of Minnesota at Duluth. She completed her doctorate at the University of Massachusetts at Amherst. She is the coauthor of *Collected Wisdom* with Thomas D. Peacock and the author of *From the Other Side of the Desk, Children's Voices, and Linguistics for Teachers.* Her research interests include the study of the interaction of affect and cognition during writing, literacy motivation, and the literacy of Indigenous people.

Thomas D. Peacock, a member of the Fond du Lac Band of Lake Superior Ojibwe, is an associate professor at the University of Minnesota at Duluth, where he teaches educational research and leadership and coordinates master's and doctoral programs. He completed his graduate study (M.Ed. and Ed.D.) at Harvard University. Peacock is the author or coauthor of several books, including *Collected Wisdom,* with Linda Miller Cleary; *A Forever Story: The People and Community of the Fond du Lac Reservation*; *Ojibwe: We Look in All Directions*; and *The Good Path*, a book about Ojibwe history, culture, and philosophy written for middle school students.

The Seventh Generation
Native Students Speak about Finding the Good Path

by
Amy Bergstrom
Linda Miller Cleary
Thomas D. Peacock

ERIC
Educational Resources Information Center

Clearinghouse on Rural Education and Small Schools
Charleston, West Virginia

ERIC Clearinghouse on Rural Education and Small Schools

★AEL

P.O. Box 1348
Charleston, WV 25325-1348
© 2003 by AEL
All rights reserved except for use by the government of the United States of America.
Printed in the United States of America.
Second Printing 2004

Library of Congress Cataloging-in-Publication Data

Bergstrom, Amy, 1970-
　　The seventh generation : native students speak about finding the good path / by Amy Bergstrom, Linda Miller Cleary, Thomas Peacock
　　　p. cm.
　　Summary: Native American youth discuss their lives, especially focusing on issues of ethnic identity, coping with problems, education, self-esteem, and finding their way to the "Good Path."
　　Includes bibliographical references and index.
　　ISBN 1-880785-25-0(alk. paper)
　　1. Indian youth—North America—Attitudes. 2. Indians of North America—Education. 3. Indians of North America—Ethnic identity. 4. Indians of North America—Social conditions. [1. Indians of North America—Social conditions. 2. Indians of North America—Ethnic identity.] I. Cleary, Linda Miller. II. Peacock, Thomas D. III. Title.

E98.Y68 B47 2003
305.897—dc21
　　　　　　　　2002192764

ISBN 1-880785-25-0

Cover art by Michael Switzer, Design Works, Charleston, WV

∞ The paper used in this publication meets the minimum requirements of the American National Standard for Information Sciences–Permanence of Paper for Printed Library Materials, ANSI Z39.48-1984.

The ERIC Clearinghouse on Rural Education and Small Schools is operated by AEL and funded by the U.S. Department of Education. AEL is a catalyst for schools and communities to build lifelong learning systems that harness resources, research, and practical wisdom. Information about AEL projects, programs, and services is available on our Web site or by writing or calling us. AEL is an Equal Opportunity/Affirmative Action Employer.

This publication was prepared with funding from the Office of Educational Research and Improvement, U.S. Department of Education, under contract number ED-99-CO-0027. The opinions expressed herein do not necessarily reflect the positions or policies of OERI, the Department, or AEL.

To the Seventh Generation:

Survive

Keep hopes and dreams

Take care of yourself

Remember your spirit

Be there for each other

Respect courage

Share knowledge

Always keep learning

Remember your true values

—Message from Native elders given at the
"Strengthening the Sacred Circle: 2000 and Beyond"
Conference of the National Indian Council on Aging

Contents

Acknowledgments xi

Chapter 1. Introduction 1
    The Story of Our Research 3
    An Overview of the Book 3

Chapter 2. Stories, Stories, Stories 5
    Maria's Story 5
        What Are You Watching Us For? 6
    Sunshine's Story 10
        Live One Day with Me 10
    North Star's Story 13
        You Just Have to Go with the Program 14
    Quoetone's Story 16
        Instead of Just Pumping Gas 16
    Sipsis's Story 20
        We Consider Life Differently 20
    A Message from Elders 24

Chapter 3. Just Be: Knowing Who You Are 25
    What Is Identity? 26
        A Coat of Armor 27
    Some Challenges to a Healthy Sense of Self 29
        Effects of Colonization and Oppression 29
        Racism and Internalized Racism 29
        Blood Quantum 30
        Skin Color 30
    Voices of Harmony and Balance 32
        Spirituality 32
        Culture Connection 34
        Pride in Being American Indian, First Nations, or Alaska Native 35
        Connection to Place or to a Healthy Person 36
    Full Circle 37

Chapter 4. When Life Gets Tough ... 39
- Things We Have to Deal with in School ... 40
  - Gordee's Story ... 40
- It's Coming from All Directions ... 44
  - Curriculum and Teaching Practices ... 44
  - Discipline Practices ... 45
  - Peer Harassment ... 46
- Things We Have to Cope with in Our Communities and Families ... 47
  - Oppression ... 47
  - Contradictions ... 48
  - Community Problems ... 49
  - Dysfunction in Families ... 51
- Coping When Things Get Tough ... 52
  - The Beads of the Eagle: A Teaching Story ... 55
  - When Life Gives You Lemons, Make Them into Lemonade ... 62

Chapter 5. Bouncing Back or Reaching a Breaking Point ... 63
- Resilience ... 64
  - Jamie ... 65
- Things That Can Lead to Giving Up on School ... 66
  - Absenteeism and Tardiness ... 66
  - Anger ... 67
  - Teen Pregnancy ... 67
  - Alcohol and Drugs ... 68
  - Sexism ... 69
  - Living Out the Low Expectations of Others ... 69
- Things That Help Students Be Resilient ... 70
  - Strength in Culture ... 70
  - Turning Things Around ... 71
- A Teaching Story ... 72
  - Season Spirits ... 72
  - Discussion Questions for "Season Spirits" ... 84
- A Review ... 84
  - Questions for Educators ... 84
- Full Circle ... 85

Chapter 6. Honoring Our Gifts ... 87
- A Hunting Metaphor ... 87
- Jeremy's Intelligence and How He Learned to Use It ... 89
  - In Jeremy's Own Words: "I Had Art Going for Me" ... 89

Contents

So, What Are Your Gifts? 91
Intelligences That Lead to School Success 91
    Linguistic (Language)-Verbal 91
    Logical-Mathematical 92
The Other, Often Extracurricular, Intelligences 92
    Bodily-Kinesthetic 92
    Visual-Spatial 93
    Musical 94
    Interpersonal 95
    Intrapersonal 95
Emerging Regard for Other Intelligences 96
    Naturalist Intelligence 96
    Spiritual-Existential Intelligence 97
The Interrelatedness of Your Gifts: Holistic Approaches 99
Cherishing Your Intelligences and Developing New Strengths 100
So, What's the Connection with Learning Styles? 100
Attention and Intelligences 101
You Can Develop Many Intelligences 102
    Believing in Yourself: A Personal Story 104
A Quest: How to Use Your Intelligences to Chart Your Future 105

Chapter 7. Making It in School 107
How Your Family Can Help You Make It in School 107
    Adult Family Members Serving As Role Models 108
    Mutual Respect among Students and Parents/Grandparents 108
    Family Expectations 109
    Family Goals for Children Once They Finish High School 109
A Kaleidoscope of Student Motivators 110
    Sports and Physical Activity 110
    Effort and Responsibility 111
    Grades as a Motivator 112
    Future Goals and Plans 112
    Friends for Personal Support 113
What to Do When Motivation Isn't There 114
    First Step: Let Teachers Know How to Help 114
    Getting and Giving Help: A Circle of Help from Peers 115
    Help from American Indian Education Counselors:
        A Tribute to Melvin and Ms. H 116
    Doing Assignments in a Way That Interests You 117
    Finding Someone to Learn From 118

  Finding Extracurricular School Activities, Cultural Programs,
    Clubs, and Support Groups to Keep You Going 118
  Finding Alternative School Settings 121
  Resorting to Homeschooling 121
  Taking Advantage of the GED 122
 How to Keep Motivated in Reading, Writing, and Standard English 123
  Reading 123
  Writing 124
  Do You Speak Rezbonics? 126
 How to Keep Motivated in Other School Subjects 126
  Having a Positive Attitude and Caring about School 127

Chapter 8. The Good Path 129
 The Good Path 130
  Honor the Creator 131
  Honor Elders 132
  Honor Our Elder Brothers: The Plant and Animal Beings 133
  Honor Women 134
  Keep Our Promises and Uphold Our Pledges 135
  Be Kind to Everyone 136
  Be Peaceful 136
  Be Courageous 137
  Be Moderate 138
 A Teaching Story 139
  Sara's Song 139
  "Sara's Song" Discussion Questions for Youth 152
  Chapter Discussion Questions for Teachers and Educators 152
 Full Circle 153

Chapter 9. Lessons for Educators: Teaching, Curriculum, and Research 155
 Literature on Native Resilience 155
 Connections That Foster Resilience 158
  The Importance of Family 158
  School Connections 159
  Individual Factors 159
 Good Teachers, Teaching, and Curriculum 160
 Characteristics of Good Teaching 161
  Having Cultural Knowledge 161
  Using Encouragement 162
  Using Explanation 162

Using Examples and Analogies	162
Having High Expectations	163
Being Fair and Insisting upon Respect	163
Being Flexible	164
Being Helpful	164
Being Careful Not to Single Students Out	165
Being Interested in Students	165
Listening and Understanding	166
Using Multiple Approaches	166
Using Collaborative Approaches	167
Personal Characteristics of Teachers	168
Being Caring	168
Being Fun	168
Being Mellow	169
Being Open Minded	169
Having Patience	169
Respecting Students	169
Staying	170
The Need for Native Teachers	171
Toward an Indigenous Model of Education	171
What Might an Indigenous Education Model Look Like?	174
Towards an Indigenous Model of Research and Its Dissemination	176
Methodology	177
The Rationale and Mode of Reporting the Research	178
The Limitations of the Discourse of the Dominant Research Community	179
Collected Stories	180
Using Students' Voices	180
Using Case Studies	180
Using Researchers' Voices	181
Full Circle	182
Appendix: Interview Questions	187
Background Information	187
Interview One	187
Interview Two	188
Interview Three	188
References	191

Acknowledgments

Without the remarkable students who lent their voices to this book, it would be empty of the real feeling that makes us pay attention to it. We acknowledge their huge contributions to this book and see them as the hope for the future.

We are deeply grateful to Betsy Albert-Peacock, Robert Peacock, Bonnie Sutliff, and Alex Wilson for their assistance in interviewing the students. Emilie Buesing, Helen Coleman, Karen Duffy, Kristin Hanson, Heather Miernicki, and Suzanne Wopperer kept our data in order and did the transcriptions and technical parts of data analysis. Special thanks go to Anna Ahlgren, who stepped in at the last minute to solve our technical problems. We also would like to acknowledge the many school administrators and guidance counselors around the United States and Canada who connected us with the 120 students interviewed.

A number of individuals reviewed this manuscript in its several stages: ERIC reviewers, Elizabeth Mouw, Mary Kay Rummel, Valerie Tanner, Betsy Albert-Peacock, Linda Grover, Sonny Peacock, and many students from the Fond du Lac Reservation School in Minnesota. We also would like to thank our editor, Patricia Cahape Hammer, whose suggestions took us beyond our original hopes.

Chapter 1
Introduction

Linda

Many American Indian, First Nations, and Alaska Native cultures have prophecies saying that unless the youth of today act in a way that plans for the future, there will be no future for the children and grandchildren to come.

The Seven Fires prophecy of the Anishinaabe (Ojibwe) oral tradition is a set of predictions about the Anishinaabe future. When the Ojibwe people still lived on the Eastern Ocean, seven prophets came among the people and foretold the future. Each of these prophecies, or Fires, refers to a particular period of time. The First Fire foretold that the Ojibwe would follow the sacred shell of the Midewiwin (spiritual teachings) in a great migration from the Eastern Ocean. The Second Fire predicted that the people would move away from their spiritual ways for a time but that a young man would lead them back to the Good Path. The Third Fire foresaw that the people would move to a place where food grew on the water (wild rice). The Fourth Fire predicted the coming of the White race and forewarned our ancestors to be wary because the White race would show two masks, brotherhood and death, whose appearances would be nearly identical, making it difficult to tell which mask was which. The Fifth Fire foretold of the people following new ways and forgetting the sacred teachings. In the time of the Sixth Fire, the prophecies told of the people being lost, both culturally and spiritually. Many would lose their languages and old ways of being. Communities would be disrupted by material and spiritual poverty.

In the time of the Seventh Fire, a new generation of young people would have an awakening of the spirit, and a young person would find the sacred teachings written so long ago on birch bark scrolls and hidden away for countless generations. This young generation would lead the people out of darkness, making our nations strong and whole again:

The seventh prophet that came to the people long ago was said to be different from the other prophets. He was young and had a strange light in his eyes. He said, "In the time of the Seventh Fire a Osh-ki-bi-ma-di-zeeg (New People) will emerge. They will retrace their steps to what was left by the trail. Their steps will take them to the elders who they will ask to guide them on to their journey. But many of the elders will have fallen asleep. They will awaken to this new time with nothing to offer. Some of the elders will be silent out of fear. Some of the elders will be silent because no one will ask anything of them.... If the New People will remain strong in their quest, the Waterdrum of the Midewiwin Lodge will again sound its voice. There will be a rebirth of the Anishinaabe nation and a rekindling of old flames. The Sacred Fire will again be lit."[1]

Many Anishinaabeg believe that we are in the time of the Seventh Generation and that the youth who will lead may be the children and grandchildren in current villages. If, indeed, this is the time of the Seventh Generation, the finder of the sacred scrolls may already walk among our villages. Other cultures have similar prophecies that herald this as a crucial time for humankind. Humbatz Man said the following about the beliefs of the Mayans of Mexico's Yucatan Peninsula:

> The Maya do not see God as wreaking havoc, but rather the people who are, after all, part of God, destroying their mother. If we continue, it will happen. Our mother has a blanket to protect her. If we peel it off, she will catch an illness. Then big problems will come.... We are the ones who are responsible, and we can change that. If we wake up, it is possible to change the energy. It is possible to change everything. ... For the Maya it is the new age–time to give away the knowledge again, to raise the frequency of the global mind. Now the world has a dark civilization, a dark culture. We need to reestablish a high culture. The prophecies say big changes are coming, and that the Sun is going to help us. We cannot say whether the change will be good or bad, but we can influence it. When we make ritual in front of the Sun, the frequency changes in a good way for everyone. We need a big change now.[2]

It is not our place to tell many prophecies of North American people, but you might be very interested in what your nation's stories, oral histories, and carvings prophesy. If you are Wampanoag, you might want to search for the prophecies of Weetucks and the carvings in Dighton Rock. If you are Seneca, you might want to look into the Seven World prophecies. If you are Hopi, you might want to hear the prophecies of the world wars, inventions, and warnings beyond.

In many prophecies, there is an urgency. Either we begin to live in concert with the earth and get others to do so as well, or the consequences will change life as we know it. If we don't repair our actions towards the earth, its living things, and ourselves, and if we don't return to the role of the protector of the earth, there will be a terrible result.

You may be among the youth who will lead the regeneration of the nations and of the earth. As Native youth of the Seventh Generation, your communities need you, and they need committed educational and spiritual guides. The task is too daunting for just one person. There are many villages and many scrolls to be discovered. Does your community have similar stories? Are there such prophecies in your community? Who

---

[1] Benton-Banai, *The Mishomis Book,* 91-92.
[2] Man, "Reconsecrating the Earth," 232-41.

Introduction

is preserving them? Who might you ask to find out if you don't already know? What part will you play in the Seventh Generation?

This book honors the Seventh Generation. It is written for and about those stepping into the Seventh Generation, using the words of American Indian, Alaska Native, and First Nations young people. As Native youth, you may bring about the dawn of the Seventh Generation, finding in your own villages the wisdom to carry on. This book also is intended for the educational and spiritual guides in your lives so they can know what you are thinking about your schooling and your community.

The Story of Our Research

Some years ago, two of us, Tom Peacock, an Ojibwe teacher, and Linda Miller Cleary, a White teacher, wrote *Collected Wisdom*, a book for teachers about American Indian education. In writing that book, we interviewed teachers and realized, too late, that we should have also included the voices of young people. Who could better tell us about education than those experiencing it at the moment? We also began to understand that the problems that Native students live with in one region are similar to those experienced by other Native students all over North America. Students needed to be heard. We asked Amy Bergstrom, a young Ojibwe teacher, to help us interview American Indian, First Nation, and Alaska Native students.

We found 120 Native youth who shared their stories about how life is and how it should be. Between 1997 and 2000, we collected stories from students in the northern Midwest because they were close at hand. We also traveled to interview Abenaki, Aleut, Choctaw, Cree, Dakota, Hoopa, Innuit, Karuk, Lakota, Mohawk, Navajo, Oneida, Penobscot, Seneca, Ute, Wampanoag, and Yurok students. They attended public, tribal, federal, and alternative schools in cities, on reservations, and near reservations.

As writers, we thought it only fair to report what we had discovered back to the students and to their peers across North America. Too often, research never gets reported to the people who had been studied. We have tried to write this book so that all who care about Indigenous education will be interested and informed.

An Overview of the Book

The strong voices of Native youth speak out through the pages of this book. They relate the joys, frustrations, and dreams of their generation; their insights weave together answers to some of the problems afflicting their people. In listening to the students, we found that certain themes emerged. Each chapter is centered around one of these themes.

Chapter 2. Stories, Stories, Stories. This chapter introduces some of the different Native students featured in the book and provides a glimpse into their lives.

Chapter 3. Just Be: Knowing Who You Are. This chapter discusses the various factors that influence how students develop an identity as Native people.

Chapter 4. When Life Gets Tough. It isn't always easy being a Native student. In this chapter, students talk about the things that make life and school difficult.

Chapter 5. Breaking Points. Students talk about ways in which they handle difficulty.

Chapter 6. Honoring Our Gifts. Students consider how they can use their different intellectual gifts to help their people.

Chapter 7. Making It in School. Students give advice about how to find the help and motivation they need to make it in school.

Chapter 8. The Good Path. Students talk about how they found the Good Path and where it has taken them in their lives.

Chapter 9. Issues of Teaching, Curriculum, and Research. This chapter reviews research on resilience, relates what Native students had to say about good teachers and teaching, informs readers about a move toward an Indigenous epistemology, and describes the research.

This isn't an easy-answer book. We have included the stories of students who are making it in school, who have struggled and quit, and who have quit and tried again. We know there aren't easy answers, but we have found students who have some great advice about getting along in schools; in their villages, reserves, and reservations; in cities; and even in the White world. Along with the stories of the young people, we have included stories from our own lives and several that we made up to generate discussion.

Chapter 2
Stories, Stories, Stories

Linda

The first stories in this book will demonstrate that you probably have a lot in common with a great variety of Native students in North America. The first student you will meet chose to be called Maria.[1]

Maria's Story

I interviewed Maria on her Ojibwe reservation in the Midwest on three different occasions. You may find yourself in parts of her story, even if you are male. If you have ever experienced racism or struggled with school, you will relate with Maria. If you worry about your friends or get angry about the hard parts of life, you will find yourself in Maria's story. A single day in Maria's life may make you feel like your memories are wrapped in her experience.

Short and strong, Maria is full of spunk. I first met Maria in her American Indian counselor's office, a place of refuge in a public high school that was uncomfortable for her. A few of the schools we visited were comfortable places for Native students to learn, but this one wasn't. While Maria and I discussed many topics, the excerpts published here were selected to depict what her typical school day was like. The day she described was interwoven with stories about her past and future.[2]

---

[1] We gave the students we interviewed the choice to be called by their own first names or to choose pseudonyms. We made up names for students who weren't sure what name they wanted to be called.

[2] The appendix provides a list of all interview questions. In Maria's story, quotes from three separate interviews are woven together. To create the passages from Maria and the others, whole pages of interview material, sentences within paragraphs, and even some words have been deleted; however, the remaining text is true to everything the students said.

What Are You Watching Us For?

What's a typical day like? We all have to walk to the end of our road and stand there early, by the highway, until the bus picks us up. It's almost an hour bus ride. I don't like high school that much. When the kids from the reservation get off, the teachers watch us when we walk in. It's like, "What are you watching us for?" and we get treated differently. You can't even stand in the hallway in a group of friends without the hall monitor wondering what's up, like you're going to fight somebody. One of my friends got suspended like for wearing bandannas, for trying to recruit gang members. It's got us really hypered up. We know that something's going to happen. One friend got beat up, so he came to school, and we were trying to find him. When we are in a big group like that, they always watch us. I don't know how to describe it; you just feel bad, and it makes me mad. Like, if the other kids came out in a big group and stand by their lockers in their big groups, [the hall monitors don't do] anything to them. So, we just go about our business and put up with it. I always get a hard time about wearing this jacket, but I see these other kids all wearing jackets, and no one says anything to them. I was going to stop wearing it just because I hated getting the hard time, and I thought, "Until they stop wearing theirs, I'm not going to stop wearing mine."

First, I go to English. I like doing the research part of writing. We had to write down three topics that we were interested in. I had the Mafia, teen pregnancy, and gangs. [The teacher] wants me to write about gangs. I had to look [at] all these books. There was an article in there from the *New York Times* about gangs moving to the reservations, so I'm going to do it on that. It was talking about kids on the reservation. They might get sent away [to jail]. What they learn is how to start a gang; they come back and make everyone look up to them. It's a way of getting their own respect. Other kids move up here from the city; it's new to everybody on the reservation, so they want to follow it. I don't care to hang around those people. Like, on my road there's all these guys that used to hang out. They had this board, put all of their names on it, and they had my name on it. I had no idea about it. They got into so much trouble. They were like stealing cars and busting in houses. I was with them one time, and I left. Some cops came and found that board; I was caught. My cousin was here for the summer, but he doesn't go here anymore [because of gang activity]; he stays with his mom in the city. So, I'm interested in this paper.

Second period, I go to Biology. In the beginning of the year, we had to go outside and catch things. That's the only thing I liked about [the] class was going outside. Some of my teachers are racist actually. The Biology teacher's been like that from way back. He had my dad, my uncles, everyone [from the reservation]. I don't know why he is still here. He tries to crack jokes, but he's really a jerk. He started pointing me out right in class, and I was like really uptight. I was like in the middle, and everyone else was talking [around me], and he pointed to me and called me to the front and said, "What's your name?" He said he was going to give me detention for talking, and I wasn't even talking. And he was asking, "Well, are you a straight-A student?" and I was like, "Yup." I don't take every situation as a racism situation, but with him, I might have done that. But I just let him say what he has to say, and I sit down. Like, yesterday I had a pass to class. I was not even two minutes late, 'cause I was talking to the American Indian advisor. I showed him my pass [and said], "I had to take care of some stuff." [He said], "Well, why weren't you able to get to class on time?" I guess it's really hard to get an A out of him. I had a C first quarter, B out of him my second quarter, C my third quarter, and, right now, I got an A! I knew I'd get a hard time in Biology [about the jacket]; he had to call the principal, and it was a big debate. [The teacher said], "It's like you could be hiding weapons or something in there." Yeah! Like I'm gonna hide a big weapon in there!

I think that even if you hate school, you've got to go. I just hate dealing with all this pressure, but I want to graduate. This one teacher hated us and said, "I'm going to tell you something." He didn't make it like a challenge or anything. He just told us like flat out, "Half of you kids aren't going to graduate from high school, about half of you girls are going to get pregnant. The boys, you'll be fathers." And he was saying this stuff, and I was like, "No way, man, I'm going to graduate." I love challenges, but he was like not optimistic at all. If you hear something so many times, you are going to start to believe it and give up. I feel kind of down, but I try to ignore it. I try to calm myself down, but if I really, really get mad at something, it just like upsets me for the rest of the day. I can't think about school. My ma said sometimes I can have a little chip on my shoulder. I just sit by myself because I'm afraid that if I see somebody I don't like, I'll just snap at 'em. I've tried to come down and talk to the counselor, just so I can get away from everyone. I try to get a pass, and they try to give me this big fight about "you're going to miss class."

Third period is cool; it's Choir and Study Hall every other day. When I came here, I made friends really easy, but I don't get really close to them. I thought I'd get a hard time 'cause there were no reservation girls in the choir. I hate it not knowing anybody in class. Some of them acted stuck-up, but I get along with a lot. They were taught that [Native students] are so mean, so they actually are scared of us. I was talking to people last year, and they thought we were out to hurt them. Some of the kids around here are racist, and I can't stand them. I'll let them be. I don't sit there and judge them whatever until I get to know them. When I was young, I went to different schools [in the city]. One school, there was a lot of Black people there; another school, a lot of Mexicans and Blacks. I got along with all of them too. I think I was more open to everything, like different kinds of people. Last year, there's this one guy. I used to stick up for him, but a lot of people tease him. I actually get after people who are teasing him. He doesn't have any clothes, and he smells bad. So, he was sitting there talking really bad about Indians in front of us. [I told him], "I can't believe you're saying like we're lazy and stuff, and we get what we want, like we just lay around, like all the times I stuck up for you." He just turned around and said, "Just shut up," and I said, "You shut up." He said he was going to get his dog after me. I said maybe I'd get my brother after him.

I brought my beadwork in to my Choir teacher today, and she was all amazed with it. It's all beaded. I got the yoke done, and I have one legging done. I'm hoping to have it done by May 17; there's a contest powwow in St. Croix. My Choir teacher is trying to find something for me and like three other girls, like a cultural song. Solos are usually like for seniors, so I'm like, "I don't know about this."

I really hate [going to] Geometry. I wish I was in the Algebra program. I hate what we're doing. I like having a little more action than just reading out of a book. We learn better by watching, at first, and then trying, instead of just being told and then get tested. Everybody in this school has this idea that Indians are not smart, and all they want to do is fight. It's not really like that. Some of my friends, they [fulfill] the expectation, and I just get so angry. It's told to them so much that they just kind of believe it. If you think for yourself, you are stronger in the long run. That's what I'm trying to do.

At lunch, they watch us like hawks 'cause we are all together. We are under constant eyes. We can walk in the hallway, and they still stop you for a pass. They are supposed to stop anyone, but they always stop us, and they never stop any others. My [White] friends are like, "Well, you won't need [a pass]; they never stop me." And I'm like, "Well, they always stop me. Always!" And then I get smart with [the hall monitors] sometimes. I was walking in the hall, and I had my pass tucked into my notebook, and there was a kid in front of me, not too far in front of me, he didn't have anything. He walked by, and I was walking, and [the monitor] said, "I'd like to see your pass," and I just stood there, and I'm like, "What about him?" And he said, "I'm asking you for it." I said, "There is someone right there who you didn't even stop." Finally, I showed it to him. After, in American History, a White friend asked me what was wrong, and I said, "I can't really talk about it right now. I just gotta calm down for a little bit." Even when I told her, she said, "They never, never stop me." She felt bad, and it was upsetting to me.

Then, I have American History. [The teacher] gives you chances, but he keeps on top of us. He takes classes on Native Americans, like in the summertime, and I seen him at powwows, and he was talking about [how] he likes to go to powwows. . . . He likes the fry bread stand. It makes a difference because he tries to find ways to bring it into class everyday. He jokes around; he teaches us, but he jokes around at the same time. He lets you laugh in class. I made this trip out to South Dakota at the beginning of the year. I seen all kinds of things, like the Crazy Horse monument. I seen the Badlands, and I got back, and he was really interested. He let me talk about it in class, and I brought pictures. Other teachers, they just don't understand.

Spearing season is coming up. They've already started negotiations. [Some] kids actually think [there] are Nazis here, and they write stuff in the bathroom, and some of the kids got hateful notes left in their lockers, through the little slots. We're afraid of being in school [during spearing season]. It scared me when my cousin, [a] big guy, muscular and stuff, was walking through town on his way home, and somebody pulled up [in] a car and asked him if he wanted a ride, and they hit him over the head with a crowbar, and he ran and ran, and they were swearing. He was in the hospital for awhile. We walked down to the hospital, and he was glad to see us. Spearing season gets really bad here. It's like they don't say it to us in school, but they get us in other ways, write it down in the lockers. Like this year, I was looking at an English book, and all of a sudden, there was like this Indian lady in the book, and [she] said, "Stop treaty rights, save a walleye." I tore the page out of the book. I came down and showed the counselor, and he's like, "Well, go get the book." It was the end of my period, and I went to tell the teacher that I was going to take this book, and I showed her, and she was like, "Oh, my goodness." She was amazed too—stuff about Black people in there too—and it just got me so mad.

In Spanish, my teacher's like very cool. He wants us all to get A's. We have a book, and we only used it like on Mondays, and he actually collected them. Now, we are done with them. I think [it] shows they care if they take time to do stuff with you.

In Pottery, I like to make things, like designs and glazes and stuff. I made this one pot, and I glazed it, dipped my own fingers and put my fingers in there, and it has like little fingers in there.

After school, I have track. I just recently made State. The American Indian counselor was so happy. He said it's been a really long time since one of us [a Native student] made it. . . . So, my friends all thought it was really cool. I have school, and then I have track, and on top of track, I have this dance outfit that I'm working on. And my ma's pressuring me about my grades and to work around the house, and I'm like, "Would you let me be?" Most [Native] kids don't know any other way to prove who they are, but I go to powwows and dance and stuff. Like, at my age, there is me and maybe two other girls. A lot of my culture is lost; nobody is doing anything to bring it back. Now, there's a drum group in the grade school again. It's not cool [for Native students] to learn about [their] culture, [so] they learn about other things like gang activity. Maybe by the time they reach eighth grade, [Native students should] know where they are coming from. I think it would help a lot. I think a lot of us are just lost, searching for something to belong to. I used to spend summers up here with my grandma. It made me feel special. Like, every weekend we were at a powwow. A lot of these girls, they've hardly ever left the reservation. My grandma is part of the Midewiwin Lodge, and I really, really want to become part of that. I guess in Canada, they've got some really good ones up there. So, I'm trying to get her to go up there so then she'll know, and then she can bring me along after awhile. I'm trying to learn this stuff. When I go off, Grandma says, "You're off your road," and Grandma pulls me back. I'd like to see more of the Native American ways taught in school, all the way through schools. Then [those ways] would start all over again.

Maria has been lucky to have both a spiritual guide in her grandmother and an educational guide in her Native school counselor. She sees the road she wants to take, and her grandmother pulls her back to it when she starts to go astray. As in the Seventh Generation prophecy, Maria's steps take her back to her grandmother, an elder, when she trips along the way. The way is not easy. Have you had any of the same difficulties Maria has had? So many Native students have a hard time staying "on the road" they want to be on. Others haven't yet found the road they want to follow; they may not even have begun the quest to find it. Is there someone in your community who helps you keep "on the road" or seek the way you want to take?

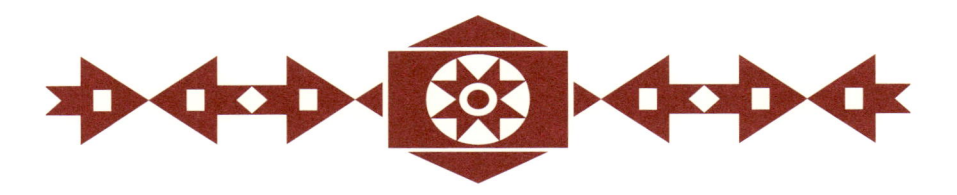

Sunshine's Story

Life hasn't always been sunny for Sunshine. As a member of the Seventh Generation, she has had to find strength within herself, as she has had less family support in the past than Maria and many of the other students we interviewed. Sunshine is a young Ute woman, only 14, but her self-reliance attests to the strength and resilience that provide new hope for her own future and that of her baby.

Live One Day with Me

You think it's just a game, but it's hard. Live one day with me, and you'll see what I go through just to try to make my child safe, make sure he's not sick, and make sure he's fed, make sure he's clean, loved. You're going to be there by yourself, and some people just run out on you. I'm lucky I have a mom that watches him. I'm lucky that my boyfriend's there too, and his family. You have to see the whole other side of it before you start [fooling around]. My average day is hard. I have to get up around 5:30, wake up my boyfriend. He gets ready for work, leaves. I give my son a bath, take a shower, get him ready, get myself ready, and make sure everything's organized. I have everything that I need for the day for him, and since we don't have a vehicle right now, I have to catch a transit. I usually get to school around nine. I take my son to day care, and I go to class. Then, lunchtime, I pick him up again and take him back to day care, go back to class, and have to wait for the transit, and I go home.

My boyfriend watches him on his days off, so we can spend time [together] on the weekends. Sometimes, he gets home from the oil fields at 6:00. He dropped out when he was in 10th [grade], but he went back and got his GED. He's there for me. He's my main friend. It's kind of hard to keep up with school now that I have a son, and you have to think about your child first, and sometimes, teachers get mad because you're late. But it's like you have a child to take care of. Maybe there's a time when your child's sick, and you have to stay home or take him to the doctor. I knew it was going to be hard. I thought having the baby was going to be the hardest part, but taking care of him is. Babies are cute but not all that fun. Sometimes, they are [fun] when they get older. When they're newborns, it's hard; you have to give them 24-hour attention, just can't walk away from them. They get you frustrated; you can't just slap 'em around and say, "I don't want to take care of you!" You made that baby; you have to take care [of him]. . . . [You should] think about it first. If you're going to have a kid, you're going to regret it. Use protection or don't have sex at all. So, I'm not saying that I regret having my son, but I'm not going to say he wasn't a mistake. He's all that I need in life now. If I had a job, had a good house, had a car, had everything I needed, then it would have been nice.

Now, I'm trying to struggle, and my boyfriend's struggling, trying to get his diapers, baby wipes, clothes, shoes, socks, everything he needs. I used to drink, before I got pregnant at least. I used to drink a lot, never be home, never wanted to go home. I'd be put in a shelter because my mom would have problems with me. Having my son actually settled me down quite a bit. It made me realize what I was doing, how much of life I missed.

When I had both parents, I didn't have to worry about nothing. [Since that time], I've been moved to a bunch of different schools. The longest I've stayed in a school was probably two years. When I was around six, my mom and my stepfather were getting a divorce; they had been married when I was one. So, I only knew him as my dad. They were fighting over who would have custody of me. So, it was kind of hard moving all over. I'd come down here and then go back up north, back and forth all the time. My mom made me lie too—well, my stepdad and my mom. That's when they were going through the divorce; he wouldn't let me see my mom at all. And he said the only way you can see her is [if] you live in the house with us. Well, she ran [away] with me down here and got custody of me. . . . She made me tell the judge that I was being sexually abused by my stepfather, but it wasn't true. [She said], "If you want to live with me, then you're going to have to say that." My mom, after she got divorced, she did drink a lot. And she'd leave me home alone, but I wouldn't know why. I was about six. My cousins would stop by and say, "Where's your mom?" So, they'd take me and feed me after I'd be home for like three days with no food. That [is] the reason I hate my mom. She did that to me.

Up north [with my stepfather], some kids would treat me ugly because I was Indian. Then, down here, they call me the "White girl" because I'm light complected compared to these guys. My own cousins would call me dirty names, and I didn't even do or say nothing. So, either way, I'm kind of like in the middle. With my stepfather in the north, it was hard 'cause I used to fight with his wife. I'd get into fistfights with her; I'd have assault charges on me. Luckily, they're all dropped. But, she laid a hand on me first, and I said nobody touches me like that. If you're having fights at home that could disrupt your education, you probably won't want to learn. My stepdad, he used to pay more attention to her kids than me, [and] after he found out I was pregnant, he didn't talk to me. Now, I just have my mom and my boyfriend and his family.

I never went to one school more than [two years], and some of them were better than other ones. In third grade, I did have a hard time with [a] teacher who used to yell at me a lot more than the other kids, when I never bothered anybody. I was the kind of person that kept to myself. When my mom and my stepfather divorced, I didn't want to talk to nobody, never understood why I was the one always getting yelled at. It was kind of hard to concentrate. Sometimes, teachers would [ask] things about your family, and you didn't know the answers. And you can hear everybody else saying, "Well, my dad's this and my mom's this, and they've been married forever." And it makes you feel kind of ugly, want to just sink down in your chair. It's kind of hard to concentrate 'cause that's stuck in your mind, especially hard on the real little kids 'cause they can't understand what's going on. [That teacher] tried to fail me a couple of times, just because I was the only Indian kid in that whole school, and I never experienced anybody being racist against me. Then, after my mom had a talk with her, she was a little bit better. I'd feel like maybe it's true—maybe they're just better than I am. But now that I think about it, some of them aren't so bright, and I'm maybe brighter than some of them! So, I just don't think about it. It could be from the way their parents talk about other races. When I was in fourth grade, I seemed almost like a bookworm, but when I got older and I started switching from all different schools, I didn't really like to read, sloughed off.

Mom's been sober for almost four months now. The experience I had with drinking was one summer. It was a way of me running away from things. I didn't really care, and my mom was looking for me, and I would say, "So, she doesn't care." And that's when I just didn't want to go to school either. I experienced almost every single thing that you can think of. [In the future], I'll say to my son, "I'll tell you a story, what [drinking's] really going to do to you." [Now that I've] stopped, even if my boyfriend wants to drink, he's not going to drink around me. [I tell him], "You go drink somewhere else." I'm not going to deal with that. I was having problems in schools, so she sent me back up north. Last year, when I was in eighth grade, I was going to school and kids from [the community] were—I don't why—but they were trying to fight with me. And I was pregnant, and I didn't know what to do, so I just dropped out of school then.

My mom says, "Don't be like everyone else. Don't drop out of school even though you have a baby." 'Cause up north, it's pretty common that they just drop out. But most people who finish school go on to college. I think everybody needs an education; that's how you survive in life. I want to work helping people. Or I was kind of thinking [that] I could go around telling kids how it really is, tell a true story about how it is to be a teen parent. It's not easy. But all that is important to me in my life is my son. My boyfriend helps me with our son. Right now, my boyfriend and I are planning on getting our own place because, after the divorce, my mom's not really a happy person. She's real mean to me. I used to run away from home 'cause I didn't like being with her, but I learned to accept it. I wish I wasn't here because of all the things I have to put up with everyday. My mom's always saying that a reason why I can stay in her house is because [of] my son; otherwise, she would have got rid of me. I wish I was never here so I wouldn't have to deal with this.

I was actually kind of surprised that this school down here accepted me even though I didn't complete eighth grade. If I was going to a regular high school, it would be harder. You have to be there on time. It'd be hard. Plus, not having a vehicle's hard. You can't stay after school, can't make up your work. There's four of us moms here; they're all older than me, and they're having a hard time too. Most of the time, they're not here. You can tell the teachers care because they say, "Tell your teacher where you're going if you go," "Try to be on time," or "Come to school, even if you're late!" If this school was bad, I couldn't take it anymore. I don't have to worry about my son being in a bad place; he's right here. I can just walk over and check on him, go back to class. My son sees me going to school. I'll make him see that education is important. Plus, other kids see, "She has a baby; she's still going to school."

Sometimes, I'm so exhausted I can't go to school because I'm sick or he's sick. It kind of goes back and forth. Sometimes, I go to school all week if everybody's not sick. At school, they're pretty understanding, but there are things I can't make up. And it's so hard to make up the work if you miss. My son's the one that's keeping me going right now. I'm having a hard time not having a job, not having a vehicle. A good education brings those.

Sunshine has goals in life and could play an important role in the Seventh Generation: being there for other teen mothers. Have you had to deal with some of the life problems Sunshine has had to deal with? Do you have friends with similar problems? How have they coped? What kind of support have they had? In what ways can you support yourself or friends who are coping with hard problems? How important is your family in the bad times? The good times? How have family and friends helped or hindered your school experience?

North Star's Story

North Star is a First Nations Abenaki young man from eastern Canada who is trying to put a life back together for himself. He was unlucky because school didn't honor his strengths as a more hands-on learner. Bored and alienated at school, he went down what he called the "wrong road." But North Star was also lucky. He was lucky, perhaps, in that his body was allergic to the very drugs he escaped to.

You Just Have to Go with the Program

I was okay and passing grades until the day I went into high school. If you go past the bridge here, school's on the other side. When you're younger, every time you would finish [your work], you could go play. Every time you would pass a test, every time that everybody would do good, you could go on trips, so that was really fun. So, in your head, you would want to learn, and, at the same time, you were having fun. And you would do things. I would rather do the experience than read the experience. I don't really know my teachers. I go into the course, I do my things, and I leave. In high school, you can't go play. And at noontime, . . . kids can leave school, and they go smoke in the woods, and they come back, and they're high. That's what we would do, and that didn't help me. And that's when I was starting to do bad at things. I would steal with kids, but I was never the one who would steal. I would just be there. I was about 13, and they were about 17. The rottenest time in school was when police would come and get me in school for doing things. I would have to go to the police station; they would ask me questions. That's when things weren't going well. I was hanging around with the same kids.

When you get down in your life, you can stay down a long time. But when you come back up, you can stay up too. I was down; now, I'm up. Now that I am 17, I'm never going to do the same things I did when I was younger. I started hanging around with kids here [at the reserve], and some of those kids went [to] the same high school as me. You hang around with your race, more comfortable with your own kind. Now, I don't care. The color doesn't count. I was never racist. It's just I was born with people from here. We always loved each other, [better than] hanging around with White people [who were] saying, "You don't pay tax." We would go to school, and then, we would smoke and do chemical stuff. Then, I had secondary effects, and I couldn't take drugs anymore; so, I've been two years sober now. My mother and my ex-girlfriend helped me. If somebody smokes a joint and they don't like it, well, then they know they're never gonna have to smoke another one because they know it's not good. But some, they'll smoke the first joint, and they'll love it and never stop, and things will [get] bad, and that's what happened with me. Then, when I started feeling bad, I would smoke. Now, when I start feeling bad, every time I hurt, I know what it is—living. Before, I was always high; I didn't know what things were. Now I understand things. I look at things now, and I see that things are really beautiful. I didn't have no choice about healing myself. Every time, I wouldn't feel good. I knew my time was up, but I was lucky because I stopped. Else I would probably be a vegetable today. I still got a good brain, though it took a good hit, and I'm still pretty healthy. My body saved me. . . . Then, my mother helped me. I owe her my life. People, when they take drugs, you think you're really a man. I was the only one [of my peers] that quit. They don't pressure me; they don't force me to do nothing. They know that what I did was good. I wanted to live my own life.

Now that I stopped, my twin brother's starting. [When] I used to take drugs, he didn't take any. Now that I stopped, he's taking some, just smoking now, 'cause he thinks he's tough. I think what would help my brother is, he likes mechanics. He likes to fix bikes.... If there would be somebody who would give spare time to teach a course that would teach kids how to fix bikes, [my brother] wouldn't think about smoking anymore, and he would probably be able to stop. It would pull him out of the circle that's not good. He's not going to school. He's super active; he can't sit for like five minutes. He's a good person, but I'll never see him in school. I go, but I have trouble. It's hard going back. The head took a good hit.

School now is hard. If I wouldn't have done my stupid things when I was younger, I would be finished high school today. Let's say I don't understand in school. There's too much. It's almost like I'm scared that the kids are going to laugh at me if they see me go in the front 40 times a day for help. So, I stay at my [desk], and I try to understand. Sometimes, it works; other times, it doesn't work. A good teacher really would continue until I really know the question. It would be somebody I'm not shy with, [someone who knows] how I learn. I don't have trouble with writing in English or French. It's easy when you're writing about what you want to write. The words, I don't have trouble; but the grammar stuff, I have trouble. When I feel down, I write what I got in my head, and that helps me for the next day. Let's say my brother's a mechanic. He'll write about mechanic things. [Teachers] should do things like that, [assign] things that you want to do, not things that you have to do. But you just have to go with the program. In the morning when I get up, I [don't] think about school; I ... think about my friends. I'll see my friends today, so it will be less boring. That's what ... [keeps] me in school. I'm just doing school because I need to.

The tribe gave me a job. So, let's say they would make you work, make you go to school six months, and [then] they would make you work six months. Do that every year [until you graduate]. I'm a lumberman, and I did do forest fires too. They teach you about your culture if they see that you're not doing nothing good with your life. They'll give you a job because they know you won't do stupid things.

The past helps you for the present. The things you did before, you never [have to] do them again. You just got to believe in yourself and understand that you can change if you really want to. I want a future, and nowadays, you have to have a diploma to have a job. I don't want to be on welfare. I want to have a job, and I want to have a wife; I want to have kids. I want to have a real dream with somebody. And I always wanted to be a sports teacher, and, in that dream, I would want to help kids. If there would be a kid that would have trouble, they could call me.

I would tell teachers to try to understand people 'cause people learn different—unique, but in our own ways. [Teachers] should try to understand, listen to [students'] hearts, make them ... comfortable where they are, and they'll pass the year with success instead of passing the year with obligations. What I hate the most is that they think we don't care about [stuff] because we're Indians. We want a life, good things, as much as them. But, sometimes people live difficult things; teachers got to understand that.

What role might North Star play in the Seventh Generation? North Star is perceptive about how schools work, and he has learned to play the system. He also has a clear idea of the way many schools fail to honor the strengths and gifts of the students. He wants to be a sports teacher, and with his hard-learned understandings, he will be a good one. Do you have any ideas of how you might give back to your people when you have finished your schooling? Life may not always be easy for North Star, but some important people in his life have helped him through a hard time, helped him believe in who he is. With his experienced realizations, he can be a leader for his people. He has chosen to persevere.

Quoetone's Story

I interviewed Quoetone in the inner-city parking lot of a restaurant with railroad tracks next to it. We had to prop the tape recorder on the dashboard, and I probably missed a few great quotes as trains went by. Quoetone is more interested in learning than schooling, so he has run into some stumbling blocks in his progress towards a diploma. As I write this, he is still working his way through school, insistent that he not lower his expectations for himself in gaining knowledge. He keeps at it with his integrity intact. Quoetone has had the family resources and an almost personal stubbornness that helps him manage rich learning.

Instead of Just Pumping Gas

I'm three cultures actually. I take care of my Kiowa culture when I go down there. I dance down there with that family, remembering their history, their stories, their songs. And the Ojibwe part of my life, I was seated on the big drum a while ago, learning those stories, and that's a lifelong commitment too, learning their stories and songs. Kiowa and Ojibwe, the songs are different, but they are very close in values. And my third culture, I don't have much time to do anything about it. I don't live with my father.

I started school in a little town kindergarten in Oklahoma. It wasn't bad because I had cousins [from my Kiowa family] there. I learned to gourd dance, and I learned their stories, some of the language, to sing from my grandfather, that kind of thing. When I was in kindergarten, they gave me a worksheet that had a circus scene on it. I drew the circus scene just right, [thinking about] the movie . . . Dumbo, and there was rain outside, so I drew rain all over the place, and they said, "You just scribbled."

And I said, "That's how it was!"

"No, you scribbled."

"No, that's how it was in the movie, the one with the elephant that can fly!" I sat in the principal's office for that one.

Then . . . I went to [a Catholic school], and the only other Indian kid there was Beau. And so, we used to get into a lot of trouble because everybody knew I was Indian, even though I kind of didn't look like one. I had some problems, especially when I was little. I was told animals had spirits in them, and my first theological argument was over that with my first-grade teacher. We were having a discussion one day, and the Sister was telling us how they used to sacrifice lambs because lambs don't have spirits. . . . It's like, "But animals do have spirits. I know they have spirits because they are living, right? Everything has a spirit inside it, some kind of will for life." She goes, "Oh no, they don't go to heaven. They don't have a spirit." I got really mad, and they had to take me down to the office. It blackballed me pretty well.

Me and Beau were pretty good kids, but we used to get into some trouble now and again. [Some students] used to make comments about the reservation, how people don't have to pay taxes, stuff like that, that they heard from their parents. I used to tell them, "Just think about it this way: you're living on our land." When I look back on it, ignorance is the main problem. When you're an Indian kid out there, there's not much you can say about it. In hockey, my friend Beau had to do push-ups on the ice and throw hockey sticks as far as [he] could down the ice, and the coach said [to him], "You should be pretty damn good at this," [meaning] throwing a spear. Beau just kind of looked like, "What are you talking about?" When you're an Indian kid out there, there's not much you can say, but I [feel] even worse for the people saying that kind of thing because when you dehumanize somebody, you lose your own humanity, really. It's the mentality. It's comments they heard from their parents, like [reservations] are hideouts from the state taxism. I try not to let it affect me; their ignorance is the main problem.

I grew up going to ceremonials on that reservation. I used to go maple sugaring with my mom, but I didn't think there was anything different about it until I moved down here in the city. I learned a lot of my core values there, and that helped a lot. In the beginning of eighth grade, a teacher of mine was teaching a unit on American Indian history, and so I offered to bring in some class materials, and she had a bit of a problem with me correcting her in class. I had a bit of a disagreement with her, so I left the school and went to an open school, and I didn't accomplish a lot academically that year.

They thought it would be good if I went to the Indian magnet high school in ninth grade. I never had any other Indians in my class in the city until I was at that Indian magnet school. I actually had three American Indian teachers there, and I took Ojibwe language, American Indian history, and American Indian literature. I got to read Momaday, Alexie, Silko. I think there was a hundred Indian kids in the school, good mix of tribes. Most kids didn't know anything about their own culture. You've got a lot of different tribes [in the city]. They group you all as "Indians." You have people losing their culture, some people learning more about it, and [others] mixing the cultures, Pan-Indianism. Gang [members] don't really care about the culture; it's doing their own thing. While other militant bunches are so into the culture, they're anti everything else. I know a kid who won't eat white flour or white sugar because that was given to us to kill us off. That's fine. I have a kind of different view of things. They're going to push Highway 55 through this supposedly sacred grove of trees. Like some [Natives] are trying to save these trees, jumping in the tracks of one of the bulldozers, sitting up in a tree with a noose around your neck or something, and I was the first one to say, "Well, I have a dream, I [wanna] cut down the trees and make a drum barrel!" But I can't say somebody's ways are wrong or right. Who am I to say?

Some kids say, "I can't stand it up there on the reservation. There's nothing bloody flippin' to do up there." [But] the reservation isn't sometimes the best place to get in touch with your culture. It's up there, and it's available, and a lot of people up there don't take the opportunity. The reemergence of culture has been happening a lot more down in the city. People down here want to get more in touch with their culture because they realize it's not around. I've taken some of the guys I sing with up with me when we go to ceremonials, and they think it's pretty cool. They got kind of in touch with it there. People who are more in touch with their culture still carry a lot of good cultural traits, like respect for elders and teachers.

When I was a ninth or tenth grader, I didn't particularly like school. I ditched a lot of classes.

A lot were boring, [just filling out] handouts.... So, they put me on a truancy intervention program, and I was sick during that time. They were going to take me to court when I was still 15, before [you] could drop out at 16; now, it's age 18. I was pretty pig-headed at the time. Pretty much what I did was sleep, just let your whole body shut down and sleep for awhile—kind of fainting on a long-term basis. It's a coping skill I can handle. So my mom said, "I'll tell you what. I don't want to put you through the legal system, so I'm going to homeschool you."

That was a rough period. I went down with my brother in Oklahoma and kind of worked things out. I decided I really needed to buckle down because high school is jumping through hoops anyway. I really admire people that really try. They put as much of themselves in as they can, working really hard for the grades. For me, it was just a kind of jumping from hoop to hoop. When you've lived on a reservation and you move to the city, it's harder understanding how to do things; but, if you never lived on a reservation and you're an Indian in the city, you're more used to it. I think it's an advantage having been both places. That kind of worked. I went back to school the following spring. I decided to go to a kind of alternative school because I was behind credits from the time I missed, but I still stay with the drum group. That transcends school. At the alternative school, I can go in at 1:00, and it's open until 7:00. It works for people who actually want to learn and get their credits to graduate.

I have a teacher who's somebody you can talk to, and he's like also the librarian, and we talk about books, philosophy, anything. And his first wife was Indian; [he] knows where I'm coming from. [I'll] come in about 3:00, and we'll sit and have a discussion about what's new in the news today. He'll ask me some questions about some of the papers he's writing in school and get on my case a little bit, "Hey, you turn that paper in yet?" But it's him respecting my intelligence, treats you not just as a pupil, but there's also this pupil-teacher thing going on. I like wood shop, then a good conversation with this teacher, and then with my art teacher, see if he's got any field trips going to the museum or anything like that. Here, it's so mixed that you can't really be a racist. The other school was different, outright race wars there, big fights between Hmong kids and White kids or Black kids. You have some skin heads; some people are just flatout bigots because that's the way they were raised. You got Indians that are bigots against all other cultures too. It didn't really bother me so much because I could pass [for White].

I used to [accept] what was good and what was bad about schooling. I just kind of took over because to learn, if you're not motivated to learn yourself, then you're not really learning. When students are empowered to take part in their own curriculum and in how their school runs, that's an important thing. They'll take it upon themselves to push themselves further to learn, and they'll like school. They need a sense of community. I think deep down everyone wants to learn something. It's like work; if you're not empowered in your job, that's a job. But, if you're empowered in a job you love, that's a career. School right now is not 45 minutes, do something, 45 minutes, do something else, like a factory. School now takes more. By sophomore, junior, senior year, we should have a lot more freedom to work on independent projects and have them count for something, encourage people to reach out with their studies. I get credit for a lot of self-teaching at the alternative school. I'm thinking of going back to the high school next year. After more concentrated learning, it's a lot easier to get through over there. There is a good support group, a lot of activities, counselors who understand a little bit more. Personally, I'm hoping for a better future for myself, chance of going to college, doing something instead of just pumping gas.

At the time of our interviews together, Quoetone had found ways to work through school, skirting the normal path. He had dropped out and found a school he could deal with. After taking a breather and building up patience for a more traditional route, he was thinking of moving back into mainstream schools. Do you know students who have dropped out of school? Who have returned? As in the Seventh Generation prophecy, Quoetone goes to elders for advice, and he harkens to the drum.

Sipsis's Story

When I interviewed Sipsis, we had to struggle a bit with language. Her French was considerably better than mine, and because she was going to talk and I was going to listen, we decided on French for the interview. When she became excited or passionate, I stopped being able to understand. I didn't know what a wise young woman she was until a friend translated the interview for me. Sipsis and I met in a workroom of her tribe's museum, as tourists were touring below.

We Consider Life Differently

There has never been a school on my reserve, so I was in elementary school in the next village. We were not accepted very well. I used to be bugged, called a savage, things like that, because there were not many people who knew us. It was like that. In high school, I'm the only one from my nation; it's a school outside of the reserve. I'm alone, so it's hard to be with all White people, except one student who is from another reserve. Teachers respect us, but the students don't at all. If we [visit] a school on a bigger reserve, it's completely different because we hear of First Nations people and history, but in French Canadian schools, we hear of French Canadian history. They say, "You don't pay taxes; we pay for you." They have much more prejudice. It's difficult to live with that. They will judge you without knowing who you are. They will say, "Oh, she is an Aboriginal." They will look at you with a snobbish eye. You cannot open yourself; you rather try to hide what you are. I myself speak a lot with the other First Nations students. We exchange information [on Aboriginal topics], but otherwise, we don't speak because people are not interested.

I feel a little apart, a little rejected, even though I was there before them [in history]; it makes no sense. They speak about French history, but they have trouble talking about us, even a little bit. It's as if we are not there. What is wrong is that people from Quebec are the least informed about Aboriginals. Most people from Europe [even] know more than what Québecois know, and it brings on prejudice.

We have to accept [being away for weekdays]. It's a little difficult because it's [living in] another world. Here, I sing, I dance, we can do some Indian handcrafting—baskets, for instance. There, it's living with books, no stories, nothing. I am not living according to my nature; I am not with people who understand me. We are very few. I am there by myself, and they consider me as strange, and my name sounds strange. I still succeed, but my motivation in classes is lower.

Other people are not interested in the same topics as I am. What interests them in History is the history of the atomic bomb, not [my interests of] Mayan history or in my nation's history. [Learning about] Hitler annoys me.

Every year, reserves have powwows I go to. Because their reserves are bigger, they have their own schools, so their classes are completely different. They won't have the history of the French [coming to] America; it will be what was going on in America and what happened with the arrival of the French. [In my school], in a class of Quebec history, we are rarely mentioned. They try to give at least one class about Aboriginals; the rest is about the French. I learn much more on the reserve than during a history class; I succeed in finding the truth. I want to tell my history, and they will tell theirs, and we can exchange. We find a connection, but it's a little one. The territory of Nunavut has just been declared; still, at school, there was a lot of prejudice: "They had nothing to do with making a territory there." It's as if the Natives had no right to be there, no right to live in Canada, as if we were immigrants in our own country, coming from abroad.

I like writing. I try to express myself in writing essays, tales. It's the only way I can express myself. I write a lot, and the stories are always interesting and contain a lot of information. I live close to the museum, so I know a lot. In Religion class, we had to speak about symbols like water, fire, air, cross, those symbols. I spoke about water but not in a religious way, not the water we would bless. I spoke of what my tribe would think of water: water as our means of transportation, water as our survival—a completely different use compared to a religious one.

I have a Web site, and I speak of who I am on it. I write about dancing group, trips I made; I write on what I feel during my shows and what I feel during everyday life, like the clothes I wear every day compared to my dancing clothes. I explain those and what they mean, to give more information. Friends will read my site. Most Innu people have their own Web sites which speak about them. In French class, I write essays in which I express what I experience, like when a friend commits suicide. I like writing.

[At home] I am surrounded by Aboriginals; I prefer being with these people. All my life, I have danced and sung. I like to be with people like me, not different. At school, it is different. I am a student; that's the only reason which makes me stay there, not because of friends.

There, I am reserved. I don't speak; I just do my work. I have friends who are not Indians, but I won't speak of my nation a lot because they won't be that interested.

With my friends here or who live in another village . . . we are able to exchange more. If I speak about dancing, they know what I am talking about. At school, I have to explain what I do. It's boring, so I don't [explain] it much. Here, I will speak about who I am more deeply. It's like having two personalities. At home, we speak French. We watch English TV, we read English books, but we speak French. My Aboriginal language is almost lost; we don't really speak it.

I want a school just for ourselves, with French, English, Math, Biology, but which would have our language. Instead of playing soccer, we should learn games like lacrosse [and] how to survive in the woods. The more we lose our history, we are going to be like French people from Quebec. We should have language classes, craft classes, learn how to make a peace pipe, how to dance, how to sing, to know what it means. If I have to give up these, I would not have any motivation to be at school; I would lose all my resources. Most of those who quit school either have a baby when they are too young or have a problem in balancing their schoolwork and their interests; they have to give them up to do their homework. If you have to do all things you don't like much, [you want to give up]. I don't like working with wood; that's me. If I had to do it without having time for my activities, it would be impossible. My family [supports me with school]—my brother, my father, my mother too. One of my brothers couldn't stand being away, had a hard time, fell in love, so school was hard. He didn't have any spare time to do what he wanted, so he gave up. They had compulsory classes that didn't have any motivation [for him]. He skipped once or twice, and after that, he never went back. And now, he cannot go back anymore. If you don't do it, you fail. If I have children, I want to raise them in my culture and not in the culture of Quebec people. I think it's important to be able to tell what you really are without having to hide it. But I don't want to be obliged to practice only Aboriginal stuff; I think I am able to work with computers, or do technical work, or practice psychology. I want to be able to do both, my interests and my job, work outside the community and live in the community.

I wish all teachers would try to know who we are, understand the fact that we are living far [away from home] and that we consider life differently. Most teachers want to know who we are. They say, "You are Aboriginals? Where do you live?" They want to know a lot, and I am pleased with it. It means I am not so lonely after all. Some teachers are interested, understand me, and will try to give the students from the other village and me some motivation. Now, I don't think there are teachers who don't like me.

Sipsis manages to move back and forth between a small eastern Canadian village and the global world without leaving behind who she is and where she comes from. She is Abenaki and has a Web page that boldly announces her presence to the larger world, honoring the people from whom she comes. Sipsis has discovered how to make school interesting for herself. Have you found any ways to make school a little more interesting for yourself? Sipsis may or may not have heard of the Seventh Generation, but perhaps she is speaking forth as a scroll holder to the larger world.

Stories, Stories, Stories

In the summers, I live on a coastal river in southern Maine. When I work in my garden each summer, I find more clam shells than can be naturally explained. I now know the Abenaki people lived near the mouth of the river and harvested what the river and ocean had to offer, to be dried and stored for months to come. I understand that some families camped on the river where my garden offers up zucchini. My life mingles with the past in ways that are hard to understand, yet I appreciate the gift of the clam shells, which provide some good nutrients for my now flowering zucchini. Perhaps the zucchini will give me the strength to return to the shed where I write and finish my contributions to this book. Downstream from my writing shed, the river empties into the Atlantic Ocean, and where that happens, there is now a pier that used to be an Abenaki encampment into the 1930s. Older residents still call it Indian Canoe Landing. After awhile, the tepees came down, and junk wood shanties took their place. These were offensive to those who were vacationing in the area, but the Abenaki themselves were welcomed as guides, as sellers of sweet grass baskets, and as canoe builders and repairers. They were usually the winners in canoe races that took place during carnivals on the river. The land around the river mouth was developed, and the number of Abenaki who made the mouth of the river their summer home became fewer and fewer.

When I first moved here in the 1960s, Abenaki people came from the north to sell sweet grass baskets to summer people and to pick blueberries on the plains in West Kennebunk. One older Kennebunk man told me, "They were eased out." They no longer come to the coast in southern Maine, but they haven't disappeared. They joined Abenaki relatives on Indian Island in the Penobscot River or possibly even further north in Quebec. Sipsis is probably related to them in some distant sort of way. Sipsis is not about to be silenced or "eased out." She is taking advantage of the great equality of the Internet to make her presence known. She convinces her teachers to let her write about topics that are meaningful to her. She is determined to hold on to her own way of being. Like many of the students we interviewed, she could be considered a discoverer of the scrolls.

Chapter 2

A Message from Elders

In August 2000, elders gathered in Duluth, Minnesota, to discuss the new millennium at a conference titled "Strengthening the Sacred Circle: 2000 and Beyond." In his invitation to the elders, Frank Chee Willetto, chairman of the Navajo, said:

> We are the First People of this land. Our young people are looking to us with questions about the future. They want to know how to protect our lands, how to treat each other, and how to deal with change. Let us come together with good thoughts and provide the next generation with a message they can use. Let us confer some of the strength that has brought us this far to them in our messages. Let this message be a legacy that can live beyond the bounds of time and have meaning for generations of our people long into the future.[3]

At the conference, the elders bid the youth of the Seventh Generation to do the following:

To the Seventh Generation
Survive
Keep hopes and dreams
Take care of yourself
Remember your spirit
Be there for each other
Respect courage
Share knowledge
Always keep learning
Remember your true values[4]

In interviewing Maria, Sunshine, North Star, Quoetone, Sipsis, and the other 115 students, my coauthors and I were struck by the many examples of youth actively trying to turn things around for themselves and for others. If you think about the five stories you have just read, Maria, Sunshine, North Star, Quoetone, and Sipsis are fighting to hold onto a good path. They are in the process of finding their own way. All five students are surviving, holding hopes and dreams, taking care of themselves and others, remembering their spirit, learning, and keeping values to guide them. We thank them for sharing their knowledge with us. We appreciate that they are still making their way through school because, from our perspectives, we know well the influence of diplomas in this world. They will give young people the power to make a difference for generations to come. These students are finding ways to do the things that the elders bid them to do. If the prophecy holds, our youthful readers are also part of the Seventh Generation. Our older readers will learn from the younger how to lend them support in making the decisions about the future that they need to make. As Maria said, if students believe themselves to be what their worst teachers think them to be, that will become a self-fulfilling prophecy. But, if we believe the revelations about the Seventh Generation, we are obligated to help these young people fulfill the prophecies. We are all part of a much larger story of our own weaving, a story where we are both the actors and the storytellers, and the ending is up to us.

---

[3] Willetto, "An Invitation to Elders."
[4] Ibid.

Chapter 3
Just Be: Knowing Who You Are

This chapter is about *identity* and how Indigenous youth from across North America describe all the different things that make up who they are. The chapter discusses what identity is, beginning with Amy Bergstrom's story of her own identity quest. In the remainder of the chapter, students talk about the challenges that directly affect the way they think and feel about themselves. The students' desire for harmony and balance centers around four consistent themes: understanding and connecting to *culture*, having *pride* in being Indigenous, connecting to *someone healthy* or to *a place,* and maintaining a strong sense of *spirituality*.

How do you do?
No, I am not Chinese.
No, not Spanish.
No, I am American Indi-uh, Native American.
No, not from India.
No, not Apache.
No, not Navajo.
No, not Sioux.
No, we are not extinct.
Yes, Indian.

From "Sure You Can Ask Me a Personal Question" by Diane Burns[1]

Does the poem carry any meaning to you? Have you been questioned about your identity, based on the way others see you? Based on the way you look or don't look? Stereotypes can be hurtful and make you angry, and they usually are untrue. When we believe them to be true, we limit ourselves and all that we can be.

---

[1]Burns, "Sure You Can Ask Me a Personal Question."

What Is Identity?

All of us have an *identity*. Identity is defined in the dictionary as "the distinguishing personality or character of an individual." What is your distinguishing personality or character? What are the things that make up your personality and character? It is our hope that you will hear stories that you can relate to and that seem familiar. As you read, try to answer the questions about yourself—what makes up who you are.

Many scholars have studied what they call *identity development*. The studies examine how human beings determine who they are and how their experiences help shape them.

One of the reasons scholars are so interested in adolescents is that we go through more changes—both physical and emotional—in our teenage years than at any other time in our lives. It is not unusual to feel angry, happy, and sad, and gain or lose friends, all in one day's time. No wonder we can become confused! Physical changes include skin problems, awkward feet size, weight gain, and body odor. These changes span all races, classes, and genders. In addition to changes in our bodies, our social and emotional lives broaden and grow. We experience more emotions and also work to understand them. Often it feels as though nobody understands what we are going through. Many Indigenous people face all these changes plus issues of racism and alienation. We also live in a society that does not always respect, understand, and honor our culture, spirituality, family life, and community.

Identity development from an Indigenous perspective has less to do with striving for individualism and more to do with establishing connections and understanding ourselves in relationship to all of the things around us. This perspective of the world is the basis for a strong sense of self.

Many Indigenous people aspire to live in harmony and balance, believing this is how the Creator wants us to live. Living a life in harmony and balance leads to a feeling of wholeness and completeness, which is a way of connecting with our spirituality. Harmony and balance require individual wellness in all aspects of our being, including our mental, emotional, physical, and spiritual dimensions.[2] This means it is important to pay attention and try to understand how each of these four dimensions affects the other. Our *mental* wellness hinges on what we think about. Are we learning and seeking to understand the world we live in? How do our thoughts affect our *emotional* well-being, or how we feel? Do we know how to express anger, sadness, happiness, or grief? What are healthy ways to express these kinds of emotions? Our *physical* well-being depends on how well we take care of our bodies and the earth, which supports life. Do we eat healthy foods? Do we get enough rest and exercise? Do we live in environmen-

---

[2] Cleary and Peacock, *Collected Wisdom*, 25.

tally friendly ways? Our *spiritual* well-being is based on recognizing a Creator or Great Mystery and spending time in prayer or meditation. Some of us believe in a god—Jehovah, for example. For the Anishinaabeg, we believe in Gitche Manidoo, the Great Spirit or Creator. What are your spiritual beliefs and how do you recognize and honor your spirituality?

As students across North America spoke, we saw through their eyes that they understood these connections. We heard about responsibility to community, family, and tribal nation, which gave them a sense of hopefulness and belonging. Strengthening these connections also helped students understand and accept themselves. In her work, Alex Wilson, an Opaskwayak Cree scholar, reflects on this notion of interconnected-ness—especially with nature— and the importance of relationships: "Each of our traditional world views recognizes the deep interdependency between humans and nature, that our origin is in the soil of the land, and that we are bound to each other in an intimately spiritual way. This shared understanding of the world shapes the life experiences of North America's Indigenous peoples and, in turn, their identity development."[3] Listening to stories from this perspective allows the students' voices in these pages to be heard clearly. Their stories tell about their growing understanding of who they are as Native persons—in other words, their identity development. The following story is about my own adolescent struggle with identity.

A Coat of Armor
by Amy Bergstrom

We were the second-to-last stop the rez bus made before getting to school. It was called the rez bus because it mostly picked up the reservation Indian students who were bused into the public school. We were the only Indians picked up so close to town on that route, a mere two miles east of the school, three miles west of the reservation. The bus was packed by the time my brother and I would make our way up the three steps onto the bus. You could always see your breath on those cool fall mornings as we boarded the bus and headed for the school. As I reached the top of the stairs, I would casually scan the bus for a seat, trying to conceal my nervousness and desperation. I never really had a place on the bus. It seemed like all the other kids did. Young elementary kids sat in front with the uncool high school kids; the cool high school kids sat towards the middle and back. I usually found a seat with the rest of the Indians about six seats shy of the back of the bus. There seemed to be a pecking order that I never quite understood until recently. The pecking order could make you feel like a million bucks or a complete loser.

Lighter skinned than most, I never felt like I belonged there among the real Indians. My hair wasn't black, my skin was barely light brown, and my home wasn't on reservation land. But there I was among them as though I belonged. I remember admiring the long, black silklike hair that cascaded down the seats in front of me. At

---

[3]Wilson, "How We Find Ourselves," 305.

that time, I didn't understand the sacredness of that hair. Some hair fell freely; some was tied back in ponytails. Others had it in a tightly braided strand that hung down their backs, always outside their jackets. This beautiful hair reminded me of my oldest sister's—long, straight, and black—the real look of an Indian I secretly admired in my sister Gail.

I also admired those who wore the jackets we received from the Indian Club at school. There, right in front of my very eyes, were these crisp, new jackets, sprinkled in the seats around me in the back of the bus. I admired them, blue with white trim or red with black trim. I didn't wear my Indian Club jacket that day, nor did I ever wear it. I simply left it hanging in my closet as though it wasn't fit to be seen. Mine was blue with white-and-blue-striped wristbands, and A-m-y was embroidered neatly in white thread across the front top left. And there on the back, outlined in bright white, was the facial profile of an Indian chief with a full headdress. All Indian students got a jacket, custom made with our name neatly sewn on the front. Who was that Indian chief so neatly profiled on the jacket? Whose nation did he belong to? Was he symbolic to all Native people or was he Anishinaabe? The Indians I knew certainly didn't look like this.

I could never muster the courage to wear my jacket in those days. I'm sorry now, but when you're 13, all that matters is the here and now. I'm sorry for the disrespect this showed my mother and my grandmothers; as a daughter and a granddaughter, I was too embarrassed to be myself. I'm sorry to my ancestors too, for what they gave to make it possible for me to wear that jacket. What mattered to me during eighth grade was how I was perceived. I was too conscious of the perceptions of others, and it affected the way I wandered from grade to grade. Finally, I graduated and left the jacket behind in my mother's front closet, where it still hangs.

I remember feeling somehow in awe of my rez bus mates. For some reason, I saw them as Indian and myself as something different. To me at that time, our external features defined who we were. In school, they were referred to as "the Indians." For some reason, I was exempt from this label in the public school we attended. The Indian Club provided services I seldom publicly took advantage of. I internalized the racist messages outwardly spoken by my classmates. Though never really directed at me, they always inflicted some type of internal wound. Today, I understand this, but back then, I was too young to recognize what was happening. I was torn between who I felt I was internally and who I acted like externally. I was seen differently by the system, maybe because I didn't live on the rez, maybe because I wasn't a full blood, maybe because I had a White father and light skin, but I'm not exactly sure why. I do know that I was ashamed—ashamed to be an Indigenous person of this country, this land. I didn't understand the great pride, wisdom, and strength my culture would come to offer me. Anishinaabeg, the name of my people, my ancestors, was a name I didn't claim as my own.

My story maps out a small portion of my identity quest and how confused I was about who I was. Confusing messages had been sent to me from all directions about who I was and who I *thought* I was. The racism of others and my own internalized racism were major obstacles in my quest for harmony and balance.

Some Challenges to a Healthy Sense of Self

Living a life in harmony and balance can be difficult, as we face many disruptions and imbalances each day. Some of these challenges we bring on ourselves; others are simply presented to us either as a natural part of human development or in some other way. *How we respond* to these challenges, however, is usually what determines whether we experience harmony and balance or an unbalanced life. The following paragraphs describe some common challenges faced by Native people.

Effects of Colonization and Oppression

When we were "discovered" and colonized, many destructive things happened to our communities. Our ways of life were condemned by authorities, and we were forced to try to be a people we were not. The federal government tried to assimilate us, which means they tried to make us be like them—White. Through this process, we have taken on many destructive practices or behaviors towards our own people. Many of these oppressive behaviors have been learned through observing what the federal government has done to our communities.

The students we interviewed spoke directly about oppression, especially as it relates to racism, as well as about issues of blood quantum and skin color. The Seventh Generation must deal with the effects of this colonization. What happened to our people is a historical trauma that cannot be forgotten. But we can overcome colonization, both individually and as communities.

Racism and Internalized Racism

Many students spoke about how the overt racism of others and their own internalized racism have affected their quests for a healthy, balanced sense of self. Examples of internalized racism would include judging one's self and others on the basis of skin color (either too light or too dark) or actions (either too Indian or too White). Maybe we think that anyone who doesn't live in a HUD house on the reservation is somehow less Indian. These behaviors are learned, and they do not reflect historically the way our communities operated.

Speashal-One (Ojibwe) talked about how racist remarks from peers in school can be both painful and frustrating:

◆ In [school] we have a few classes for Indian students cause there's only a few of us out there. And it's just hard for us to get things done because some people hold prejudice to us. My friend, she's a full blood, and she's been told to go back to her land, her country. The funny part is, we were here first! And so, you can't tell us to go back; we can tell you to go back. And I do; I hold some prejudice towards White people because of taking our land after you gave it to us, the taking of our land that you shouldn't have taken. All right, I hate you, but I don't! I got one foot in one world and one foot in another world. So it's kind of hard. I don't belong in either, really. I know how my dad felt because he couldn't bring my mom onto the reservation and she couldn't bring him off. Everywhere you go, you get shunned. It's hard for someone who's half-and-half to get through life without knowing what each half is.

Does this sound familiar to you? How might you deal with a comment like, "Go back to your land"? How do you think prejudice affects the development of identity and living a life in harmony and balance? Nahami, a First Nations Abenaki student, also spoke of racism at her school:

◆ People think you have to have dark skin to be Abenaki. They say, "You don't pay taxes" or "You don't pay your electricity." I just explain to them and it gets tiring. Sometimes, they say things like, "Oh, she's an Indian." It affects me inside, but I don't listen to them. It happened that I was made fun of a little bit. I got laughed at, but it wasn't long before I overcame those experiences.... I told them to stop. They called me names and things like that. It wasn't something we talked about in public. It was something shameful, something hidden, because children play games like that; they laugh at you. I never told anyone, nobody.

Blood Quantum

Issues of blood quantum (the amount of Indian blood we have) and tribal enrollment have sometimes torn our families, communities, and selves apart. If we think about it, these are merely behaviors we have taken over from the federal government, which tried to abolish our communities. If we aren't quite one-fourth (or whatever the blood quantum requirement for *membership* is), we cannot enroll in some of our nations. Some nations have closed enrollment while others have passed restrictive rules, such as revoking community status of anyone who partners with someone outside the nation. North Star (Abenaki) commented on this:

◆ If I marry a White person and I know that my kid won't be able to have a card and be recognized like an Indian person, well, I'll still show them the Indian way.

Fortunately, North Star is willing to overlook issues of enrollment and blood quantum. He will teach his children about his nation's and community's ways of life, not merely about blood quantum. Sherman Alexie, a Spokane/Coeur D'Alene author, writes about this in the poem "13/16":

> It is done by blood, reservation mathematics, fractions:
> Father (full-blood) + mother (5/8) = son (13/16)
>
> It is done by enrollment number, last name first, first name last:
> Spokane Tribal Enrollment Number 1569; Victor, Chief
>
> It is done by identification card, photograph, lamination:
> IF FOUND PLEASE RETURN TO SPOKANE TRIBE OF INDIANS, WELLPINIT, WA.[4]

Skin Color

Another effect of colonization that permeates our communities is the issue of skin color. Being too light or too dark seems to cause further trouble in trying to develop a culturally grounded sense of self. Megan (Ojibwe) stressed that ceremonies and other aspects of her cul-

---

[4]Alexie, *The Business of Fancy Dancing*, 16.

ture have kept her connected and balanced despite the fact that some people have judged her by her light skin color:

- I'm really light complected, so sometimes I feel like I belong in both worlds. Like, if I said I went to a powwow with my cousin, I'd feel kind of self-conscious. I know inside I belong there, but people are looking at me, walking around saying things like, "Who's that White girl wannabe at our powwow?" And I know they're thinking that, and I understand why they think that. But it's kind of hard because I know I'm not [a wannabe]. I mean like all my brothers are dark. I kind of joke around sometimes with Tom that I'm the white sheep of the family instead of the black sheep. Sometimes, I do feel like a wannabe because my skin is so light, but I consider myself an Indian. If anybody has ever said anything racist, I don't think I've really felt intimidated because I stand up to them. So, I don't really feel intimidated, but I think if my skin were darker, I might not be as outgoing. I went to look at [a university] because I'm applying there. And I met with the Native American recruiter, and she looked at me; and, because it's a public school, they can't ask you to verify that you're Native American. And she was real skeptical, and she was just giving me the tidbits, just like what she had to give me for an interview. She wasn't really in-depth until she mentioned they had someone teaching Ojibwe at [the university], and I said, "Oh, who is it?" And it was a friend of the family, and I said, "I know him!" Then we started getting into this conversation about him, and we just hit it off, and then she was much more interested because she knew I was Indian.

Have you ever thought the word *wannabe* when looking at a fair-skinned person who you know is Indian? What are some ways internalized racism has played out in your life? How has it played out in the world around you? How have you been affected by internalized racism? How have you dealt with it? You will learn more about internalized racism in chapter 4.

There seems to be a broad spectrum of opinions about skin color within our communities. Being too light is one end of the spectrum, but being too dark can also have negative effects. Having dark skin can immediately put you in a challenging position. Because you have dark skin, you can be looked upon as the "know-all and be-all" of anything Indigenous. Other times, you might get laughed at for not knowing enough about your culture. Will (Dakota) talked about this:

- I don't know anything about these ways, and they're going to laugh 'cause I'm Indian and I don't know nothing about these ways.

Having dark skin can be a tremendous challenge, living either in mainstream society or within our own Indigenous communities. For some Navajo students, being referred to as a "John" is not a very positive thing. A "John" refers to a person seen as being too Navajo, which means living very traditionally. If you are too dark or too traditional, this sometimes creates conflict between you and your peers. When this happens, it can interrupt your healthy identity development or strong sense of self.

Voices of Harmony and Balance

I didn't really know what I was getting myself into when I started writing for this chapter. When I began combing through the file folders on "Identity," I wasn't surprised about how thick it was. What surprised me was the eloquence with which students spoke about their lives and their connections. Many had become grounded and secure in who they were at this very moment in time. Their stories sing a beautiful song of harmony and balance, of wisdom and strength.

Although the students had no magic equations about identity, their wisdom speaks volumes about how understanding who we are as Indigenous people is firmly rooted in these common themes: spirituality, understanding of and connection to culture, pride in being American Indian/First Nations or Alaska Native, and a connection to a place or a healthy person.

Spirituality

Spirituality is interwoven through much of what these students have to say. Although they may not have used the word *spirituality*, they did speak of dancing, singing, drumming, and praying. These are all aspects of spirituality. Our spirituality is all around us, and there is culture everywhere we go. However, some students spoke directly about spirituality, and it is important their voices are heard. They are inspiring. The students reflected specifically on the importance of spiritual connection in their lives and how it contributes to an overall understanding of themselves.

In my literature research, I found very little that spoke about the connection between spirituality and adolescent development. In mainstream America, references to spirituality often pertain to Christianity or Judaism. This assumes that most people fall into one of those two religions. However, spirituality means different things to different people. A number of students seemed to understand the importance of spirituality in their lives and the role it plays in their healthy development. Werlth-Kerish-Nah (Hoopa) talked about how harmony and balance begin within ourselves:

◆ I had to look within myself, inner self, figuring out that these things happen. There are things in life that you'll be dealing with, and if you let them carry you and destroy you and take you down, then that's where you're gonna dwell. But if you learn and understand them, then you will gain from them. You'll gain strength. And it's helped me out a lot, mainly when I went back to the religion, the religion of the Indian people, and started understanding the meanings again, because for a period there I was blind to it. I had forgotten.

The main guy that would sit me down and tell me things was my uncle. Rather than pointing me in one direction or another, he would just make it clear what was going on and let me choose. He never preached at me or anything of that nature, but he did help me understand. I was doing the sweat house and going through the ceremonies, going through fasting, all of this looking for the answer. And in a dream, about two years into it, where I was still searching for that answer, he had been given to me in a dream, to just talk to him. When I was talking to him in my dream, it was in nothing but [my Native] language, which I speak [only] a little bit. But he was speaking to me in [my language]. And when I went to speak to him, when I went to talk to him about it, the dream, it was like he was telling me the same exact thing that he had said in the dream, but it was in English. And I could make a lot of connections now because I've learned a lot more of [my] language. . . . I can still see it really very vividly in my mind, and so I can understand the connection. And I imagine the more of the language that I learn, the more connection I will also understand.

I think it was constantly taking the wrong path that finally made me say, "Hold on, I'm going down the wrong road." I can see that now, and I know that I have to change. And the only way that I could do it was if I examined what I was doing. It's like looking at my actions from someone else's perspective. If I do this, what is that going to do to the people around me? And that had a real impact on me. I was constantly fighting and bickering with everybody. I was more along the lines of like withering away, like a flower withering away because it doesn't have the nutrients that it needs. So I had to supply myself with what I needed to revive. It was just realizing, I guess just growing up in a sense, realizing that freedom of choice was there. It was always there, and whatever path I wanted to go down was the one that I could go down if I put my mind to it.

Werlth-Kerish-Nah talked about how dreams are an integral part of his life. Dreams play a significant role in most Indigenous people's lives. In my life, dreams are a large part of who I am and what I do. I have learned to remember them and seek out their meanings. I allow them to guide me in all aspects of my life. We may not know the meanings of them for years, but figuring them out again is a part of the process. If we believe in a Creator, dreams are one way in which our Creator communicates with us. It is important that we listen.

What are some things that revive you? How does your spirituality guide you and keep you balanced? How can you learn about your spirituality? I learned that spirituality for me is about balance and connection, about understanding my relations and my responsibilities to my family and community and nation. Those responsibilities are aspects of my spirituality. Jamie (Seneca) talked about his participation in the longhouse and the strength he draws from it:

◆ I grew up by myself, actually, because I was kinda different. You know, I stayed away from trouble. I went to the longhouse, and I participated in most of our religious ceremonies. I was really the first child to do that. So, everybody viewed me as different, kinda a good kid, stayed out of trouble [by going to] the longhouse, did a lot of stuff no other kids did. I'm the oldest out of my brothers and sisters, and I'm the oldest grandchild, so I really have to do . . . everything the first. That was one of the reasons why I got so strong in my religious background was because I was by myself and I wanted to do stuff for the community, do stuff for myself to make myself feel good. And it has. Culture has played a big role in my life because I was the only child to ever participate and sing in the longhouse. So, it's kind of been a big role for me. You know, all the elders are trying to teach me so I can do it when I get their age; it's played a big role.

For many students, it was their spirituality that helped them stay out of trouble, get off drugs and alcohol, or get back on the Red Road, or the Good Path, as it is known among the Anishinaabeg. Megan (Ojibwe) went on to share how her spirituality has kept her strong, connected, and grounded in who she is:

◆ My mom, for a while before I was born, she quit going to ceremonies and going to pipe ceremonies and going to the Midewiwin lodge and stuff. . . . after her grandma died, because it was her grandma that would always take her. Her mom and dad are both alcoholics. And so, after she married my dad and after they had us—I have a twin brother, we were about eight—they started going to the Midewiwin lodge again, and that was the first time I had been introduced to it. We would just go and watch. We went every summer, and we tried to go to as many winter and fall ceremonies as we could, and we started having feasts and pipe ceremonies and sweats, and it became a more and more regular thing. It was right before I started becoming an adult, and so it's always been with me. I've grown up with it, and so it's really important to me. I think religion in general should be really important to everybody. I think that's why I've kept myself out of trouble, because of my traditional ways.

Clearly, a strong sense of spirituality is the foundation in which these students' identities are rooted.

Culture Connection

There are many different ways to find a connection to our culture even if we have not been brought up with it. For some of us it takes coming into adulthood, meeting the right person, or spending time with an elder or grandparent or auntie or uncle. Others simply are blessed with having it as a part of their home-life experience. Daisy (Yurok) explained how school was her connection and doorway to her culture:

◆ I think [culture] didn't play a part until like I moved here, because they didn't have Native American programs at the other schools. And I wasn't aware, I didn't even know I was Native American for a long time. You know, I didn't acknowledge it because so many other things are important. So when I moved here, it was important because of Indian Club. That's what really got me interested and aware. And then, moving to the reservation, I learned to fish and bead and braid bear grass, but I think Indian Club was the biggest thing that got me involved.

Listening to Daisy made me both happy and sad. Sad because, like Daisy, I, too, thought other things were more important. I failed for a long time to acknowledge my Anishinaabeg culture and all it has to offer. On the other hand, I am also happy that she has made connections and relationships that are a part of her healthy identity development and journey to that culturally grounded sense of self.

I remember interviewing Will, a soft-spoken, Lakota/Ojibwe young man who had a spark in his eyes. His eyes were not filled with hopelessness but with hope and determination. He spoke quite honestly about how his identity is rooted in his culture and observed that this link is missing in many of his friends' lives:

◆ [The elders] say you make it through school and you'll have a good life and keep practicing the ways . . . [but] it's really, really hard to keep up with these ways when . . . you're growing up. . . . So culture has really played a lot in my life, all through my life. . . . It's a lot about identity. With other kids, they don't know about their culture. . . if they don't really know who they are, they're going to go a separate way and they won't really know about their ways. . . . I see that when someone gets older and they want to come back to these ways. . . they don't know anything about it. . . . All of your life you search for an identity, who you really are. And this is who I am, and this is my identity, my culture. That is how I was born, that is how I was raised. . . . I really love these ways. That's why I live, I keep going.

Pride in Being American Indian, First Nations, or Alaska Native

Another aspect of the students' stories about identity revolved around the theme of pride in being an Indigenous person. This may have meant different things to different students, and how each student showed pride varied, but pride clearly echoed through many of their voices. When I interviewed Fred, a young Choctaw man, never before had I met someone of his young 16 years so confident and secure in understanding who he was. Pride in his family, community, and tribe shone through his big, dark brown eyes. He said: "For me, being American Indian, I like the way I am. I like who I am and wouldn't really want to change anything about me." Fred sounded content and grounded, with his feet firmly planted, and satisfied with who he is. Tom (Mohawk) continued this theme of pride: "I'm a different person from everybody else. There is not another person that is like me. It's like I'm Native and proud of it. My mother and father kinda made sure of that, made sure I was proud of being Native."

Jana (Hoopa) shared how this pride is evident in her life:

◆ Whether there was like five Indian kids in the whole [school] out of 1,000 kids of every race, we'd still be just as proud to be who we are. Some more than others, and some for different reasons. Either way, every one of us is proud.

When Jamie (Seneca) was asked why he seemed to be making it in school, his response was to the point: "Because we care about ourselves, we have self-respect . . . and we just want to see ourselves become successful." I, too, want to see our young people be successful and be filled with that pride that flows from the students' voices. That, in part, is why I helped write this book.

Connection to Place or to a Healthy Person

As Indigenous people, we have a unique relationship and connection to the land, to Mother Earth. We come from the earth. She has given us life, so, in return, we respect her and acknowledge her in our prayers and ceremonies. Joseph Bruchac describes this:

> When you ask a Native American person about himself or herself, they will often begin by talking about their family. That is because our families make us who we are. To talk about myself, about my concept of home-ground, I must talk about that land which shaped my ancestors, that land which made us and continues to make us.[5]

In addition to this land relationship, we have unique assets in our lives. Those assets include our values of extended family, respect for elders, and the wisdom of our grandmothers, grandfathers, and ancestors. This, ultimately, is an aspect of our spirituality.

Thunder, a Hoopa student, talked about connection to land, specifically his homeland and how he is unable to leave:

> ◆ When I go on the hills and I pray, it relieves me. 'Cause on my hill, there's this really big rock up there, and you can see the whole valley. It looks so nice; it relaxes me. Beautiful up there. Clears my head. You know, I tried [to go away], I went away for a little while and I couldn't handle it. This place is not really exciting. It's just, I don't know, it has the power to drive you back. I try to get somebody else to explain it to me 'cause they said they felt the same way. They tried to move away, and they couldn't. It's nice up there 'cause you can actually relax and listen to all the birds. The creek by it, it's kind of cool.

This land connection is a part of who Thunder is. It is a thread of the very fabric that holds him together. It is a relationship we were given, just by the mere fact we were born Indigenous people of this continent. Thunder has come to acknowledge and understand this relationship. In addition to his connection to the land, he talked about the sense of responsibility he has to family:

> ◆ I do a lot for my aunties, do a lot for my grandma. I kill a deer, I give them 75 percent of it and keep 25 percent for myself. When I can fish, I give, you know, whatever. And if I have jerky, I'll send it to my grandfather in [town]."

Melanie, an Abenaki student from Canada, spoke to this connection and love of her land:

> ◆ I adore the reservation. I'm proud to be an Indian. I believe that everyone who lives

---

[5]Bruchac, *Roots of Survival*, 19.

here is proud to be Indian. I believe that what makes us proud is the fact that we're here to help each other. Whenever we have a problem, we're sure there'll be someone to help. There are always exceptions, of course. I adore the reservation and the people who live here also.

What Melanie described is the deep love she feels for her community and her land. She has made the connection between place and sense of self and understands how this helps in being proud of where you come from. I have learned to listen to these things in the many different ways Mother Earth speaks to us. It is a way for me to understand my relations and my place in these relations. We must first look within ourselves. This allows us the capability to really listen. Bruchac adds:

> There is a word in the Cree language which describes the place that knowledge and stories come from. It is, it seems, the center of creativity. That word is *achimoona* and it translates as the "sacred place within." I believe that the greatest one is that we will only find peace and fulfillment when we are able to look into our own hearts while thinking of the common good.[6]

Diddems (Hoopa) talked about the strong relationships she has with her father, elders, and grandmother. When asked who she looks up to, she responded:

◆ My elders, they teach you a lot—teach you how to respect them and stuff. One thing you shouldn't do is disrespect them. Some kids just don't care, but I do. My grandma helps me with my fund-raising sometimes. She helps me make pies, stuff like that. She just helps me out a lot. My dad teaches me a lot of stuff too. He teaches me what's right and wrong, why I should go to school, get an education. We dance our religious dances together too.

Full Circle

When I asked an Anishinaabe elder about identity, she said this to me:

◆ The Anishinaabeg were born to this land. Nothing can take this away from us or change this. It is who we are. When our kids understand this, it becomes like a coat of armor. Nothing that is said or done can penetrate this. Our children discriminate against each other because of skin color and blood quantum. It's right here (she put her hands to her heart), inside of us, what's in your heart. You can't be one-fourth Indian or one-sixteenth Indian or one-half. You were born Indian, and that's who you are and always will be.

I, too, have come to realize how powerful this coat of armor can be, but it has taken me my time on this earth to do so.

I shared a personal story in this chapter of how ashamed I was to wear my Indian Club jacket while secretly ad-

---

[6]Ibid., 104.

miring others for wearing them. As I became older and sought out my true identity, I couldn't wait to have something to *show* I was Anishinaabe. I think I was the first student to pay for our Anishinaabe Club jacket my third year of college at the university I now work for. Although this jacket now hangs in my own home's front closet, it hangs faded and worn. That is where it belongs because my coat of armor now is what's in my heart, not what's worn on my back. It is more about the way I go about living my life, just being me, aspiring to make life better for the generations that come after me, so that they might find their coats of armor exactly where the Creator has put them—inside their hearts.

Chapter 4
When Life Gets Tough

In this chapter, students across North America speak about challenges they face, illustrating that we're all in this together. Amy Bergstrom begins with a story about her friend Gordee and talks with the students about the problems they encounter at school. But not all problems are based in the school. Thomas Peacock describes the internalized oppression that can make dealing with families and communities tough, and Linda Miller Cleary explains why these problems make concentrating on schoolwork hard. The chapter ends with the story of a young woman named Josie, who faced a situation she should not have had to face. It is important to hear how these various people confront their problems because the stories of others can become a sort of shield when things seem to be coming from all directions.

Life presents problems to all young adults, but American Indian, First Nations, and Alaska Native young adults often have a special set of problems they encounter in life and in school. Challenges await Native students daily, from facing racism and discrimination in public settings to the problems Native people sometimes bring upon themselves partly as a result of colonization.

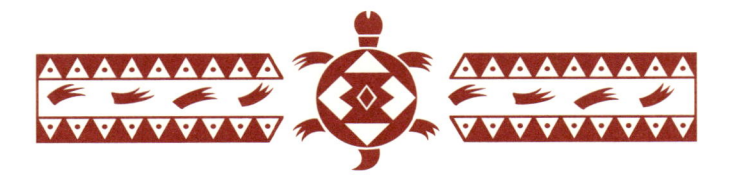

Things We Have to Deal with in School

Gordee's Story

by Amy Bergstrom

Gordee was one of those dark-skinned Indian students who rode in from the reservation to our public school on the school bus. He stands out to me now as I reflect back on my school experience and try to remember all the things that we, as Indian students, had to adjust to in the public school system. Gordee, who came from a more traditional home, had to accommodate his learning style to learn the ways in which the teachers and curriculum expected him to learn. Much of our public school experience took us out of our natural ways of being and learning. Now, as an educator, I see why we, as Native students, had challenges and struggles on a daily basis throughout our school experience. Some of us had an easier time with these challenges; some of us internalized the stuff we had to deal with; some of us fought back; and some of us simply quit, walked right out those front doors, never to return to school as a student again. Gordee was one who walked out.

Gordee was short and stocky, built like a rock. He had shoulder-length black hair, dark brown skin, and deep-set dark brown eyes. He was tough as nails and had earned a reputation as someone not to mess with. He dealt with being picked on by fighting, having been taught these skills by his older brother who had also been picked on. Gordee and I became good friends in middle school. We rode on the same school bus and had many of the same teachers in elementary school, so, by the time we hit middle and high school, we had become pretty good friends. Although there was a rough side to Gordee, he had a gentleness that made him a pleasure to be around. We stuck up for each other, and I learned a great deal about Gordee, his life growing up on the reservation, and the traditions that I had not been taught at home. I learned about wild ricing and the sugar bush, and I looked for Gordee daily to hear more and more about how he filled his time after school, living out many of our traditional cultural practices.

It was always a disappointment to me when I boarded the bus and didn't see Gordee. I looked forward to hearing a new story or his latest adventure, which he had become accustomed to sharing with me. Attendance at school was a big problem for Gordee. It seemed the farther along we got in school, the more Gordee missed. I could never quite figure this out, as I kept my sights on graduation, closer each day to getting out for good. By our 10th-grade year in high school, Gordee was missing a lot of school. More often than not, his desk was vacant, from skipping class, getting kicked out of class, or just not being in school.

It wasn't until I learned about his responsibilities outside of school that I understood these absences. Gordee was an integral part of his family's survival. Putting food on the table and keeping the house warm were responsibilities to which each family member contributed. Gordee trapped, fished, hunted, and went wild ricing. He could track animals by knowing their behaviors, which are affected by both weather and the location of the moon. He observed tracks and marks left on trees, bank, and brush. Gordee was up early many mornings, no matter how cold, to hunt, fish, split wood, or check on his traps.

Gordee would frequently skip our English class that year to avoid the hassle he faced for not having read his chapter, not having an excused absence, or simply not having an insight regarding our nightly reading assignment. On many of those days, when Mrs. R would be taking attendance, we would see Gordee walk by the classroom window to the woods, where all the skippers would go and hang out. The woods behind our school made an ideal skipping spot because if you were just skipping one class, you were within earshot of the bell and knew when to go back into the building and blend into the hallway crowd. It was no secret that Gordee missed a lot of school and a lot of our English class that semester. Our English teacher, during the course of her *My Fair Lady* unit, seemed to make it a point to let the class know when Gordee's desk was empty.

"Would everyone please open up to chapter 10? Your assignment last night was to read chapters 10, 11, and 12," Mrs. R said, looking out at us over the rims of the reading glasses perched on the tip of her nose.

Mrs. R's desk faced our desks, which were all perfectly aligned facing her, five desks per row. I was fortunate enough to have the last desk in the first row. This allowed me a bird's-eye view of my classmates, who I found intriguing. Gordee, however, wasn't so fortunate; he was put right in front, the first desk, third row, directly in front of Mrs. R's desk.

"Gordon, how would you describe the protagonist and his actions in chapter 10?" Mrs. R questioned. You could hear the rustling of pages as people scrambled to review the chapter or at least find a name they could throw out so they might have appeared to have read the assignment. The ones who had done their reading had their hands held high in the air, displaying their eagerness to answer the question. Those of us who hadn't read kept our heads down, fumbling through the soft pages of our paperbacks, anxiously looking to find chapter 10.

Gordee's book was always tucked away in his corduroy jeans. His book was bent ever so slightly to fit in his back pocket. No matter what novel we were reading, Gordee's was always in his back pocket. His paperbacks were permanently creased, and I always got a chuckle when watching him try to smooth out the fold and creases of his book so it could lie flat open like the rest of ours. Usually by the time Gordee had smoothed out his book, Mrs. R had already moved us onto another task.

On this particular day, however, something different happened when Gordee pulled the paperback out. Folded, creased, with a slightly torn cover, he gently pulled the book out of his back pocket. As he did this, something he had in his pocket pulled out with the book, and a strange noise filled the room when it hit the floor and rolled toward the center aisle. The instant I heard the sound, I knew it was Gordee's handmade cedar rice knockers. Smooth as silk from hours of sanding by hand, Gordee had shown me his finished product earlier that morning. Gordee quickly reached down to the floor to gather what had fallen, anxious to put the knockers back in his safekeeping. At the same time, however, Mrs. R swiftly walked to the foot of Gordee's desk and placed her foot firmly on his rice knockers. A tense silence filled the room as Gordee peered up at her, keeping one hand firmly on the knockers.

"What have we here, Gordon?" Mrs. R asked with a slight edge in her voice.

"Nothing, just something I was working on in shop class," Gordee replied as he continued his efforts to pick his rice knockers up off the floor.

"These look like some kind of weapon," Mrs. R continued. "What on earth are they? I'm going to have to keep these and show Mr. Johnson after class." Mr. Johnson was our principal that year, and he and Gordee knew each other quite well.

"We wouldn't want you to use these on anyone, knowing all the fighting you do out there on that reservation. Someone could be hurt," Mrs. R said, looking down at Gordee. I knew she had gone too far. Her words penetrated my soul and stung my spirit. Anger filled me as I sat silenced, witnessing yet another head-tohead confrontation between a teacher and fellow classmate.

"Get your feet off of my bawa'ganaak-oon (Ojibwe for rice knockers)," Gordee replied. His tone alone could have backed any one of us off. Mrs. R slowly rolled her feet off the knockers and moved back to her desk as Gordee picked up his beautiful handmade rice knockers. He now was backed into the defensive mode that I had seen him in so many times before.

"Gordee, you can bring your things down to Mr. Johnson's room and explain to him what it is you are carrying around with you, and then spend the rest of the hour in Patsy's room," said Mrs. R. Patsy was the Indian education teacher in our school, and we would often get sent to her room if things in class weren't going well or if our regular classroom teacher thought we should spend our class time in Patsy's room. I now see an element of racism motivating these efforts to remove us from the classroom.

Gordee gathered up his things, and as Mrs. R sat behind her desk with her arm stretched outright, holding his hall pass, he simply raised his middle finger to her and walked out of class.

This was the last time Gordee was in class, and not long after that, he left school.

Indigenous people across North America place high value on connections and relations, on connections with our families and all things around us. School immediately became an unnatural experience for Gordee, who had trouble separating out knowledge and experience. For Gordee, learning science by observing the ricing of our lakes and math by measuring or calculating the size of the harvest might have been natural ways to connect subject disciplines to tribal sources of knowledge. But generally speaking, school does not teach us in these ways; instead it separates knowledge into content areas, each topic covered in a standard chunk of time before students are moved onto the next. Further, spiritual and mental well-being are not addressed in the general education classroom. For me and many other Native students, there has been a disconnection between our daily lives and what is taught and how things are taught. This isolates many of us. *My Fair Lady* offered nothing more to us than 50 minutes of sheer boredom and resentment every day from 10:00 until 10:50 a.m., when that bell would ring and set us free. Nothing about the book or story related to the life I was leading, and now, as a teacher myself, I know none of it meant squat to my classmates either, especially to Gordee. The irony I see now is that the school and teachers were implementing many of the same practices that the main character in *My Fair Lady* was using. He was trying to change a woman into something he wanted her to be, not something she was naturally. This is exactly what was happening to Gordee. At the time, I didn't make sense of all his absences, other than attributing them to his rebellion towards school and life. I was dead wrong about this.

Gordee, like many of my other Native classmates, especially those living a more traditional life on the reservation, had certain responsibilities outside of school that needed attention, responsibilities that put the notion of teaching and learning in a different light. Those responsibilities were directly connected to who Gordee was, an Anishinaabe young man who brought a culture and a life into the classroom. His life was more seasonal. The traditional life of the Anishinaabeg did not follow a school calendar, but a seasonal calendar, one that our ancestors lived by, harvesting mahnomen (wild rice) in the fall and tapping maple trees for syrup in the spring. These commitments were great. Participating in these activities was not just a family and community event but also a spiritual one.

Each season offered opportunities for us to give thanks for the abundant gifts given us and to honor and celebrate the cycle of life. In my eyes, then as a student and now as an educator, Gordee was an untapped body of knowledge. If it weren't for my mother placing a strong value on education, I would have been right behind Gordee out those front doors.

The experience in Mrs. R's class stands out to me now as I write for this chapter and read similar stories from the students we interviewed across North America. There are still many disturbing, disrupting events we face as American Indian, Alaska Native, and First Nations students in school. I remember the anger I felt sitting helplessly, witnessing the unfairness and disrespect many teachers showed our culture, our families, and our values. This anger and emotion was there again as I sat interviewing students across North America, listening to them talk about the same challenges, the same unfairness, and the same kinds of isolation I had felt. As I sat across from these students, I thought about the untapped body of knowledge they held and about my luck in being given a part of their stories. These articulate, brilliant students spoke to me so eloquently about their schooling experiences. Painful as this was at times, their stories will help change the way our children and grandchildren experience school.

It's Coming from All Directions

Having to deal with things that bombard us during school makes it hard to learn. Challenges come at us in many different forms and through many different types of behavior and people. Pointing this out enables us to recognize the challenges for what they are and to rise above them. The students we met talked about the different forms these challenges take, including curriculum, teaching and discipline practices, and peer harassment.

Curriculum and Teaching Practices

Jaime (Seneca) commented on the lack of Native perspectives in her school curriculum:

◆ It's [English and literature] all about Americans, not Native Americans, just plain Americans. That's all. That's all they teach us, nothing about Native Americans. It's like they always talk about the wars and stuff, how the Indians did all this stuff. I'd like to teach American history. I'd like to teach it myself so that I could get up in front of the class and tell a lot of students what really happened.

Lisa (Dakota) talked about the racism embedded in required reading—racism teachers seem unaware of or dismiss when it is pointed out to them:

◆ In one of my English classes last year, there was this one teacher reading *The Light in the Forest*. It's a really racist book, and I had trouble reading it. I'd bring it home and say, "I don't want to read this." And my parents were like, "Well, you have to; it's for your class." We were in class one day, and there was this girl reading, and it said "squaw." And I know what squaw means—it's a corrupted French word that means a woman's private part—and I told that to the teacher, and she didn't really believe me. You know, and I was thinking, an educated teacher should know what this means.

Carol (Navajo), a very energetic young woman, talked about her difficulties in keeping her own culture while she learned the knowledge and culture of the school, and in rising above her teachers' low expectations for Native students:

◆ I think that at times it's difficult to be Native American in school because you're learning a lot of new ideas and new ways of doing things. And I think that it's difficult to try to keep like culture with some of those new ideas and new things that you're learning. And I think that sometimes it's hard because I wish that we could learn like things about . . . our people and about different nations, different Native American nations. And I don't think [teachers] set very high standards for you. And I think a lot of times, Native students kinda get pushed to the back of the classroom, or they're kinda put on the back burner.

When Life Gets Tough

Celeste's (Seneca) story reminds me of Gordee and how he dealt with things coming from all directions:

◆ It was American History in 11th grade, and the teacher wrote, "All Native Americans turned to alcoholism to ease their pain," and she put *all* in like big letters and underlined it twice, and I said that was f___ed up. And I walked out, and then I got suspended for three days, and she didn't even have to apologize to me or nothing. Then, when I played softball, well, I don't play anymore because I missed one practice, and they called me an alcoholic.

When we are on the receiving end of racism and negativity towards our family and community, anger often is an easy way to deal with our pain and frustration. Gordee clearly chose this way, as did Celeste when she became the object of stereotyping. The trick is to find ways to let the anger cool down and to use this cold anger to energize your efforts to overcome such stereotyping in school.[1] Oppression is wrong and unfair and should not be happening in our schools, and you have every right to be angry; but not learning positive ways to deal with these things will only push you farther down. Some teachers are open to changing assignments and other curriculum if they learn that it is offensive; others are not. Sometimes, students have to take the initiative to let teachers know.

Travis (Dakota) talked about how he took ownership of his work to teach his classmates and teachers a little bit about himself and his culture. This cannot happen unless you are given a choice over your assignments; fortunately, Travis had some choice in his project.

◆ I had a history class, and the teacher never taught anything about Native Americans, except maybe one chapter that lasted one day, when you spent weeks on other chapters. So I was kind of upset 'cause kids really didn't know what the real story was. And so, we had to choose a topic in history, what we wanted to do. Anyway, we had to get up in front of the class and explain what happened. So, everyone chose World War I and World War II, the Civil War. [When it came to] Wounded Knee, almost every kid in the class looks at me, and I was like, "All right." So I got in front of the class, and I had pictures of a Gatlin gun, [which] they used on the women and children.... I turned all the lights off, and I told them to close their eyes, and I told everyone. I told the story about what happened, some of the detail: the soldiers walked up to a baby, put a gun to his head, point blank, and shot it. And sometimes, to save bullets, they'd beat the heads in with the butt of the gun. Everyone was in tears. I guess that made me feel better because now they knew just one part of what Native American people had to go through.

Discipline Practices

Many students talked about how they had been treated differently than their non-Native peers or classmates. For example, Megan (Ojibwe) observed a clear double standard in her school:

---

[1] See Rogers, *Cold Anger* for a story about how Mexican Americans used their anger to fight against discrimination.

- Oh, I've seen it like millions of times, you know, like a Native student late for class or something, and they write that person up. They'll say, "Why are you late?" And they may give them a tardy slip to get detention, and a White student may walk in and they'll say, "Well, why were you late?" And [the White students will] say, "Oh, my locker got stuck," and the teacher will be like, "Okay, well don't be late next time!" I've seen that happen, seen Native people get yelled at more for like the same things that White students may be doing. If a Native guy's wearing really baggy pants, you know, they'll make him go home, or they'll suspend him because they'll think, "Oh, he must be in a gang. Oh, he must have a gun." And then, if some basketball players wear baggy pants, if some White kid is wearing baggy pants, he might not get suspended: "Oh, he's a basketball player. He won't be hiding any guns."

Peer Harassment

Next to family, friends rank among the most important influences in our lives. They can affect the places we go, the decisions we make regarding our bodies, whether we use drugs or alcohol, even the way we dress or the music we listen to. When our classmates, peers, or friends (or people we consider our friends) hurl insults or project attitudes towards us simply about our race and ethnicity, it is painful and can be humiliating. As Lisa's (Dakota) comments reflect, racism can leave us with feelings of pain, anger, and isolation:

- I thought elementary was really hard for me, from about third grade until I moved up here.... I used to get teased on the bus; there was this fourth-grade kid who used to push [me] down on the bus and call me "nigger." And I used to pretend I had really bad headaches, and I'd go to the nurse everyday, and I'd get sent home [to] my Aunt Kim's house or back home, and, you know, I'd be okay after I was home. I hated going to school and getting teased and having teachers be mean to me. I was still little; I didn't know what was going on.... Even in one of my kindergarten recitals, we have me on tape singing, "One little, two little, three little Indians."

North Star (Abenaki) discussed forms of unchallenged racist stereotyping:

- I hate Halloween at our school. There's a lot of people that dress up like what they supposedly think Native American people look like. Me and my friend are walking down the hallway, and there's this kid with like this big, funky, colored headdress thing and a little tomahawk. I'm thinking, "What the heck?" And like . . . no one said anything to him the whole day, and I [thought] "That's wrong. That's wrong!"

North Star summed up what he thinks is the problem with trying to educate people or correct misinformation about our culture and communities: "There's always got to be stupid people to make good people. [Stupid people] never understand. Even when you tell them, they just get more mad, and they want to kill you. It's almost like they've got cotton towels in their ears, and they don't want to listen."

When Life Gets Tough

We will never be able to change what every person thinks or does not know about our lives, our communities, our culture, and our history. We can only be sure we know where we come from, who we are, and the direction we are going. *Mino-bimaadiz-win,* "the Good Path," is what in Anishinaabeg we call "living the good life." Remaining on this path helps us dodge or deflect to some degree the many different stones that are cast our way. Freddy D (Hoopa), whom I interviewed last winter, taught me the importance of this and how he overcomes these many challenges:

◆ The thing that keeps me in school, even when things are kind of down, is probably the fact that if I don't have an education, I'm not going to go anywhere. That's what keeps me going. I know there are a lot of days that I wish I could just stay home and sleep and just hang out and not come to school at all. But then I realize that if I do that, I may be having a good time at that present time, but later on, down in the future, when I have to collect welfare checks, have to work a minimum wage job, it's going to be a whole lot worse. And so, I'd rather stick to school and get the education that I need to go on. That's basically what continues keeping me in school, even though there are times when I want to give up.

Things We Have to Cope with in Our Communities and Families

Tom

We can better understand the troubling issues facing Native people—including you, as young people—by comprehending the nature and extent of the dysfunction that plagues many of our families, communities, and tribes. This begins with understanding the nature of our oppression and the ways many of us have internalized it, or taken it inside of us—a process that works against us. First, we need to identify what an oppressor and oppression—both external and internal—look like.

Oppression

What is an oppressor? An oppressor could be someone who abuses others physically, psychologically, or sexually. These individuals tell the abused they are less worthy of respect than other people. Oppressors usually ignore the fact that culturally different people have their own histories, poetry, songs, and literature, as if these things never existed. An oppressor could be someone who believes his or her own philosophy or religion is the only acceptable one and who considers the beliefs of other groups to be primitive or to be myths or legends. An oppressor could be someone who doesn't value other people's input or accept others' opinions. In their worst acts, oppressors kill or injure other people. The Jewish Holocaust, the genocide of Native people in the Americas, and the slaughter of millions of Cambodians are just a few examples of this extreme form of oppression. The

47

killing of one individual by another is a form of oppression.

Often, the oppressed eventually turn against one another. In these instances, the hatred can turn into a twisted form of self-hate, causing the oppressed to become oppressors themselves. Some of the U.S. cavalry scouts used against American Indian nations were fellow American Indians. The most feared guards in the Nazi death camps were often Jews. Young people who have been abused have a higher than normal risk of becoming abusers themselves. Negative patterns, if not disrupted, will tend to repeat from one generation to the next. For instance, children of alcoholics are more likely to become alcoholics, although this is certainly not inevitable, especially if some caring person helps break the pattern.

Without such help oppressed people eventually begin to believe all the negative things the oppressor thinks of them. Young physically abused people sometimes think they are responsible for their abuse. They might start thinking they would not get abused if only they were better people—if they would keep a cleaner room or if they would listen. Oppressed people may begin oppressing themselves through acts of self-destruction, such as alcoholism, drug abuse, and suicide. The problems with alcohol and the abnormally high rates of suicide in some American Indian communities are examples of how we abuse ourselves.

Acknowledging both the oppression we suffer at the hands of mainstream society and the internalized oppression we suffer at our own hands is the first step to freeing ourselves. Confronting ourselves is the first and most painful step to liberating us and our communities from these problems.

Contradictions

We live with contradictions, which make up the gulf between the ideal world we are led to believe in and the real world we live in. This gulf has prevented us from breaking the great cycle of pain—the generations of poverty, alcoholism, drug use, violence, and various forms of physical, emotional, and sexual abuse we have directed at ourselves and our own people.

On one hand, we have cultures of astounding spiritual and cultural depth, with philosophies and lifeways like no others in human civilization. Few know, for example, that the United States' unique form of democracy was modeled after the League of the Iroquois's constitution, the *Great Law of Peace*. The Iroquois model recognized that each of the five tribes of the Iroquois had certain powers and responsibilities but that a union of the tribes under a central government made their nation even stronger. Foundations of the United States Constitution, such as states' rights and federal rights, arose from the Iroquois model.[2] Even today, our Native communities are experiencing a great cultural and spiritual renaissance, producing some of the world's most gifted writers, renowned musicians and artisans, and compelling orators.

Yet, on the other hand, many of our people suffer from the deep multigenerational soul wound caused by colonization, genocide, forced assimilation, racism, and poverty. And so, many of us wear that wound on our hearts, and it shows

---

[2] Grinde and Johansen, *Exemplar of Liberty*.

in everything we do. Triumph and tragedy exist together. Love and self-hatred form part of the same circle. We are joyous. We grieve. My friend Linda LeGarde Grover once said that for Native people, even in times of great happiness, there is great sadness. Even in times of great sadness, there is great happiness.

I see the contradictions all around me. Gang members walk among respected traditional elders around the circles at the summer pow-wows. Some grandmas are raising the babies of their children, who have either abandoned their families or have too many personal problems to be raising children. A culture teacher who has a reputation for molesting young girls is allowed to continue working with youth. An administrator whose personnel file is filled with accusations of sexual harassment is hired to run a school. A politician who has served time for stealing money from his tribe is allowed to run for office again and has substantial community support. Some of the housing projects in my community have become breeding grounds for problems, including violence, drug dealing, alcoholism, and poverty. And just down the road is the tribal headquarters, in perfect repair, with a new fleet of government vehicles waiting to take employees off to training seminars on how better to serve the people. It isn't as if no one cares. Most of us who seek positive change are community people ourselves, and we want only the best for the people. Yet the contradictions remain, coexisting in a most sacred and beautiful place.

I ask myself how we have come to accept these contradictions. How can we have such intense beauty and such deep pain living side by side, all at the same time? And how and when will we break this great cycle of pain? When will our children stop suffering from the dysfunction in our own communities? It is the great challenge facing the Seventh Generation.

Community Problems

Later in this book we will focus on what is strong and good in our communities. But we cannot ignore the kinds of things that aren't right in our communities and how they affect young people. We heard many stories from the youth we interviewed about community problems, or *dysfunction* (when things aren't right, aren't functioning well). When did dysfunction begin? Our ancestors experienced community problems, but those weren't as devastating as the problems our people experience today. Some of the problems in our communities are directly related to historic oppression, like being forced to attend boarding schools. Fred (Choctaw) explained:

◆ I think it's an oppression thing because my parents' generation were taken from their homes and put in the boarding schools and forced to forget their traditional ways, never to speak their language, banned and punished for doing what they knew as life. And it created controversy in their minds. So, when it was time for them to teach their children, they had to choose; "What should I teach them? Should I teach the old ways or should I teach them the dominant society ways so they aren't punished like I was, so they won't have to go through what I went through?" But a lot of that generation, instead of teaching both, they chose the dominant society because it had been burned into their head so much. They no longer wanted to be Indian; they no longer wanted to have to deal with the traditional ways, because the rest of the world, so they thought, wasn't dealing with those issues. They would rather not torment their children with those issues. And it's a bad thing. It's regretful. I see it a lot today, a lot of my peers don't know what the dances are. They don't know why they're done, and their ignorance will be our demise.

When a community starts to experience problems, the issues look similar to when individuals begin to have problems. Both experience disharmony. A lot of times, the community is bound together in friendship and in harmony. But sometimes, that kind of atmosphere, drugs and alcohol, tears some of the harmony apart. And it's hard to work with people like that. And it's a shame to see because a lot of people that are in our jail, our police station, were drinking, and they have to pay fines and bail. It hurts the family. It hurts the people around them. And part of it kind of hurts the community. Unfortunately, in this community, there are a lot of people that do use drugs and alcohol.

Gina (Navajo) noted how the loss of culture, which ultimately affects community harmony, has had an impact on cultural events:

◆ We'll go to cultural events like a powwow. . . . Like, the dancers and everything and the music, it's really nice; it's a nice environment to be in. And then you look into the crowd, and the crowd is just completely opposite from what the culture represents. It sickens me to see it. In the center, where everyone will be dancing, you will just see the culture, the richness of it. But some of the things that happen in the parking lots. It's the opposite.

Dysfunction can take the form of people being disrespectful to one another, treating others badly, and not making them feel a part of the community. Chloe Blue Eyes (Seneca) commented:

◆ With the families on the reservation . . . it's all politics. My family won't even go to the [religious ceremonies] because some people would just look at us and go like, "What are you doing here?" . . . my family chooses not to go because they don't want to put up with that. . . .

Another student (who wanted to remain anonymous) added:

◆ We were having problems on the rez. There were threats to our family, about killing us, and so that was really a big worry. I would say that was when I couldn't concentrate because I only had a half an hour of sleep . . . that was a really hard time.

Kelly (Wampanoag) talked about the contradictions in the community she lived in:

◆ It's got its ups and downs. It's got its junkies; it has its bad people. But . . . everybody is so close together; they stick together, and it's just like a really tight community.

Carol, a Navajo student currently living in a city, offered a perspective on ways to heal our communities:

◆ Native American nations were able to thrive because they were communal, and they worked together. I think now, they are like, "This is mine. This is my space." It's really taken a toll on Native Americans everywhere, and I think we should go back to working together.

Finally, Bell-Bell (Seneca) spoke of the need to begin community healing and offered a pathway to begin:

◆ I don't want everybody fighting. It doesn't give the future generations a good idea of what we're all about. They are going to grow up and say, "Well, my mommy and daddy fought," or "Everybody fights, so it makes it look like it's okay." You know we can't give our next generation that outlook. We got to raise them right and show them what's right and what's wrong.

Dysfunction in Families

In many of our traditional cultures, families did not experience the enormity of problems we see today. Problems were dealt with by the community or by other family members. Today, however, the issues are more complicated. This was the case illustrated by Thunder, a First Nations Mohawk student:

◆ My mom pretty much takes care of these kids. She's trying to do what I'm trying to do—improve the community. This girl, she's only 14, and she's going out with a 40 year old, and my mom is the only person to step up and say something about it. She took it to the [authorities], and they were scared of the family. That family is like that. This girl, she ran away from home and went over to that guy's house. The mother didn't really care.

How these issues affect students shows in a variety of ways. Chapter 5, "Breaking Points," talks about the issue of teen pregnancy, demonstrating how some young people deal with it by trying to stay in school during and after pregnancy. How did it become such a serious problem in Indian country? Travis (Dakota) spoke to some of the root causes:

◆ There were three girls who got pregnant. . . . Their mom was a drug addict; their dad was who knows where, at some bar or something. These kids had no clothes. They couldn't afford a winter jacket.

Megan (Ojibwe) tied the issue to family mobility:

◆ There's a lot of families that move around a lot. . . . Their parents don't have stable jobs, and if you switch schools four times a year, what is going to make you want to stay? You can't really get going solidly and learn a lot if you're switching around so much.

As Jazzy (Ojibwe) pointed out, family dysfunction can result from a number of issues, like not knowing your ancestry because of adoption. When youth have to cope with family dysfunction, some will look for substitute families, sometimes in the wrong places.

◆ I was really confused because my grandma wasn't really my grandma, my aunt wasn't really my aunt, and I didn't know who I was. My dad wasn't around. He's Indian, and I don't know my culture . . . and I was thinking, "Well, I don't know who I am." And my mom also told us that my uncle was adopted, and so, they weren't really brothers and sisters—that he molested her. So, that really got me upset, [and] now I'm thinking, "Wow, what a big mess." And it was really hard to come here every day and deal with school issues and go home and deal with all of that. It was too much!

In families where there is great disarray, gang activity has replaced the family. A gang is a group of people who come together, and they are kind of like a family. They help each other out. They are there for each other. And people go to them, I think, because they don't have others who care or love them at home. So they find a group of people who also have that in common, and they form a family. It's not positive because they do horrible things.

We are just now beginning to heal from the dysfunction in our families and communities. And the work being done to heal us is led by people of all colors, races, ages, and both genders. It will take the efforts of many courageous people until the work is complete. Patience is the key. Like people everywhere, Native people want better lives for themselves and their children. All humans are imperfect beings. The cultures we live in are not perfect. We all stray from the Good Path. Then, we dream of better times and a better life for ourselves and all who are important to us. And we live to make it real.

Coping When Things Get Tough

One of my cousins died and then my parents got divorced shortly after. And I still had to go to school every day, and I still had to get good grades. [School] doesn't really fit with the troubles in your life. Life isn't going to stop when something bad happens to you. It just gets you a lot more stressed out when something is happening to you.

—Megan (Ojibwe)

Life can just get *too* tough. Personal problems can add up, at school, at home, and in the community. An anonymous student talked about how life can get so tough that you can't concentrate on your schoolwork:

◆ My Mom and I had a falling out, and we didn't really agree on some things, and I didn't agree with what she was doing. It was just a big clash, and it got a little hectic there, and my grades fell 'cause I couldn't concentrate, and it just really bugged me.

When we are upset, our minds have difficulty focusing on the work at hand. As human beings, it is not something we can help. The area in our brain that is used to concentrate on schoolwork is called the short-term memory. When emotions are high, circumstances that set off strong feelings simply take up too much space in our short-term memories. Even though we try to concentrate, our minds keep going back to what is upsetting. It is hard to focus on schoolwork when the upsetting things are clogging up our minds. Emotions disrupt the workings of the mind, or, as researchers might say, there is emotional disruption of cognition (thinking).[3] This also makes it harder to remember the things we need to remember for a test or other real-life situations. Fred (Choctaw) described how this happens:

◆ There are two ways to feel bad: on the outside, if you're sick, and on the inside, if you're having an emotional problem, and teachers will sometimes ignore [the inside]. If, let's say, a teacher asks you a question, and you have so many thoughts in your mind you didn't pick up on the question, some teachers will snap and get mad. A teacher needs to decipher, to watch people carefully.

In the interviews, many students talked about a time when they had upsetting circumstances in their lives. Some students talked about how they used simple and positive ways to cope with temporary or less severe emotional pain. Desirae (Aleut) said:

◆ If I'm having a hard time, I'll go do something and get my mind off of school for awhile or whatever is bothering me, and then it'll be a little better than it was, and I don't feel quite as bad.

Carol (Navajo) felt that prayer helped:

◆ It sounds kinda weird, but I rely a lot upon prayer to help me get through the days. So I think that like spirituality and prayer help.

Lola (Seneca) coped with problems by "just getting away from everybody, [to] be by myself, just anywhere, I guess, as long as nobody else is around." Rob (Wampanoag) said, "I usually just listen to music. Zone out, sleep. That's it." Jeremy (Aleut) used humor to get beyond depression:

◆ I didn't know I had mild depression until I went to see the psychologist. She was just pointing it all out—this stuff, subjects that I pretty much had in the back of my head, and why I was depressed. She put it plain and simple. [But], if I really want to talk about it, I'll talk to my friends. My friends will listen to me and just make jokes, and I make jokes about it too. It's good to have friends to really help out.

Kat (Ojibwe) found that she could get beyond the pain by writing about it:

◆ If I have a problem with something, I just write down my problem. I learned that through Alateen. I started doing [it in] my own journal.

Writing about problems sometimes helps you work past emotion to find solutions, as does talking with trusted adults or friends. Tarilee (Ojibwe) had another technique:

◆ All you have to do is try to see it from the other side of something. That's what I always try to do. It's a whole lot easier if you do it that way. And, if you are having a problem . . . [realize it] could always be worse.

---

[3]Cleary, *From the Other Side of the Desk*, 80-96.

In writing or in thinking about what's happened to you, you can sometimes look at things from different angles or different people's perspectives. This could help you solve a problem, or it could simply help you be less angry or disturbed in the face of the problem.

Most students we interviewed had figured out productive methods for dealing with life's problems, but some had adopted self-destructive ways. Quoetone (Ojibwe) found a way to cope with depression that kept him physically safe, but he did miss time in school. As he said in chapter 2, "Just let your whole body shut down and sleep for awhile—kind of fainting on a long-term basis. It's a coping skill I can handle." We heard many stories from other students about their friends who had dropped out because they were on drugs or were drinking heavily. Substance abuse, which keeps us from confronting problems, is often the most self-destructive method of coping. North Star (Abenaki), as we learned in chapter 2, made no progress in addressing his troubles when he was using drugs:

◆ When I was all drugged up, I didn't care about nobody.... Now, when I start feeling bad, every time I hurt, I know what it is—living. Before, I was always high; I didn't know what things were. Now I understand things. I look at things now, and I see that things are really beautiful.... The past is the past, the present is the present, and my past has gone away. The one thing I understand is [that] the past helps you for the present. You have to believe in yourself and understand that everybody does bad things in their life, and things can change if you really want them to change.

Clearly North Star has been doing some thinking. He has called on his ability to think about his situation and has made a better life for himself. When you really get down, it's important to remember what so many students told us: things get better. It's hard to imagine that things will get better when you are deep down because many students haven't had many experiences with getting beyond depression. But it is so important to remember that things will get better. As Shana (Ojibwe) said, you can pull yourself "beyond it":

◆ You got to get beyond it. I've messed up, and I gotta take the responsibility. I got suspended for a month, and then I got expelled for another one, and then I came back, and I was in in-school suspension. I sat in there for two weeks, and then I got to come back out, and I was on probation. I was so laid back, "Oh, I can do this next year." And then it comes down to it, and it's too late. I brought it upon myself; I have to take responsibility to change it. If you don't get your high school diploma, you're going to end up working at a cheap little store or something. Now, I'm rushing myself. Now, when my mom thinks about it or when she talks about it, she's like telling everybody she's proud of me because I came back and am doing so good, and I'm on the honor roll.

Some people are more reflective about their lives than others, but everyone has the ability to develop some of the skills that can pull them up from bad times. It's not that you don't need time to heal from the deep wounds, but it is important not to get mired. Those who love you, or who have loved you but passed on, would want you to get back on track, get back to the place where you can work for your future, for your future happiness. Sometimes there will be people you respect, family or friends or elders, to help you get unstuck, and sometimes you will have to do it mostly on your own. Sometimes the issues you have to cope with are not fair. You shouldn't have to deal with the internalized oppression that has affected those you care for and those you love, but that is the way of this world. Sometimes, even those who love you can create problems for you. And though you shouldn't have to, until you and the Seventh Generation deal with those problems, things will not be happy for you or your future children.

Gary Zukav said in his book *The Seat of the Soul* that the way you handle problems today will affect your future and that of many others:

The decisions that you make and the actions that you take upon the earth are the means by which you evolve. At each moment you choose the intentions that will shape your experiences and those things upon which you will focus your attention. These choices affect your evolutionary process. This is so for each person. If you choose unconsciously, you evolve unconsciously. If you choose consciously, you evolve consciously.[4]

The story below is about Josie, who has a real-life problem to cope with. This isn't a real story; I've used characteristics of people I have met and of some people I have heard about to create this story. It could be real, but it represents no one person that I have met or interviewed. Josie is dealing with a contradiction. As you read, think about the strategies Josie uses in trying to cope with her problem, in dealing with the contradictions in her life.

The Beads of the Eagle: A Teaching Story

by Linda Miller Cleary

Josie looked out the window at the lake. It was one of those days when the air was so cold that tendrils of steam rose off the almost frozen water, making it look like spaghetti water just before the rolling boil. There were only a few eagles left, but she didn't see them this morning; they were probably puffed up in their nests, waiting for the sun. She shivered and grabbed what she needed for school, shoved it in her backpack, hauled on her heaviest coat, hooked her dancing dress hanger over her gloved hand, and headed for the door. Just as she was about to burst out into the cold, her mother yelled from a back room, "Would you stop in and see Grandma on your way in from the bus? And don't forget your hat." Her brother would have walked on out without his hat; but, being on the dutiful side, she put everything down, pulled on her hat, loaded everything back up, agreed to stop in and see her grandmother, and ran

---
[4] Gary Zukav, *The Seat of the Soul*, 29.

out the door to the circle where the bus would pick up the reservation kids.

By the time Josie got on the bus, she was glad she had remembered her hat; the group of them had stood behind the roofless bus shelter, huddled together out of the wind, trying to avoid the cold. She had stood at the same place for years with an ever-dwindling number of her friends. There were seven of them left that took the bus to the high school, and the easy bantering that went back and forth kept the shivering down.

Usually, getting on the school bus felt like a sort of loss, but this morning, she was glad to get into the heat of the bus when it pulled up. Tara, who was a senior, dropped down in the seat next to Josie at the last stop on the rez line before the long trip to the regional high school. They both settled themselves into the homework that they hadn't gotten to the night before. As they were entering town, Tara glanced up smiling. "Let me see your dress," Tara said as she glanced down at the plastic bag that held Josie's outfit. Josie pulled the plastic up without taking the dress off the hanger. The beadwork was only a fourth done, but the feathers were already taking shape, and the tail of the eagle was partially done. She was proud of it and had worked hours with Auntie Marilyn, her favorite aunt, to make the original design and trace it on the material. She, her mother, and Auntie Malvina worked on it when they had time together: one dress, two or three laps. Each bead was like a little blessing for her. The dress was coming together from different ends toward the middle. Pretty soon their knees would be knocking, and then, only one person could work on it at a time. By then, the eagle would be done.

"Look at those feathers, great colors with the background. Is that the tail of an eagle? Will it be ready for this summer?" Tara asked. Tara had completed her dress a few years ago and had been a dancer at the summer powwow already.

"Yes, I'm working with Uncle Billy and some other dancers. He wants to see the dress after school at the center."

Tara looked down and said, "Yes, he always wants to see them. You don't have to put it on, you know; just show it to him as you're leaving, when someone is waiting for you."

Josie had been worrying about Uncle Billy. He was old enough to be respected, but she didn't like the way he touched her hair between dances. It was more than an affectionate pat, lingering beyond affection into slime. Tara said, "You're probably the one that will be his favorite this year." Josie wanted to ask questions, but it was just then that the bus pulled up to the school, and Tara jumped up saying, "Always, always have someone wait for you," and she was off the bus.

It wasn't until lunch, after her beastly History class but before her beloved English class, that Josie could snag Shana. "Stay with me after dance this afternoon, will you?" she asked her friend. "Uncle Billy wants to see my dress, and I was hoping you could stay with me for a few minutes."

"Sure," said Shana, "I know, he's way creepy, isn't he? He asked me last year, but I grumbled enough so he started on Louise instead. She isn't much of a grumbler." Louise had not come to dance this year. In fact, no one had seen much of Louise lately. She was one of the ones who didn't get on the school bus anymore.

Josie loved to dance; she couldn't imagine dropping out of her group, especially when the older dancers and singers joined them on a weekend every month with drums. She would be excited all week, and then, on the weekend when the dancing began, she was beyond the learning, beyond the caring of what pattern she was working on. She was in her feet and arms and body, and the drums seemed to be the punctuation of her steps, of her heart beating. She knew what her grandmother was talking about when she talked about the "connected times." She knew that something deep inside her was meant to dance, to celebrate through dancing.

That afternoon, there was still enough light to see the lake out the windows of the school; the tendrils of mist were gone, and it was a grey blue. The eagles were finally out, braced against the wind above the island. She liked the curve of their wings, their strength against the wind. She took a deep breath, a deep sigh, and then went off to her locker to pack her books and get ready for dance in the cafeteria. She came in as late as she reasonably could and plunked her things down on a table. Then, she hung her dress from the corner of a table that was still folded up and looked like some gawky prehistoric bird.

Others were already putting on moccasins. Today, the young ones had come from the reservation elementary school in a minibus to join them. As Uncle Billy picked up his drum, they stopped the dizzying circles they were running on the tan tiles and looked up at him. Uncle Billy smiled and patted one of the youngest on the head—just a pat—and began talking of the dance, the drums, the story behind the dance they would work on today. Some of Josie's young cousins were there, and they crowded to stand next to her.

Uncle Billy said, "Josie, show those cousins of yours that part of the dance," and he drummed. The drum was his thin, hand-held drum, but the rhythm was there, and she danced beyond the cafeteria tiles, beyond the pterodactyl lunch tables, out of the room, and into her steps, until she was dancing for herself and for something bigger than them all. She tried holding her arms like the wings of the eagle and felt some strength in them that she hadn't felt before. When the drum stopped, she was startled to see she was still in the cafeteria, and Uncle Billy was looking at her in that way she didn't like, with a bit of amazement hanging onto the edge of his leer. An hour later, they had to stop because the late bus would be leaving. Josie pulled out her dress, and her cousins and the others gathered around to see how it was coming.

Uncle Billy said, "Go in and put it on, Josie."

But Shana piped up, "We have to leave in five minutes on the bus."

Josie was quick to add, "Maybe another time, Uncle Billy, when we've gotten it farther along."

The others moved off to put their things together, but Uncle Billy moved in to get a close look at the dress. "I see the beginnings of an eagle there," he said. "That's a strong bird for a beautiful young woman like you." His hand touched her hair again, in that lingering way, and then he brushed against her breast as he bent down to touch the end of the eagle feathers. "Next month, I will drive you home and have a chance to see you in that dress."

Shana yelled out from the door, "Hurry up Josie, the bus is already loading." Josie grabbed the dress without putting it in the bag, along with her jacket and backpack and hat, and ran for the door, whispering "THANK YOU" to Shana, as she caught up with her.

They jumped on the bus and the doors closed behind them. The only seats left were at the front of the bus and none were together. Josie put on her coat, stuffed her bag under the seat, and dropped down in the seat, her hands bumping into the seat in front of her. She glanced down at her dress, at the place where Uncle Billy had touched it, at the tail of the eagle, and shivered. In the dim light of the bus, the beads didn't seem to reflect the light as much as they used to. She felt as if her breast had been bruised instead of brushed and wished she could pull her shirt off, cram it in the washing machine, and cram his fingers into the agitator with it and watch them break apart. She kicked the seat in front of her and then looked innocent when the boy sitting in it turned around.

It was dark by the time the bus let the rez kids off at the end of the line, and groups plodded off in their separate directions. John, a longtime friend who lived in her direction, walked with Josie awhile in silence. She couldn't think of anything interesting to say, and, it would seem, neither could he. It was almost a relief to turn off at Grandma's house, which was just a ways down that road. The porch had a couple of generations of kids' toys scattered around. She remembered the many days, many years, she had stopped there on her way home from school because her mother worked in the tribal office every day until 5:00 and her father was often fishing. She opened the door and walked into the warm hall, taking in Grandma's smell: rice cooking and something vaguely sweet that she had never identified. She yelled from the front hall, "Grandma, do you want me to shovel that walk? A few inches must have fallen last night. I didn't even notice it this morning."

"No, dear, come in here," Grandma called. "I'm cooking something for you to take home for your family's dinner. Your mother's going to pick you up on her way home from the tribal office. So how was your day? Help me with these dishes, will you?"

"We had dancing. And we heard the story of the drums for the millionth time," Josie told her grandmother. "But Auntie Marilyn's kids were there, and I was amazed at how quiet they were when Uncle Billy was speaking, just listening like I've never seen them do before." Up to her elbows in soapy water, Josie continued, "And Uncle Billy talked about elders and told a story about respect—you know, the one about the raccoon and the blind brothers. And then we got to dance, and you know how I love that!"

"I've seen how you love that, dear," her grandmother said.

Then, Josie asked, "Grandma, what happens if you don't like being around an elder, but they want you to do special things for them?"

"You know, it's important to respect those older than you, even though they do things that you don't agree with," Grandma advised. "Concentrate on looking hard, granddaughter, and you will find things to respect. Young people will respect you when you are old. It's the way that things work. We respect all living things, but give special respect to those who have earned it with years."

It was as if her grandmother's voice came out of the ages. It held no room for argument. Josie sighed and wondered where its meaning was for her. She had overheard Tara once grumble to a cousin, "We have no right to disrespect or anything. We're not supposed to talk disrespectfully about elders, but with everything that we know about some of them and things we even know our parents know, it makes it a lot harder to respect some of those uncles, and we could get in trouble if we went along with them." She hadn't quite understood what Tara had meant completely, had even been surprised she dared to say it, but standing there with her hands in the warm water, hands slipping mindlessly over the dishes, the words came back to her.

As Josie's mind wandered, her grandmother went on: "You'll have a grandchild someday to respect you and to shovel the front steps when you can't get to everything anymore, and you will deserve one, granddaughter. Now show me how you are coming on that dress. Your mom told me that you would have it with you. Have you done any more on the eagle since we last worked on it? I have something special for you to add to it when you are a little farther along. Your mother knows about it. And I've been working on your moccasins. You will be beautiful this summer, granddaughter."

A few weekends later, the aunties came over, as they often did a couple of Saturday afternoons a month, whichever aunties were in town. They used to go to Grandma's, but now, they would come with Grandma to Josie's house because there was sewing to be done. This Saturday, Auntie Malvina worked on the leggings of Josie's dress while Josie's mother and Auntie Marilyn worked on the dress itself. Everyone said that Josie took after Auntie Marilyn in shyness and in stature. Auntie Marilyn had plumped up a little since having children, but there was a similarity that everyone seemed to see. That morning, Auntie Marilyn was sewing the place where the eagle's tail began, and she pulled it to her for a closer look. "These beads seem dull, Josie," she said. "Did we get some bad ones? Do you want me to change them?"

"Oh, Auntie, would you? And can we work on the eagle today?" Josie sighed deeply with relief. She had pulled the plastic up on the dress two or three times since she had taken it to school, to look at that section where the black beads seemed almost dull grey. She shuddered each time, hoping it was the bad light.

"I could have sworn I did these with the right color," Auntie Marilyn mumbled, but she deftly pulled that section of beads off, looking on the back to see how the knots worked so other beads wouldn't fall off as well. "Your eagle must be magnificent. You and your dancing will have to be strong enough to live up to it, my dear. There is much to overcome here and everywhere."

At the stove, Grandma was making her famous pudding. Josie's mother asked her sisters whether they wanted her to go to the store to get some Cool Whip. There was a chorus of voices saying, "yes!" Josie's mother was glad to get away from her sister Marilyn's grandiose statements; too much heavy talk wasn't the way of Saturday afternoons.

"How's dancing, dear?" Auntie Malvina said after Josie's mother left. "We can't wait to see you in the powwows this summer."

"I love dancing, but I'm not sure how much I like Uncle Billy," Josie replied. "He's a little too nice."

Auntie Malvina said, "Oh, he's a loveable old goat! He must be over 60 now because he was able to retire on a pension last year. He knows a lot more about our culture than we remember. Wish I had listened to him and the other elders years ago. He's the only one left that really knows how to make the canoes. Back then with him, you learned how to dance, and you learned how to stay away from men! The years have probably tamed him some by now."

Auntie Malvina and Grandma laughed and laughed. Auntie Marilyn didn't. She looked into Josie's eyes and then back at her work. Tears threatened in Josie's eyes as she realized that Auntie Marilyn had understood, and she felt a tightness in her chest and jaw from holding the tears back. But the women were concentrating on the next bead, and Grandma was off at the stove, so no one noticed her in the next minute. And then, her mother was back, and there was the pudding, and there was Cool Whip, and the eagle was almost done, and the warmth and care of women swept Josie back to the safety of her own home.

The seasons were changing. There was light in the east when Josie got up in the morning. Water was melting out on the lake, and she noticed some of the eagles had returned. They were out looking for breakfast, banking against the wind, their wings set strong. She could almost feel that spring wind under their wings, holding them aloft, powering their intentions. There was dance at school today, and she felt a combined anticipation and anxiety. She'd had trouble studying for the English test last night. The last two times they danced, Josie had conveniently forgotten the dress, and a time before that, she had really been sick. This morning, her mother had left a note on the table: "Uncle Billy called to remind you to bring your dress. I finished the eagle last night, so it is almost ready to go. Uncle Billy said he'd drive you home. And don't forget your hat." Josie's stomach felt queasy. Maybe she could be sick, she thought, but she had an English test she had really studied for. Why did she have to do things she didn't want to do, like wear the hat and try on the dress for Uncle Billy? Her brother had always called her a "Goody Two-shoes," always doing what the grown-ups wanted. Maybe "wimp" was a better word. Maybe she should be rude, rebellious, tough, more like her brother—or maybe just strong, so strong that no one would want to mess with her. "The eagle," she thought, "I need to be like the eagle."

When Josie arrived at school, with her dress on a hanger and her hat on her head, she looked for Shana, who didn't come in on the bus anymore, now that her mother worked in town. Josie didn't find her until the end of the school day; by then, the anticipation had worked its way into full-blown anxiety. "Shana, will you stay after dance for awhile?" she asked her friend. " I have to show Uncle Billy the dress, and I want some company."

"Sure," said Shana, "I think my mom is going to be late anyway. Plus, I want to see your dress."

Josie walked to the cafeteria feeling better. Her cousins crowded around her as she hung the dress on the gawky folded table. Josie asked for help in putting on her new moccasins, gritting her teeth so she wouldn't pay the inevitable price if her cousins were to ever learn she was ticklish. Uncle Billy came in with a big drum, so the kids left her and crowded around it. And so began the stories; the young ones had to learn how to respect the big drum. She sat relaxing into the familiar rhythm of his words, waiting for the drum to pull her into dancing. And when her legs were in tune with the song that Uncle Billy sang, when the drum took up the beat of her heart, she felt herself slip off the words and beat and into her dance. She held the image of the eagle from that morning, and it was almost there, almost freeing her from her feet. She stopped dead with the drum, knowing internally when the last beat would occur. The younger ones danced on a few embarrassed beats, surprised when the drum stopped short.

There was laughter and joking going on when Shana's mother stuck her head in the cafeteria and motioned for Shana to come with her. Shana said, "Just a minute, we want to see Josie's dress," trying to stall for her friend. But Uncle Billy waved her away, stopped the class, and said, "I'll drive Josie home tonight. I left word with her mother, so go on, Shana. Kids, you can get ready. The van will be leaving in a minute. Also, the late bus will be loading in a minute. Josie, use the women's room across the hall to try on your dress." It was all so quick, and there was no arguing with the tone of his voice.

Josie picked up her dress with a grim resignation and took it into the bathroom. The light was so strong there that as she slipped the plastic off the dress, the eagle looked out, reflecting brilliance that took Josie's breath away. Strong like the eagle. She could dance that way; she could feel the strength developing in her shoulders. She slipped on the dress, feeling worthy of the respect it conferred upon her.

Josie left the well-lit bathroom, heard the drum beating, and realized the lights in the cafeteria had been dimmed. She slipped into the phone booth in the hall and called Auntie Marilyn, her words barely audible above the beat of the drum. She hung up quickly and continued on. As she entered the cafeteria, Uncle Billy looked up towards her, his eyes filled with her worst fears, hands not missing a beat. She wasn't going to march in front of him modeling the dress; an eagle wouldn't do that. Instead, she took up dancing as she crossed the threshold. She concentrated on the eagle, the one she had seen that morning on the wind, pulling in its strength, its self-determination, its swooping motions, its invincibility. She let it take her. It was as if the drumming was keeping up with her instead of the other way around. She knew this wasn't a dance that she had danced before, but she danced on, beyond her old self, and beyond his reach . . . until she felt a sudden tug of the earth.

The lights flashed up to full power, and she turned to see Auntie Marilyn in the door. "Ah, good, I was afraid you were going to have to go out of your way, Uncle Billy," she said. "Thought I'd drop by and pick her up since I was going out to my mom's house anyway."

Both Josie and Uncle Billy were drawn from somewhere far away, and Josie felt a sudden rush of affection for her auntie. She would have been okay, she knew, but there was relief in her auntie's presence. Her cousins, hovering around Auntie Marilyn, stared at her dress. Then, drawn by the empty shiny floor space, they recommenced their racing around on the still-cleared cafeteria floor, completely, joyfully breaking the mood. Josie said, "I'll just change, Auntie Marilyn." She dashed into the bathroom, threw on her clothes with a bit of a defiant air, and only took time to put the dress, the accumulation of her female family's love and work, back on the hanger. She stuck her head back in the cafeteria and asked Uncle Billy if he needed help with the drum, and with his "No, thanks," she said a quick goodbye and left with Auntie Marilyn.

Auntie Marilyn said, "You would have been fine, Josie. You've found your strength at a younger age than I did. He wouldn't have bothered you after he'd seen you dance like that. You will be fine, Josie; you won't have to worry about him. I could see it in his eyes."

These questions can be used to write or talk about "The Beads of the Eagle":

1. What family values had Josie learned that were contradicted in real life? How are these similar to or different from the values with which you have been raised?
2. In what different ways did Josie actively try to overcome her problem?
3. How did Josie's problem affect her schoolwork?
4. Should she have tried something other than what she did?
5. Should Josie have taken her problem to the principal?
6. Have you or someone you've known had a similar experience in your community? What did you do about it or what could you have done?
7. What are some other sorts of contradictions between the way people should act and the way they do act? What might you do about those contradictions?

When Life Gives You Lemons, Make Them into Lemonade

In some ways, this has been a painful chapter to write, and a painful chapter to read. You will want to read on to chapters 6 and 7 to find many good suggestions for maintaining your dignity as an Indigenous person in a world that doesn't always value it. "When life gives you lemons," the saying goes, "it's time to make lemonade." Part of the process of dealing with challenges is to face them, to acknowledge and learn from them. Adults and friends who you respect can help you carry the burden. As Auntie Marilyn helped Josie, you will help young people when you gain elder status, or before. We cannot ignore the bad in this world, but we can be active in trying to make it better. You might ask yourself, "How can I make such situations better for myself and for my children and grandchildren? How can I be an agent of change for myself, for my community, and for the Seventh Generation?"

Chapter 5
Bouncing Back or Reaching a Breaking Point

Most young people tend to possess remarkable resilience—the ability to bounce back or adapt—when faced with adversity. While the Native students featured in this chapter have responded to challenges in different ways, they all possess a common inner strength that has helped them handle life's successes and failures. But how did they develop this strength and resiliency? In this chapter, we begin to explore some answers to this question in a story about Jamie, a Native student from the Seneca Nation (New York) who exhibits great determination in overcoming the challenges in his life. We also will take a close look at how some people find it impossible to bounce back and instead reach their breaking points. The chapter ends with a short story, "Season Spirits," which portrays how even small decisions can lead us to either a breaking point or to the strength and resilience needed to face life's challenges. Later chapters will explore resiliency in more detail.

The Class of 1968

Ten little, nine little, eight little Indians,
seven little, six little, five little Indians,
four little, three little, two little Indians
one little Indian . . .
And that left me, the last one
of the bunch, kindergartners of 1955
our teachers, the shade of our skin, our histories
those random chances, silent banshees, chasing children
one by one out of our parents' dreams, 'til I was
the only one left, and the one perceived as leaving,
leaving Vicky, pregnant in the 8th grade, who never came back
Vernon and George, nomads between rez and town 'til they were forgotten
Wanda, always sick and agonizingly shy, who disappeared

Birdeen, who went to work after her father died
Percy and John, expelled for fighting
Susan, for skipping school to take care of the younger kids at home
Jim, who studied incorrigibility at juvenile hall
Pete, who perfected that art at Red Wing
Eliza, who never learned to read and waited for her 16th birthday
Bonita, who almost made it but "had to" get married, as we said in 1968
and that left me, the last one
the forgotten, the untouched, the protected
the bookish, the lucky, the lonely
the pride of her family
the last one.

—Linda LeGarde Grover (Ojibwe)[1]

Resilience

What helped Linda LeGarde Grover stay in school and graduate, often with much difficulty, no matter what? What caused her friends to drop out of school? What has caused you to stay in or drop out of school?

Resilience is a quality that enables children and adults not to give up despite the failures that school and society lay out for them.[2] Resilient people can bounce back after setbacks and difficulties, while others faced with similar circumstances reach their *breaking point* and fall along the wayside. Some of us commit ourselves to succeed in spite of racism, while others respond by becoming so angry they drop out of school. Some young people fall victim to the pressures of alcoholism, drugs, and poverty so typical in our communities, while others overcome these pressures and emerge stronger. Many Native young people manage to avoid problems such as absenteeism and excessive tardiness in school, dropping out, teen pregnancy, and substance use and abuse. They also are able to overcome other problems such as anger, gender inequity and sexism, and the low expectations of schools, teachers, or society in general.

---
[1] Grover, "The Class of 1968."
[2] See Finley, *Cultivating Resilience*.

Being resilient can help you with all of the issues we talk about in this book, including developing your identity—your own strong sense of who you are (chapter 3), coping with things that make life tough (chapter 4), honoring your gifts (chapter 6), making it in school (chapter 7), and following the Good Path (chapter 8).

Jamie

Sometimes you meet someone whose voice flows so meaningfully and powerfully that you don't want the conversation to end. Their words seem precious and almost sacred. So it was with Jamie. A Seneca student from New York, Jamie has learned to face personal challenges and overcome them. He was an 11th grader when I met him at his high school just a few miles from the reservation.

In many ways, Jamie's story has common threads with the stories of so many young people I talked to: a commitment to making it in school and in life; resilience; his use of the advice and assistance of others, especially his elders; and a growing self-confidence. What most impressed me was his knowledge of and belief in Seneca ways. As a young man, he is well on his way to achieving the harmony and balance we all seek in our lives.

On that late spring day when I first interviewed Jamie, he had recently lost his grandmother, the most influential person in his life. Now, more than ever, he believed he had to make it on his own, in a sense, to do right by her and for his people. He felt he was different from his peers because he was so strongly connected to the longhouse:

◆ I grew up by myself, actually, because I was kinda different. You know, I stayed away from trouble. I went to the longhouse, and I participated in most of our religious ceremonies. I was really the first child to do that. So, everybody viewed me as different, kinda a good kid, stayed out of trouble [by going to] the longhouse. [I] did a lot of stuff no other kids did.

There was a long period, however, when things didn't go so well for him in life or in school. He didn't do his schoolwork or feel good about who he was as a person. He was, as he termed it, a "fat kid." His grandmother influenced him to lose weight and get on with his life:

◆ She passed away 'cause she had diabetes. And she always told me if I took care of myself, ate right, then it wouldn't happen like that [to me]. She was only 50-some years old. I started working out a long time ago 'cause . . . I used to be a heavy-set kid; but then I started working out, started lifting weights, and I lost like 60 pounds, gained a little bit of muscle mass. That's another thing I like doing when I feel bad. [I] just go lift weights or else work on my hotrod.

And what did his friends think of this? He responded, "I think they're kinda jealous, actually, 'cause I went from dud to stud, I guess. I never used to be before. I always felt rejected. But it feels good, actually."

Losing weight exposed a new person inside Jamie, the person who was always there, just waiting to be uncovered.

◆ I started working out, and my grandmother told me . . . what to do, and that's when she gave me the strength to do it. And I've done it.... It's kind of a good thing because I can play a lot of sports. I'm really good at things that I never used to be. That's what's made me kinda popular among the community. I can do all these things that I never used to be able to do, and I can do them better than some of the kids today.

Jamie was making it in school because he had focused on the future and was determined to succeed, no matter what.

◆ When I look at the kids who have dropped out, that have a job to just buy drugs... I thought about dropping out; But like I said before, if I want to [finish something], then I'll do it, not because I have to do it, but I want to do it because I want to have a good future for myself and my kids.

Jamie's grandmother and grandfather passed on before I had the opportunity to meet them and tell them how impressed I was with this young person. My wife, who accompanied me in interviewing Jamie, said what I felt that day: "It looks like they each left you a little of their spirit." He replied, "Yeah, [that] can help you make it through life."

Things That Can Lead to Giving Up on School

The factors that can lead to either giving up on school or sticking with it are present at the same time, creating a push-pull effect. The negative things push us away from school, while the positive things tell us to stick with it, no matter what. How young people deal with these positive and negative influences seems to determine if they drop out or successfully complete school. First, we will look at the negative things.

Absenteeism and Tardiness

Many schools have adopted attendance policies that have a heavy bearing on whether a student passes or fails. Students who miss too many days, including excused and unexcused absences, are not allowed credit for the term. Does high absenteeism directly cause students to drop out? Or is it an effect of something else, like working too many hours at a job, not getting enough sleep, not doing homework, partying, or having to deal with family issues? Our sense is that absenteeism can be both a cause and an effect. We know that students who are absent a lot don't feel connected to school, and those who are chronically tardy often have difficulties with their schoolwork. Frequent absences have a negative effect on the ability to be resilient, and can be a big factor in students' decisions to give up when they are too far behind or when difficult situations arise. Chronic absenteeism nearly pushed Will (Dakota) into dropping out:

◆ See, my 10th-grade year really brought me down. That year was really bad for me. I'd be sick, and I'd want to come back to school and try to get my grades up. And then, my friends weren't there so I just got really lazy-minded, and I stayed home. Plus, I was feeling sick all the time too, and I'd have to stay home 'cause I was sick, 'cause I didn't want to get anybody else sick at school. It was just a really bad year for me; my grades were really down. I missed almost 40 days of school. A couple of times, I was thinking about dropping out. I don't know what kept me from dropping out.

Sometimes, as in the case of Quoetone (Ojibwe), the issues of boredom and undiagnosed depression affect attendance:

◆ I went through kind of a depression there for a while. And I was sick during that time too. I had like almost pneumonia and stuff like that. I didn't particularly like school. I ditched a lot of classes. A lot of them were boring. Like a 10th-grade English class, I'd go in and he'd give us maybe 50 pages to read by the end of the week, and maybe a couple of handouts you had to fill out by the end of the week. And so, I'd sit and I'd do them during the class, and I'd have half the class left plus the next two days of nothing to do. So I'd show up late or not go to class, or whatever. And I just got behind in my work because I wasn't going. And so, I got bored with it. I was depressed at the same time. So they put me on a truancy intervention program because I was truant.

Anger

How we deal with anger has a bearing on our ability to be resilient. People with low breaking points sometimes allow anger to consume them and lead them down a destructive path. More resilient people turn anger around into something positive, using it as motivation to change the conditions that caused the anger. Initially, being angry is the result of something else, whether it is feeling unaccepted at school, having to deal with racism, or living with painful issues at home. As Fred (Choctaw) realized, unresolved anger often contributes to other problems:

◆ I was in a state of bitterness because I was an outcast. There are a lot of people who are out there that are in that position. They're being pushed out by society. Society has had that attitude: I don't want you; we don't want you in this crowd or anything. They've allowed that bitterness to build up because no one has paid attention to them. . . . A gang has that feeling [of acceptance], saying, "We want you, join us. . . . We'll do everything together, we'll always stick together, we're brothers." And that's how a lot of Choctaw kids join gangs.

How we deal with a moment of rage also can affect us for a long time. Whether we decide to walk away and calm down or to confront the person or situation making us angry can either defuse or accelerate the situation.

Teen Pregnancy

How might the issue of teen pregnancy be related to resilience? We know teen pregnancy is the most common reason Native females drop out of school. The responsibilities of caring for a baby can be overwhelming, so schooling must inevitably move to the back burner as a priority. Sunshine (Ute) shared her experience:

◆ Last year, when I was in eighth grade, I was going to school, and kids from [the community] were, I don't know why, but they were trying to fight with me. And I was pregnant, and I didn't know what to do, so I just dropped out of school then.

Jazzy (Ojibwe) witnessed similar problems:

◆ Sophomore year, a friend of mine got pregnant. She said she was going to come back, and she never has. Another girl just kind of drifted away. She just didn't come to school anymore, and then we just never heard from her. Some go to [an alternative school]; some other people, they were here freshman year, and we had classes together, and then they were pregnant.

Boys also drop out to support a baby coming into the world, as attested to by Dee (Ojibwe):

◆ There's a lot [of dropouts], boys and girls. Some of them drop out to get jobs; some of them drop out because the girl's pregnant and the boy's got to get a job for the girl.

Alcohol and Drugs

Alcoholism has had a devastating effect on Native people and communities since colonization. The misuse of alcohol and drugs is the result of bad things happening to people: abuse, neglect, racism, genocide, poverty, powerlessness, or insults. Most people who get drunk or high feel like they are on top of the world for just a while. Then, they use it to lessen the pain. Students like Lisa (Dakota) have seen the tragedies of alcohol and drug abuse all around them:

◆ There's people that go through the same problems as Indian people, but I don't think there's as many. All my Indian friends have like really bad family lives, and it's just really sad. Some of them don't, but there's abuse, there's violence, there's sexual abuse, [and] it all relates to alcohol, I think. . . . My dad's side of the family, my Indian side of the family, they're all really bad alcoholics. And I just see how that kills people. And it changes like when they stop. I know people that have stopped drinking, and it just changes the total person that they are.

We know that having good connections to family and school influences whether a young person will misuse alcohol and drugs. As individuals, however, we all make choices about whether to use alcohol and drugs, who our friends will be, and how much they influence what we do. Along the way, especially with a bit more maturity, some young people, such as Kelly (Wampanoag), begin to see their decisions in a different light:

◆ My first two years of high school were really bad. I was on drugs and into bad things. So now I have to finish all my work, which is like catch up in school, so it's really horrible. I was stupid, pretty much. That's all I can explain. I was stupid back then.

Peer pressure can influence drug and alcohol use, a fact pointed out by Blue (Ute) when asked why fellow Native students drop out of school:

◆ A lot of peer pressure, I would have to say, because everybody likes to drink around here. And you know, it's really hard to get away from drinking. I don't really think it's fun because I've seen a lot of my family members die from it.

Sexism

Sexism, like all forms of bigotry, can wear people down. If you are already dealing with racism, sexism can only add to the burden. Native girls, like all other girls, notice that the mass media seems fixated on the selling of sex. How do you think this affects girls' development and the ways they see themselves? Carol (Navajo) was disturbed by the media's portrayal of female role models:

◆ We were discussing how . . . the media places women kind of less, and how that they have to be pleasing to men. And so, I really thought about things like the Spice Girls and how they . . . have this idea of like Girl Power.

. . . I think Girl Power is about . . . being talented and being smart—being able to do lots of different things. [But] . . . the message that [the Spice Girls] portray is that you need to be sexy . . . I saw these pictures of little girls that were trying to imitate the Spice Girls, and I think that it sends such a horrible message to young girls, to all different races, that they're less . . . .

Living Out the Low Expectations of Others

A lot of research supports the idea that when others don't expect much from us, we live down to their expectations. Conversely, when people expect great things from us, we tend to rise to meet their expectations. When we live out the low expectations of others, we confirm and solidify their bigotry. Carol (Navajo) has seen Native students begin to embody the negative perceptions teachers have of them:

◆ I think my sister and I were kind of treated a little bit like, "Well, since you're Indian, you can't know [or] do anything." And I think that's how a lot of other Native kids [are treated]. They're kind of told they can't do anything, so I don't think they try. . . . I think the majority of them have the skills that are necessary, and I think a lot of them are really bright children that are capable. But they just don't try.

Things That Help Students Be Resilient

Students talked about what had helped them turn things around when they were not doing well in school. These times of decision turned out to be important life events for them, what some would call *epiphanies*. Students drew the strength to stay in school from many things, including their tribal cultures and the desire to live up to the expectations of adults, particularly family members. Others had their own ways of being tough, sticking to the business of attending school, and turning things around for the better.

Strength in Culture

Feeling good about who you are as a Native person and being connected to your Native culture will help you make it in school. We call this being *culturally connected*. A very important finding of our study is that culturally connected students do better in school. Why? They seem to share three positive characteristics in particular:

1. good self-concept (feeling good about oneself as an individual)
2. a strong sense of direction (having goals for schooling and life)
3. tenacity (finding the strength to deal with all the adversities that school and life can offer)

Feeling good about one's tribal culture showed up in many ways. The youth we met talked about their

- ability to feel more comfortable with living in both worlds (the Native community and mainstream schools)
- participation in cultural activities, such as powwows and singing and drum groups and ceremonies
- strong, positive feelings of belonging to a Native community and family
- respect for the influences of traditional people, especially elders, grandparents, and parents
- participation in a school curriculum that included Native history, language, and culture

Feeling good about their Native culture fostered the traits that made them resilient and strong.

Sometimes, it's just feeling so proud of being who you are: a Native person. Karonhiakta, a First Nations Mohawk student, understood this:

◆ I would say you carry on your culture and your beliefs and traditions everywhere. It's not just that you come to school at 8:00, and at 3:00 you pick it up again. It's an ongoing thing; it's what you stand for and what you believe. And I'm just so proud that I'm here today. I know the background, and I know the people, and I know who I am, and I just have to accept that and am proud of who I am, and I go to school and learn—learn things that keep me educated.

Some young people have acquired some of the wisdom of the old ones. Margie (Hoopa) heard the stories of her ancestors and wanted to live up to her father's high expectations for her:

◆ I know a lot about my culture, and it kinda helps me—what happened to my parents, to my great-grandparents and my great-great-grandparents, when they didn't go to school. . . . And if they didn't want to learn, they got beat for it. But look at me, I have the chance to learn. And when it comes to culture, it's like [Dad] always said, "No matter how many times you get beat or locked up, as long as you know something, they'll never be able to take it away from you."

Turning Things Around

Bell-Bell, a Seneca student from upstate New York, talked about how she turned things around for the better. As with so many students, maybe she simply needed to grow up a little, to mature and realize that schooling was important. Maybe it was having some success, whereas in the past, there had been mostly failure. Maybe it was playing sports and having the internal motivation to work harder.

◆ I was really excited because I never [made merit roll] ever before, ever, even when I was doing good in elementary school or middle school. I've gotten awards [for] going from being a really bad student in 9th and 10th grade and then accomplishing something that big. It wasn't even like that big; but just to pull an 85 average, that felt like a really big accomplishment. I think I just concentrated a little bit better, worked my hardest, and got along really well with my teachers. . . . I was playing sports last year too, so I think that kind of motivated me.

Shana (Ojibwe) told a similar story:

◆ I got suspended for a month, and then I got expelled for another one, and then I came back, and I was in in-school suspension. I sat in there for two weeks, and then I got to come back out, and I was on probation. I was so laid back, "Oh, I can do this at this time or next year." And then it comes down to it, and it's too late. I can't. When I first came back, it was like the teachers just looked like, "What are you doing here?" Kind of like, "Why is she here?" And then it was just a normal thing. [I] proved myself. . . . Now, when teachers sit down and talk about me, or like the principal does a checkup on me or something, he sits there and says . . . , "Oh, she proved herself. She can do it. She don't need to fight. . . ." I just sit and think about that stuff when I get mad or something. You know, you can't let anybody down, and that just brings me right back up. From what I've done, I'm proud of myself.

A Teaching Story

"Season Spirits" is a fictional story about Ron Andrews, a young Ojibwe man who, along with his friends, attended a special summer math and science program for Native students. In some respects, the story is about how seemingly little choices can have a profound impact on our lives. We try in school, or we give up. Sometimes our culture is important, or it isn't; or it is, but we don't live it—we just talk about it.

"Season Spirits" is a metaphor for the two kinds of spirit in each of us. One wants us to give up; the other wants us to finish things. One is positive; the other takes us down the wrong path. In Ojibwe oral tradition, the seasons are controlled by two spirits: Bebon (the spirit of winter) and Zeegwun (the spirit of summer). They are very different. Bebon is a being of great endurance and strength as well as intensity of character. He has control over the cold, causing sickness and making plants and their leaves and fruit wither, and he has the ability to cover the earth with snow and ice. He is not afraid of anybody. Zeegwun is a rather meek and docile young man, shy and introspective. Zeegwun represents life and growth. He brings the birds in spring, makes the trees bud and flower, and works for all life to be reborn again.

Each of these spirits struggles to control the seasons, and the struggle has gone on, and will continue on, forever. When Zeegwun is winning, we are bathed in the warmth of spring and summer. When Bebon is winning, we are chilled by the cold of fall and winter. The same is true with our character and the decisions we make.

Season Spirits

by Thomas Peacock

The rez kids first heard a rumor about a new summer school program during sixth-period study hall. With only two weeks of school left, all the high school kids from the rez had been thinking for a long time about what they would do during the summer. The study hall kids had even more time to wonder. The study hall was where many rez kids were confined for long-overdue library books, unfinished assignments, or misplaced textbooks that had disappeared into black holes. This time of year, the study hall seemed to hold rez kids like prisoners of war—prisoners who always sat in the back of the room while the town kids had passes to go to the library, see a favorite teacher, or clean out their lockers. *Exceptional* students (those who were exceptional at brown-nosing the study hall teacher) were given passes to go outside, sit on the lawn, or visit with other *exceptional* friends.

Julie Loons, a niece of one of the Indian social worker aides, told her fellow study hall students about a deal that couldn't be passed up: "I heard there's this grant from the NITS or NSF or something like that to have a summer school program for rez high school kids—field trips and stuff like that, math or science something or another. And I heard they're gonna pay us five bucks an hour for 30 hours a week. It's supposed to last a couple of weeks. Geez, man, that's a couple of hundred bucks—serious coin."

"Sign me up," echoed a chorus of rez kids from the back of study hall. Most of them had long ago been relegated to general math and environmental science, also known as "idiot science" because all the class did was go on field trips and watch videotaped reruns of *Nova* and *Nature*. Most had barely passed these classes but couldn't wait to make some *junia*, Ojibwe for cash money. Junia is a word that could only be said when a person was rubbing the thumb and fingers together for emphasis.

Sure enough, rumor evolved to form and substance when Ron Andrews, one of the study hall kids, received a letter from the Indian education office that included a program description and application for the Red Cliff Summer Math and Science Program. It began, "The Red Cliff Summer Youth Program, in cooperation with the University of Minnesota at Duluth, will be jointly operating Project Bizindun (to listen), a summer math and science program funded by the National Science Foundation." It went on, and Ron read it aloud, "Blah, blah, blah . . . blah, blah, blah . . . and participants will receive $5.25 for each hour they attend, up to a maximum of 30 hours per week for the two-week program."

Ron read that part over again several times. Surely, this was manna from heaven. He spent a good part of Sunday evening filling out the application form and turned it in to the Indian home-school coordinator early the following Monday. He commented to Julie as he passed her in the hall, "Good rumor about summer school, Julie."

"Oh, sad," she said and just smiled and walked away. "Oh, sad" is one of those traditional/contemporary rez sayings. Ron wondered about Julie's smile all day.

For the rest of the regular school term, the rez kids—including Ron, Julie Loons, Jenny Shaugobay (called "No Neck"), Joey Ainawash (called "Ain't Ever Washed"), and all their high-school-aged cousins, nephews, brothers, and sisters—waited in anticipation for their acceptance letters for summer school. All of the prisoners of study hall waited for the final bell to signal the end of another regular school year so they could walk as free young men and women out of the school. For the first time, though, they looked forward to returning for summer school.

Then, three days before the end of school, the students received their letters: "After a thorough screening and selection process, we are pleased to announce that you have been selected to attend Project Bizindun (to listen), a summer math and science program to be offered by the Red Cliff Youth Program and the University of Minnesota at Duluth. Participants were selected based upon their mathematics and science grades, potential for success, and recommendations from teachers and Indian education staff."

Whispers of "Get your letter, neej?" (the Ojibwe word for friend) echoed throughout the rez bus, in the school halls, in the back of every classroom, and, most loudly, in the study hall.

"Uh-huh."

Everyone who applied got the same letter. Even several of those who didn't apply got the letter, especially those who were related to tribal council members or the Indian home-school coordinator. There were lots of happy Indians in school that day.

On the last day of school, an excited group of kids climbed into the rez bus and headed down the highway back to Red Cliff. The bus seemed to almost dance down the road with a special glee, filled with the kind of happiness that can only be brought on by surviving yet another school year. The kids were filled with anticipation for the summer school that paid cash money, the powwow season, fishing out on Lake Superior, babysitting jobs, and partying. Who would ever have known that life could be so grand? On a warm, early summer day with the deep blue sky and puffy, happy clouds, Ron sat with his cousin Jayhog in his favorite bus seat, on the side closest to the lake. The bus kept dancing up and down dirt roads, a whole busload of rez kids bidding a warm and hearty farewell to one another as they were deposited into dusty driveways, calling "See you in September!" The phrase sounded like an old and tired song sung long ago in some ancient generation, but this time it had a certain gusto.

When it was time for Ron to leave the bus, he had to run a gauntlet of cousins and nephews, large and small, all filled with the spirit of the last school day, happy Indians all. Before he left the bus, he turned and bid farewell to Julie Loons, saying "See you on Monday at summer school. Remember?"

She just smiled back, and there was a special twinkle in her eyes. He thought of that smile and that twinkle all the way up his driveway, all the way past the junk cars and satellite dish and fish boxes, all the way until Monday.

Ron was up early that Monday, the first day of summer school, to take a long Ivory soap shower. He combed his flat top, no tail, as straight as he could. He brushed his teeth with baking soda and a clean index finger. He put on his favorite cut-off jeans and No Fear T-shirt. Then he trudged his way down the hall to the kitchen, whistling under his breath something from an old Jimi Hendrix song he'd heard the night before on an MTV special. He dished himself out a large bowl of oatmeal, added some sugar and hydrated powdered milk, and sat hunched over at the table, like a bear eating blueberries, breathing through his nose.

His mother was sitting across the table watching her only son, her only child, with a mix of bemusement and pride. "You certainly are focused today, Ronnie," she said. "I didn't even have to wake you up. I wish the rest of the school year would have been this way." She had learned the importance of getting *focused* while taking classes during the past year from Mt. Scenario College's continuing education and extension division.

"Gonna make me some coin, Mom. Gonna make some junia," he said, his left thumb rubbing against its neighboring fingers for emphasis, his right hand jamming oatmeal into his mouth at the same time. She just smiled back. When he was done, he bounded out the door and down to the end of the driveway to wait for the bus.

Soon, down the hill came a large, 15-passenger blue van bearing the name "Red Cliff Head Start" on its side. It lurched to a stop, and

Bouncing Back or Reaching a Breaking Point

Ron climbed aboard a van full of cousins, nephews, neighbors, and fellow Red Cliffers, most of whom were happy to see him. Driving the bus was Ruth Copes, the Indian home-school coordinator known lovingly as "Ruth Can't Cope" by all the rez kids, except her closest relatives. The nickname accurately described her. She was constantly frustrated by the unwillingness or inability of Bayfield Schools to teach the Ojibwe history or culture, or even to pretend to teach the language. Ruth was seemingly oblivious to the failure and dropping out, to the drugs and drinking that claimed at least one Indian student each year, and to the fact she was totally and completely and forever ineffectual.

"Hi, Ronnie," she said. His fellow summer school classmates mimicked Ruth Can't Cope as he found a place to sit, chorusing "Hi, Ronnie."

They worked their way up and down the dirt roads of Red Cliff, occasionally stopping to pick up a passenger. Sometimes Ruth had to send a runner in to awaken someone, but, for the most part, each driveway contained at least one shiny Indian face. They continued down past the federally approved pastel-colored HUD (federal Housing and Urban Development) houses to the Head Start Center, their home base for the next two weeks. The van lurched to a stop alongside another large, 15-passenger blue van fresh from dispatching the other load of rez kids. There, in front of Red Cliff Head Start, stood 23 rez high school kids—23 of the 37 selected for the program. "Not bad," thought Ruth Can't Cope, counting the number who had shown up for the first day. "Not bad at all." Ronnie stood there amongst his peers—Hoops, Frog Eyes, No Neck, Jayhog, Snowball—they were all there, and in the back of this odd collection, whispering and giggling to one of her friends, was Julie Loons.

"This is going to be totally cool," he said under his breath.

Ruth Can't Cope was accompanied by some strange White guy no one had ever seen before or would ever see again after the demise of the program. She herded the eager learners into the building and told them to have a seat. Have a seat they did, with some of the larger students completely overwhelming the tiny Head Start chairs, their knees up almost over their shoulders. Far below their knees were tiny kidney-shaped tables.

"Now, we tried to get the science lab at the school for this," yelled Ruth Can't Cope, as she tried to get their attention, "but you know they start their summer cleaning as soon as you kids leave the building. So, the tribal council offered us this. Don't get all worried. We won't be here much. Just consider this home base."

Everyone knew the public school officials didn't want a bunch of Indian kids running loose in their building during the summer, especially in their science lab. Everyone knew except Ruth and that strange White guy standing next to her.

"This is Michael Stone," she said and motioned with her lips toward the stranger. "Mr. Stone is a graduate student at the University of Minnesota at Duluth in the education department. He is going to be your teacher these next few weeks. Mr. Stone?"

The strange White guy stepped forward, put his hands on his hips like a coach pretending to assert his authority, and said, "Hi, folks. As Ruth said, I'm going to be your teacher for Project Byzantine. We're going to be doing what I hope will be some really interesting stuff these next couple of weeks. We'll be working on projects that combine math and science concepts in a thematic way—a practical, hands-on, activity-based learning approach—real-life, high-interest stuff."

As Mr. Stone mispronounced the word *Bizindun,* there were a few giggles from invisible Indians somewhere in the room, and one snort. Like most non-Indians, he mispronounced the Ojibwe language.

True to stereotype, 23 Indians sat in stone-faced silence as the strange White man told them of the great adventure that lay before them. Some were beginning to wonder if it would be worth $5.25 an hour. Finally, one invisible Indian elbowed his invisible companion and whispered, "What's he saying, neej (friend)?"

"Who knows."

It didn't take long for Michael Stone, the strange White man from Duluth, to notice he was losing his audience. So, he quickly cut to the chase. "This week we'll go out on the lake aboard the Wisconsin Department of Natural Resources research boat, *Wenonah,* to study the fish population in the Bayfield area. We'll take water samples while we're out there and analyze them for pollutants. We'll also dissect some of the catch and take it over to the Environmental Protection Agency lab in Duluth to see what foreign chemicals and pollutants it contains. You'll get a tour of the lab, and we'll do some fun stuff while we're in Duluth, like visit the zoo and have a picnic at Bayfront Park."

Snowball, alias Vernon Smith, interrupted the speaker. He was not shy, so he spoke for the group. "Hey, can we go to the Grand Slam video arcade?" he wanted to know. "Man, that would be fun."

The speaker completely ignored Snowball and continued, "We'll go down the road to the Bayfield Fishery to see how they raise trout and salmon for stocking the lake. And we'll go over to Bad River to the Great Lakes Indian Fish and Wildlife Commission to talk to some people about their research projects on the effects of the spring spearfishing harvest and the effects on people of eating fish from Lake Superior. We'll go kayaking over near Cornucopia and learn about rock formations and wave action.

We'll then go over to Madeline Island to learn about plant identification, and while we're there, a tribal elder will talk to us about tribal history and culture. If it's not cloudy, maybe we'll do some stargazing and identification of stars, galaxies, constellations, and all that stuff. And we'll camp out at Big Bay State Park on Madeline."

"OOOOhhhh!" Invisible but very audible teenage hormones were speaking from the back of the room.

"So, as you can see, we have a lot of things planned for you this next couple of weeks," Michael Stone concluded. "And to top it off, you're going to get paid for it."

Everyone listened to that last sentence. Everyone listened to their new teacher, "Michael's Stoned," the rez name already given him by the odd collection of rez kids who had now become his students.

Then it was Ruth's turn. "I get to be the bad guy," she began, and started reading the rules. "First of all, in order to get paid, you need to complete the entire two weeks here. You can't just come here a week or every other day to get paid. This is like a job—you show up, you get paid."

That virtually eliminated a substantial number in the room, enough that everyone was confident the rule wouldn't hold.

Ruth continued, "Now here are the rules. No smoking."

"No smoking" groans arose from the smokers in the room. This was going to be hard, they were thinking. Real hard.

"No booze or drugs. No fighting or goofing off," Ruth went on. "You will listen to Mr. Stone. We will all help with setting things up and cleaning up after we are done. When we go out in public, you will conduct yourselves as ladies and gentlemen. We will have zero tolerance. You screw up, and you're out of here. Now, does anyone have any questions?"

She peered down her nose like the nuns who used to teach summer catechism at St. Mary's Catholic Church—nuns who told them they were all sinners, nuns who specialized in terrorizing little Indian kids with stories of hell and damnation, and who knew all the good nerve holds. After hearing Ruth, Joey Ain't Ever Washed was already planning on leaving, although he would wait until after lunch, if it sounded good enough.

For the next three days, 17 of them—6 didn't return after the first day—did all the things their teacher told them they would do. All 17 were survivors: some with alarm clocks or parents who acted as alarm clocks were able to wake up and get on the van every morning; others could last half a day until they were able to sneak off into the bushes for a quick smoke. They survived by keeping their eyes on the prize and reassuring themselves with visions of cash money.

It turned out, to most everyone's surprise, that Michael's Stoned was a pretty good teacher. Doing things was fun—much more fun than sitting in a classroom all day. He found a way to make science and math come alive. He also had a good sense of humor and soon accepted his rez name. He called his students by their rez names, and this personal and informal manner of teaching soon gave him quite a following. In the first couple of days, they learned things they should've learned in math and science a long time ago. They did things they should've done during the regular school year. The kids started asking themselves, "Why can't regular school be more like this?"

It also turned out that Ruth Can't Cope was adept at making edible lunch meat sandwiches, and although some of them were dry around the edges, the students would race to them like hungry puppies when it was time to have lunch.

Many of the students even practiced math after they got home. Ron would sit at the kitchen table each night after school and do multiplication: "Let's see, $5.25 an hour times six hours a day times three days . . . ."

On day four, some of the students began to notice one another in hormonal ways, an inevitable result of spending so much time together riding in kayaks and dissecting fish. Ron, of course, had noticed Julie Loons long ago when they were 14. There was something in her dark and laughing eyes, the way her black hair shone in the sunlight, the way she said "Sad," and the way she pointed with her full and kissable lips. Julie noticed Ron's quiet and gentle reservation English voice. She liked the way he looked at her. So, it surprised no one that, by day four, they were sharing lunch meat sandwiches.

Day four was quickly followed by day five,

and Michael's Stoned was looking forward to the weekend. He checked out of the motel room he'd called home for the past week and hit the dusty trail back to Minneapolis, where he would tell unbelieving relatives what a joy it was to teach Indian kids about math and science. He couldn't wait to tell them about his new rez name and about Snowball, Hoops, Frog Eyes, No Neck, and the few kids like Ron and Julie who had yet to acquire rez names.

That weekend, Ruth Can't Cope had serious bingo evenings planned at the rez casino/bowling alley; Ron was going to help his father and Uncle Eddie pull and set fish nets out on the lake; and Julie, Ron's sharer of sandwiches, was hitting the powwow trail. For a weekend, everyone planned to return to their real lives, which somehow seemed disconnected from Project Bizindun. That Friday afternoon, as Ruth unloaded Ron at his dusty driveway, she reminded him that they would be going over to Madeline Island and staying overnight on Monday: "Remember to bring a sleeping bag. And you promised you'd bring a tent. Now don't get into any trouble this weekend, and we'll see you on Monday."

The weekend passed without incident for most of the 17 survivors, all except for Hoops, alias Moses Brown, who decided being a summer school dropout was an okay way to be. He could never explain why he didn't finish Project Bizindun, except for the fact that he had trouble finishing anything. Finishing something now wouldn't be good for his image. Maybe some time that same weekend, he decided regular school wasn't that hot either because he didn't return to Bayfield High School in the fall. It was one of those spur-of-the-moment life decisions that are often made in a trivial manner. So, Hoops didn't return on Monday, but 16 eager learners did, climbing aboard two blue Head Start vans, fully loaded with sleeping bags, tents, food, and other camping gear. Down the highway they went to catch the Madeline Island Ferry, which would take them two miles out into Lake Superior.

Two vans full of rez kids made some tourists on the ferry nervous that morning. Women hid their purses, men hid their cameras, fathers protected their daughters, and mothers practiced phony smiles to the Natives. Frog Eyes pretended to push No Neck over the rail out into the lake. Ron sat with Snowball, ogling Julie and No Neck. They both agreed Julie was good looking, but the jury was out on No Neck, alias Jenny Shaugobay.

"She needs a neck," concluded Ron. Snowball reluctantly agreed.

Ruth couldn't cope with it all, but every one of the rez kids knew the whole story of that. Michael's Stoned disowned all of them and wondered who had fed them red candy for breakfast. The 15-minute ferry ride became a metaphor for summer life in Bayfield. Cowboys and Indians stuck with one another on the ferry of life, back and forth, on the hour, every hour.

When they pulled into the dock in the island community of LaPointe, all the other vehicles drove off in the opposite direction of the rez vans. First stop for Project Bizindun was the LaPointe Museum, where a National Park Service guide told the rez kids about the lives of early settlers on the Apostle Islands. The students toured an old cabin and got to see how settlers lived: old butter churns; washboards; and pictures of pale, homely, stone-faced settlers. The men all had handlebar moustaches, and the women had their hair in buns. The men always leaned against an axe or some farm implement, while the women held washbasins or stood next to clotheslines. The rez kids were good listeners and equally good observers. But Indians usually are. They especially noticed that the guide said nothing about their people, the Ojibwe, who had lived on the island for hundreds of years. It was as though they never existed. It was as if the guide was just talking to air.

Then, it was off around the island to learn plant identification from some White guy from Minneapolis. As strange as that sounded, none of the rez kids would ever forget that day, learning about the food and medicinal value of plants in the ancestral homeland of the once great and powerful Ojibwe nation. Yet, not a single soul noticed the tragic comedy being acted out: Ojibwe people being taught their culture by a teacher whose race had forcibly taken away that culture in boarding and mission schools.

After a long day of ducking under bushes, fording swamps, slapping mosquitoes, and doing all those other things one does on plant identification day, the tired group settled into Big Bay State Campground on the northeast side of Madeline Island. They picked out two adjoining spots, one for the girls and one for the boys. Theoretically, at least, that's how it was supposed to be. Their equally tired chaperones, Michael and Ruth, tried to keep all of them busy setting up tents, fetching firewood, and getting water. That took a half hour, then the group slowly dissipated to explore the wonders of the park. Most ended up down on the beach, a beautiful stretch of sand that made them wonder why their ancestors ever moved from this place. The kids clearly made the tourist beachcombers and sunbathers nervous, some of whom thought they were being invaded. It was one of those events that rez kids sort of get used to, but sort of don't. White folks seem to be experts at staring. The rez kids retaliated by being loud and obnoxious teenagers— something *they* were experts at. For the rest of the afternoon, until Ruth summoned them back to their camp spots for dinner, everybody had a good time playing stereotypes.

After dinner, the mosquitoes came out. Everyone rubbed down with repellent and then teased one another about being "shinier than before." Indians are always teasing one another about being shiny. Then, it was back to the beach for the nonsmokers, back to the bushes for the smokers.

"You kids be back here in an hour for our speaker," hollered Ruth, as she tried to get a blackened skillet off the fire with a stick. Ruth looked and acted the part of an overnight camp chaperone. There she stood in all her glory, frizzy hair, faded pink sweats, and an equally old and faded T-shirt emblazoned with the motto "We car about kids." The letter *e* in the word *care* had worn off, but the word *car* was just as appropriate, since her main role was to transport the kids to and from school. Michael hadn't been any help in making dinner or cleaning up afterwards. He was out exploring too. After all, he'd never been on Madeline Island until this day.

By about 9:00 that evening, most of the kids had returned to camp, and those who didn't answer Ruth's persistent calls soon were found by the runners she sent out. "Our speaker's going to be here soon," she said.

Sure enough, at 9:20 or so, an old pickup pulled into camp. It was Ron's Uncle Eddie. "That's my uncle!" proclaimed Ron to his fellow campers.

"Duh!" said an invisible Indian from the back of the group.

Eddie quickly became part of the campfire crowd. Ron poured him a cup of coffee. Ruth cleared a place at a picnic bench for Eddie to sit and asked for his social security number so he could get paid. Michael shook his hand and said he was pleased to meet him. They visited for a while, and Michael noticed how all the rez kids treated the old man with great respect—this man with a mischievous twinkle in his eyes, who wore a flannel shirt and green work pants, but who carried himself with such dignity.

Ruth started the program by formally introducing Eddie. "We're really privileged to have Eddie Bainbridge here tonight to tell us the history of our Ojibwe people," she began. "Most of you know he is one of our elders. He still fishes commercially out of Red Cliff. He is a renowned storyteller, and some of you might remember that he has come to Bayfield High the last couple of years and told legends. So, without saying anything else, our speaker, Eddie Bainbridge."

Eddie threw a twig in the fire and began. "Now, this time of the year, you know, we don't tell certain stories. Certain stories are meant for winter," he explained. "But I'm going to teach you your history. That I can do. In the old days, you know, when we used to have the old people come to us and speak, we used to give them tobacco and ask them to tell us things."

He looked toward Ruth, and she immediately knew she had made a serious cultural error. Obviously, he meant, "You should have given me tobacco when you asked me to come here tonight." She knew enough about her culture to realize his comment also meant, "If you ever ask me to do this again, you need to first offer me tobacco, and if you don't, I'll make up some lame excuse and not show up."

Ron knew what was going on right away. He nudged a smoker for a cigarette and whispered, "Daga sagaswayzhun? (Do you have a smoke?)" He handed it over to his uncle, who took it without reaction and continued. It was expected.

"I'm going to tell you the history of this place," Eddie began. He told them how the Anishinaabe (Ojibwe) people had lived for countless generations on the Eastern Ocean in what is now known as Newfoundland. The spiritual people of the tribe had a dream in which a *megis*, a sacred shell, appeared in the ocean and moved inland. The people followed the shell, which eventually appeared for the last time on Moningwanakaning, or Madeline Island. The whole Anishinaabe nation had lived there for several hundred years until the coming of White traders and missionaries. Then, starvation and sickness came to the people, and there were even rumors of cannibalism during this time. He used voice inflection when he said "cannibalism."

It was one of those defining moments when everyone, just for a split second, was absolutely terrified. All of them looked like fireside raccoons. The fire popped.

"OOOhhh!" cried multiple frightened voices from the darkness.

Eddie continued, "So really, you know, we *Indins*," meaning *Indians*, "shouldn't be camping here because all our ancestors left this place. There was too much evil here."

Bouncing Back or Reaching a Breaking Point

Eddie knew he had the crowd in his hand. He could take them anywhere he wanted now. But, because of his nature, he wanted to leave them in a nice place. He smiled and continued.

He told them how the people had branched out from Madeline Island and now occupy most of northern Wisconsin, Minnesota, and parts of North Dakota. "And we're all over Canada," he added.

Because of the time of year, Eddie told them the whole story of Zeegwun, the guardian of summer, who always battles with Bebon, the guardian of winter. "They battle all the time. Sometimes, Bebon has the upper hand, you know, so we have winter, but this time of year, Zeegwun is winning. That's why it is summer. These are the season spirits."

It made perfect sense. Michael wanted to believe the story, even knowing it defied all scientific principles. A gifted storyteller talking to eager learners, Eddie held the young people's attention for nearly two hours. Then it was time for him to leave. "The last ferry runs at 11:00, and if I don't get my butt in gear, I'll get stranded here overnight," he told the group. "And I don't want to have to put up with all of you noisy kids."

They all laughed at his teasing. Then he was gone. His noisy old truck puttered down the road, its taillights winking goodbye through the bushes as it disappeared around a corner.

After Eddie left, Ruth told the group they could stay up until midnight, but that was it. They would need to get up early in the morning and head back to the mainland. With that, the group dispersed. Snowball, Ron, Julie, and No Neck found a quiet spot to talk.

"You wanna go down to the beach tonight?" asked Snowball, the planner of adventures. There was nothing like a little adolescent rebellion to liven things up. Snowball said he needed to get something from his pack.

Down the trail to the beach they went, quietly, so as not to draw the attention of the other campers. They stepped into the clearing and out onto the long stretches of sand. The half-moon offered partial light for their walk. There was something about how the moon shone off the lake, the way the waves took the light and made art of it. The four took off their shoes and walked for a long time, finally stopping to rest on a log that had washed up in a spring storm.

They sat and talked. No Neck told them about when she lived in Superior, Wisconsin. There were a lot of positive aspects to living in a big town: going to rock concerts, carnivals, shopping malls, or the theater just down the street. She missed living there and was bored in Red Cliff. "Geez, there's nothing for kids to do there," she said.

"We could go to the movies anytime we wanted in Superior."

"I like living in Red Cliff," said Julie. She reached down and held Ron's hand. Ron felt awkward and couldn't speak. He only knew that tonight he would kiss her for the very first time. He knew it because he had been planning it for years, ever since he was 14. It wasn't like it was the first time he had kissed a girl. He had dated before and felt like a seasoned veteran. But this was different. He was completely sober, and there was a half-moon and a warm gentle breeze that kept the mosquitoes at bay. And there was a girl named Julie, whose soft and gentle hand was touching his.

"You guys want a pull?" Snowball pulled a pint bottle out of his back pocket. He opened it, took a tug, and handed it to Ron, joking, "You notice the way it speaks to you when it goes down? Good, good, good, good, good."

Ron laughed and took a tug of courage. It spoke to him.

He handed it to Julie, who said something like, "Sad, you guys, I don't drink that stuff."

She handed it to No Neck, who mumbled, "Ish."

Back to Snowball. "Good, good, good, good, good." It spoke to him too.

Back to Ron. Back to Snowball. Back to Ron. This went on for a while until the boys could hear flies buzzing inside their heads and everything was funny. Snowball began singing a song of enjoyment:

I like whiskey, ya way a hey yah
I like whiskey, ya way a hey yah
Hey oh, hey oh, hey oh, hey yah a hey yah
way ah hey, way ah hey, hey ah

Suddenly, a shadow appeared out of nowhere, a shadow whose initial darkness quickly became form and substance, a shadow whose voice sounded frighteningly familiar. It was Michael.

"Busted," everyone thought at the same time.

Snowball and Ron marched with heads down back to camp. Snowball told Michael the girls were innocent. This was confirmed by Ron. The girls begged Michael to be lenient on the boys, but he reminded them that they had all agreed to no booze, that there was to be no tolerance, and that the boys would probably be expelled and sent home from Project Bizindun.

They arrived in camp to find Ruth sitting on top of a picnic table, her frizzy hair wild against the firelight and shadows. "These boys have been drinking whiskey," said Michael, handing Ruth the remains of the bottle.

Ruth was livid. "Julie and Jenny, you get your little butts in that tent," she said, "and I don't want to hear a peep out of you. I'll talk to you two tomorrow." She pretended this had never happened before, but she had chaperoned many field trips and there was always something like this—always some minidisaster, and sometimes more than one. This was something she was good at.

Before Julie disappeared into her tent, she approached Ron and kissed him on the lips. Ruth gave Julie that disapproving look Ojibwe aunties give their nieces. Then she turned to Snowball and Ron, saying, "You boys get to bed. You're both going home tomorrow."

Snowball and Ron both slept very well, considering they had just been expelled from summer school and would have to face their parents in the morning. In Ron's dreams, he and Julie were sitting on a log out on a moonlit beach. He kissed her just the way it was supposed to be, the way it happens only in dreams.

The next morning the whole group broke camp. There was a hush, as everyone knew that two of their compadres were rolling up their sleeping bags for the last time, at least for this summer school program. Ron was sick. His tongue felt like he had been licking pool tables. Drums pounded in his head and his eyes wanted to stick shut. He saw Julie but couldn't look at her, couldn't talk to her. They loaded the vans and headed for the ferry landing. As they waited, Ruth called the boys' mothers from a public phone.

Bouncing Back or Reaching a Breaking Point

The ride back on the ferry was so quiet even the tourists wondered what was going on. Rez kids sat in the back of the boat, where Indians always sat. The two boy casualties of contemporary war sat with heads hung—and hung over.

After the ferry was secured to the dock in Bayfield, the vehicles were allowed to unload. The kids piled into the two blue Head Start vans, which headed out down Highway 13 toward Red Cliff. It was a quiet drive. Ron sat on the lake side where he always sat.

They pulled into the Head Start Center. All the passengers disembarked, except for Snowball and Ron. Michael poked his head inside the van to bid farewell to two rez kids he'd never see again. He was a good teacher, one who Ron would always remember. He was one of those good people who pass before us in the circle of our lives and then are gone forever.

"See you guys," he said to them. The rez kids said goodbye. No Neck and Julie just looked at their guys. Ruth jumped back into the van and fired it up. It lurched like some ancient horse, then down the road it went.

Snowball was dropped off first. He sauntered down his dusty driveway, lighting a cigarette as he went. He was an expert at getting into trouble and at being confronted by angry parents. Little did he know this expertise would be tested in the future when his own children would saunter down his dusty driveway to be confronted by him. The great circle of life travels in many forms.

Ron sat in the rear of the van as it turned up the dirt road to his home. It lurched to a stop in front of his driveway. He swallowed hard and climbed out, grabbing back at his tent and sleeping bag. There, in the yard, was his father, who was mending fishnets. Ron walked toward him not knowing what would be said. He came within a few feet of him, but his father seemed to look right past him.

Ron climbed the steps to his house, opened the old wooden screen door, and walked inside. It slammed hard. His mother faced away from him as she washed dishes at the kitchen sink. He put the tent and sleeping bag down and walked past her toward his room. She looked toward him, but as he walked by, she seemed to look beyond him too. In fact, she ignored him as if he were invisible.

He remained in his room for much of the day, almost afraid to go out. He was thirsty and in need of aspirin. He knew that he had shamed his parents and that he was being shamed in the old way of the People.

He would come out only when the coast was clear, when his parents were in their room or when they were outside. When all was clear, he gathered some food from the refrigerator and brought it to his room to eat alone. He could hear his mother answer the phone occasionally. Sometimes, it was for Ron. His mother always said, "No, Ronnie can't come to the phone right now." Her voice was gentle. And sad.

He slept, but it was a restless sleep, and he had to get up often to get a drink of something. He was overcome by thirst.

He awoke the next morning and came out of his room, padding down the hall to the kitchen. His mother sat at the kitchen table, and his father was in the living room reading the morning paper.

As his mother looked at him, Ron noticed she could see him again. She said, "Your father wants to talk to you."

Ron looked toward his father, who continued reading his paper. Then his father's voice spoke from behind the paper, strong and even and clearly understood by everyone in the room. "You aren't going anywhere for a while," he said.

Mash-ka-wi-sin (Be strong). Mi-i-iw (That is all).

Discussion Questions for "Season Spirits"

1. How might the decisions that Ron and Snowball made affect their schooling and, ultimately, their lives? What do you think happened to Ron? To Snowball?

2. Why do you think some people give up and others complete things? Are there good reasons to quit sometimes? Are there not-so-good reasons to finish sometimes?

3. What are the season spirits that affect the decisions you make? What voices tell you to give up, and why? What voices tell you to finish school and, ultimately, succeed in life?

A Review

A number of things keep young people from developing resilience. All of these things affect our breaking points, those moments when we make decisions to give up on something or complete it, no matter what. Any of the following can negatively influence a student's decision making:

- experiencing the cumulative effects of absenteeism, tardiness, and school attendance, which contribute to giving up on school
- being overcome by anger caused by many life frustrations
- becoming pregnant while still in school
- using alcohol and drugs
- having to deal with sexism
- internalizing and living out the low expectations of others, particularly teachers

Conversely, there are individual traits that foster resilience:

- being well-grounded and connected to one's tribal culture
- trying to live up to the high expectations of influential adults, particularly family
- tapping into one's inner strength and maturity to stay motivated when things aren't going well

Questions for Educators

1. What concrete things can schools do to reduce chronic absenteeism and tardiness?

What could be done to lessen the negative effects of mandatory attendance policies on chronically absent or tardy students?

2. How can schools identify and address the root causes of anger in Native young people?

3. What can schools do to help reduce teen pregnancy?

4. What school programs effectively deal with alcohol and drug use in Native young people?

5. What is the role of schools in assuring that students are well grounded in their tribal cultures?

6. What can schools do to nurture students' inner motivation?

7. How can schools reinforce the high expectations of families or promote high expectations?

8. What are the coordinated roles of schools, parents, tribes, agencies, and communities in dealing with these issues?

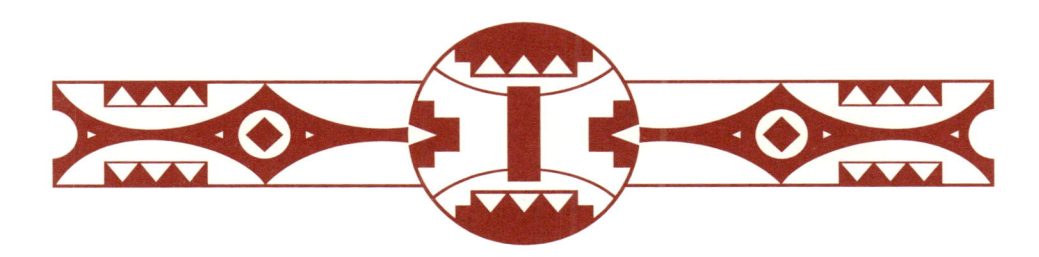

Full Circle

We began this chapter wondering what had helped Linda LeGarde Grover make it in school when most of her Native friends had dropped out. So many Native young people have a difficult time in school and in life as well. The reasons are many, and what helps one person will not always work for another. And there are always intangibles, including luck, timing, circumstances, happenstance, and, from my own perspective, divine intervention (the Creator's will).

Linda LeGarde Grover overcame her breaking points and grew up to be a caring person to the People, serving them as a wonderful poet, mother, grandmother, and teacher. Having a noble life purpose to serve the young, those in need, or the elderly is intricately woven into the great circle of these things. To learn to serve the People in the unobligated manner of our ancestors—not expecting or desiring anything in return—is to achieve wisdom.

Chapter 6
Honoring Our Gifts

This chapter examines how you can uncover the inner strength to help you cope in school. We look at the full range of intelligences that you and your friends might have. By reading about the abilities that some of the 120 students have found in themselves, you might identify some of your own strengths that have not yet been recognized or rewarded by your school. After reading this chapter, hopefully, students will more fully understand their likes and dislikes about school, and educators might begin thinking about multiple ways to approach Native learners.

A Hunting Metaphor

Linda

Before the federal government took charge of education for Native people, one of the things that young people did to gain status among their people was to hunt. In many Native cultures, both males and females contributed to the good of the community by hunting, and many different talents were needed to make the hunt successful. The young hunters needed sharp eyesight and observation skills to see the slightest movement on the horizon or in the woods. They needed spatial gifts to use the lay of the land to hunt effectively. They needed logical and mathematical gifts to consider the numbers in herds and figure out possibilities in the hunt. They needed physical gifts to move as graceful and powerful hunters. And they needed the gift of language to learn from the stories of past hunts, told by their elders around campfires.

But even these skills were not enough for a successful hunt. Hunters needed to have a keen knowledge of the others in the hunting party to figure out when silence was necessary, when words were not possible. They needed the gifts of understanding and predicting nature in order to tell the difference between a dust whorl and dust raised by a herd, to read clues in animal tracks, and to listen to the wind and know how its direction might affect the hunt. Some hunters needed musical intelligence to sing the songs of the hunt and discern the meanings behind the songs of the birds. And they needed spiritual intelligence to understand the meanings in their dreams and the guidance of their ancestors. Finally, they needed self-understanding to recognize their own individual strengths and know when and how to use them to best benefit their tribe. A hunter with a particular strength needed to know when to stay in the background until his or her particular talent or leadership was needed.

Hunters used these gifts in harmony with one another. Not all hunters had the same strengths in particular skills; the tribe naturally drew on the different gifts of each hunter. One hunter might be able to remember configurations of hills hundreds of miles away and know where and when the herds would gather. Another hunter might have a good sense of numbers and be able to calculate the efforts necessary to get game back to camp. Still others might have intuitions or dreams trusted by the other hunters, who considered these messages advice from the ancestors. Hunters didn't learn these skills by sitting in classrooms. They observed their elders, listened to the stories and songs, visualized the tales of great hunts of the past, assisted in chores preparing for the hunt, and, when old enough and skilled enough, joined in as assistants, learning in real situations and for real purposes.

The purpose for learning was compelling: survival of the tribe. There was no problem with motivation. Hunters used many different intelligences, and youth and elders held status for very different strengths. For nations and tribes to survive today, they still need everyone's gifts to be used in harmony.

Life today favors people and their skills less equally than it did when survival meant successful hunting; but, as peers and educators, we need to value what everyone has to offer. This chapter contemplates the gifts, or intelligences, we all have and how we can use them in different combinations for ourselves, those we care about, our communities, and the larger world.

In our schools today, status and eventual economic gain generally have been awarded to students who have developed strong language and mathematical skills early in life. They end up as good students and later get jobs that allow them financial security and some power in their worlds. Others, relatively few, earn respect and money for their physical skills and persistence (i.e., NBA players, gold-medal skaters, and runners) or for their musical intelligence (i.e., recording stars). Other gifts often go unacknowledged until success is earned based on them.

In recent years, more has been discovered about intelligence. Researcher Howard Gardner rejected the previous notion that humans can have a single intelligence score for *smartness*. Looking at a broad range of human abilities, he also rejected the notion that a human being has or is able to attain only one set of gifts.[1] While we collectively have a full range of different intelligences, each of us is unique in that we have a distinctive combination of those intelligences.

We are so unique that even the intelligence categories defined by Gardner and others are useful on the one hand but limiting on the other. Hunters on the Plains knew this before psychologists were certified. They balanced their community's needs with the abilities of their members to get the work accomplished, honoring each contribution.

Jeremy's Intelligence and How He Learned to Use It

In his early school years, the only way Jeremy (Aleut) felt exceptional was in his ability to beat up the kids who teased him. His physical agility and weight kept him sane in a world that didn't look kindly on his different ways. The irony is that he used physical violence as protection, even though he didn't like using his weight and coordination in that way.

In Jeremy's Own Words: "I Had Art Going for Me"

I like art, and, hopefully, that's what I can take up when I get out of school. Comic book art, that seems to be it. That's how I [finally] learned to read. My parents didn't really like [me being artistic] at the start, but they found that was the only way to keep me in check. I was a really bad troublemaker. Because of my weight, kids would make fun of me, and I'd take it out on them physically, beat up kids. There were some kids that [I] hurt. I was really sensitive about my weight in elementary school. It was like I was an alien, a sideshow freak. When my cousin was here, we used to always hang out . . . we hung around with a group, [but] we were the outsiders.

But then I got into art, a special class, because I had a learning disability. I pretty much focused on my art, and then I focused on controlling my anger. After a little while, I just sort of went, "The heck with it; all my anger's doing is getting me in trouble." In sixth grade, Ms. C used to help me. I'd go to her class, and she'd find another angle, do different things like building, drawing, reading books. We actually acted good and got good reports from [other] teachers.

One time, a kid slammed my head against the wall, and I lost it. That seemed to be the only one time where I really, really got mad. Tenth grade, it pretty much ended right there. I usually don't do anything until someone provokes me, making me hit something hard. Other than that, they can call me all the names they want. I say,

---

[1] See Gardner, *Frames of Mind*.

"Sit down, little man," 'cause I really don't care anymore. I just pretty much put it all out of me.

When I moved to the city from the village, everybody treated me with mutual respect and stuff, all different kinds of kids, and I had art going for me. I was taught at an early age to respect my elders, my grandpa, some of my uncles. You can just walk in and learn a lot of stuff off of them. And teachers should [use respect], treat students equal, like my grandpa. If they treat everybody equal, then that will teach students to treat everybody equal later on in life too. If a White teacher treats a Black kid [badly] in front of [a] White kid, then the White kid goes out in the playground, and he's ragging on the [Black] kid because maybe he looks up to the teacher. Next thing you know, the [Black] kid is a complete outcast.

And if [special education kids] are supposed to be in the grade where the others are actually doing algebra, the [special education] teacher should at least teach them a little bit of algebra. I mean, don't keep them back [from things]. If other kids find out [the special education kids aren't doing algebra], they'll crack on them, make fun of them—sort of lowers their self-esteem.

You feel bad, really bad, but I pretty much got over it. I've had this through my whole life. I used to use my weight against all the little kids 'cause they were afraid of me. I was trying to be all hard. Then, after that, I pretty much mellowed out. Now, if I hit a little kid, I'd probably kill him. I ain't doing that. Just get out of my face and back off.

[When I was young], I felt inferior, "You're special ed., ha, ha, ha." But when I got into art, a special class because I had a learning disability, it focused me on my art, and then I could focus on controlling my anger.

If Jeremy had been in a school that valued only weight, physical agility, and artistic talents, he would have received all A's. But he wasn't. Jeremy discovered his artistic abilities, with the help of his special education teacher, and managed to get beyond the anger and pain of being overweight. If Jeremy had lived in Italy when the de Medici family supported artists financially, his skills would have been valued and rewarded. Schools in North America aren't particularly good at recognizing, using, and rewarding differences. Many students with skills that aren't cherished by schools find themselves designated as "gifted" or "special ed." Jeremy had been designated as special ed. before I interviewed him at the end of his high school years. Both federal and state governments give extra money to schools that have high numbers of students designated in this way, so identifying students as "special" brings in much needed funding for operating costs. This is good for the schools but probably unfair to many students who possess unique talents and intelligences. In a way, "special ed." and "gifted" are great descriptors, but they also have taken on meanings that aren't as "special" as originally intended.

So, What Are Your Gifts?

In this chapter, you will probably find out that you are smart (intelligent) in more than one way. Most everyone is smart in a complex combination of ways. A few people are extraordinarily smart in one way and have to work hard at being smart in other ways. For those of you who are educators, you may be interested in how these intelligences play out in the lives of Native people.

The Western world hands out money and power, to a great extent, based on two skills: linguistic-verbal and logical-mathematical. You probably are somewhat familiar with these areas because of school. Are these intelligences special strengths for you? Ask yourself the questions in the next sections and then listen to some students who have these strengths. This chapter goes way beyond these two kinds of intelligences. Don't stop reading when you determine one of your strengths because you are probably smart in a number of ways.

Intelligences That Lead to School Success

Linguistic (Language)-Verbal

Do your thoughts come out easily in words? Do you enjoy reading and writing? Do they come easily for you? Do you enjoy hearing stories? Do you enjoy telling stories to get your points across? Do you like the sounds and rhythms of the words you or others speak or write? Do you learn new languages easily? Do you enjoy speaking about your thoughts and beliefs or reading about those of others? Do you learn by listening to people? How do you show a teacher you know something? By writing or talking about it or in some other way? Do you like books? Word games?

As you ask yourself these questions, remember that you do not need to answer each one positively to indicate that you have a special strength in this area. Different strengths play out differently in different people's lives. Through the years, Quoetone, the Ojibwe student introduced in chapter 2, learned that he had strong linguistic-verbal skills; reading and talking about thoughts were things he did for fun:

♦ In sixth grade, I learned the whole human anatomy with the rest of the class. There was one thing we had to do. We had to take a test at the end of the year. We all had to keep these notebooks, so you could use them when you took your test, writing everything down from the board. I didn't write down a note all year, and then I scored highest in class. [The teacher] said, "Where's your notebook?" I said, "I didn't use one; I just listened to you all year."...

Taking notes interrupts your thought process. I can usually recall, if not verbatim, at least very close to it, and that helps in school.

Logical-Mathematical

Do you enjoy working with numbers? Do you enjoy using logical step-by-step reasoning? Does school math come easily to you? Can you apply math easily to shopping, doing tasks, playing cards, building, cooking? Do you like to solve problems, fix things, plan outcomes, etc.? Are you interested in science and its new explanations for things? Do you like finding logical flaws in speeches or writing? Do you enjoy measuring and analyzing with numbers?

Dee (Ojibwe) has found something he likes to do that keeps his attention and he knows he's good at. Mathematics comes easily, while computer drawing, which probably taps skills that aren't in his areas of strength, is hard:

- I like math, and it seems like all the math teachers that I had like me 'cause I like that subject. When I'm in math class, don't matter what kind of mood I'm in, I just like solving like algebra. I like algebra. Right now, I'm on the computer for math class. That's kinda hard, I think, 'cause we're drawing stuff on the computer, have to use commands that just draw it for us and do all this and that. I think I'd like to be an accountant 'cause we have accounting class right now with the math teacher; he's teaching two of us, and that's pretty fun. All the stuff in that class interests me.

Linguistic-verbal and logical-mathematical intelligences are often the most honored skills in schools. Of course, many rich and famous athletes, musicians, artists, and dancers have been successful with limited linguistic and mathematical skills, but only a few make it to the place where sizable rewards come their way. It's useful to develop the verbal and mathematical skills you have, but to judge your entire worth by them (as many Canadian and United States schools tend to do) is wrongheaded. This system is unfair, but, just now, that's the way it is. While most schools excel in developing linguistic and mathematical skills, they should never ignore the other gifts you might have. And, if they do ignore your other gifts, you should not; instead, seek out ways to develop them.

The Other, Often Extracurricular, Intelligences

Schools frequently encourage students with other intelligences to take electives or participate in extracurricular activities. Read how other students discovered their particular intelligences and see if you recognize some of the same skills in yourself. The first intelligence we will explore is actually required in most states as a regular part of the school day, but it's most apparent in after-school sports.

Bodily-Kinesthetic

Do people consider you well coordinated or skillful in using your body to meet your personal goals? Does your body pay attention to what your mind wants from it? Do you learn well when you can work directly with the objects or materials about which you are learning? Do you enjoy sports or dancing or crafts? Would you rather be doing things than sitting still? Would you be good at assembling small computer components or sewing up a wound? Can you work with machines that need coordination of different pieces? Can you figure out what something is or does by touching it?

Jamie (Seneca) had pride in his own physical talents and in his Native peers:

◆ The reason our basketball team is going to the semifinals is because of the Native Americans. . . . [A Native American kid] took the basketball team to the semifinals. You know, some kids look at Indians as being good athletes, and, you know, it's kinda cool they just look at us like that. They always try to be as good as us, but they can't, and they always wonder why.

Bodily-kinesthetic skills play out in many ways other than sports. Like Maria in chapter 2, many Native students find they really enjoy dancing, and they look forward to powwows and powwow season. Other students find themselves adept at fixing things, as North Star's brother enjoyed fixing bikes.

Visual-Spatial

Do you have artistic skills? Can you think in three dimensions, as a sailor, architect, or moving-van packer might? Can you pack a lot into a small space, knowing how things should fit together? Can you see things in visual images? Do you picture things in your mind as you would like them to be in the real world? Are you one of the people who does not get lost easily, knowing where you are after several turns? Are you good at puzzles? At drawing? At doodling? Can you tell how something might be fixed by looking at it, or by watching someone else fix it? Are you good at reading diagrams or maps? Was geometry easier for you than algebra? Do you prefer books with pictures and diagrams?

Carol, a young Navajo woman, realized how important it was to have visual components as well as other ways of learning:

◆ I like to see visual things. If I had a history teacher, I'd want to act out the roles of the people because what I'm trying to do is like imagine them as real people in history. It's a lot easier to learn things if it means something to you. In math, if you're just given a lot of formulas, it doesn't make any sense. But if the teacher applies it, gives you examples of how you can use it in your life, then I see it and retain it a lot better. I have this teacher in chemistry, and she always makes up these funny voices and different stories, and I can remember it a lot better when I associate it with a story.

Because so many students talked to us about valuing visual components in the classroom, we will say a bit more in this section. Some time ago, I interviewed a young man who wanted to be called Hobbes. He told me that visualizing events while reading helped him to remember them. He pretended his mind was a VCR, transforming textbooks into pictures and movies that played out in his head. Then, at test time, he'd push "rewind through the pictures in [his] mind" to get to the place that had the answer.[2]

---

[2] For more from Hobbes, see Cleary, Hudson-Ross, and Casey, eds., *Children's Voices*.

Rob (Wampanoag) had a teacher who helped him remember science material:

◆ He'd put up a couple of elements on the board, show us how to make them a compound, stuff like that.

As soon as science became visual, Rob could remember.

Movies were favorite learning experiences for students. Many said things like Dee (Ojibwe):

◆ I like English teachers that show you, that might pick someone out of the classroom and have them come up to the board, do something. That's what you need, visuals, or something you know. Anything will help. Like in English class, we read *Geronimo,* and then we watched the movie. Then you can tell the differences between the book and movie, and it's fun 'cause you can watch the movie.

Musical

Are you sensitive to the melodies and rhythms of songs? Can you sense what people mean by the tone of what they say? Do you enjoy music? Listening to it? Playing it? Singing it? Drumming it? Are you drawn to the drums and songs of the powwow or other ceremonial music? Do you sense how music affects others? Do you hear music that others don't always hear, in nature or in the sounds of people going about their lives? Can you sense when music is off-key? Do your feet move, tapping to music when you aren't even aware of them? Do you surround yourself with music whenever possible?

Travis (Dakota) found out he had a natural gift for drumming and singing, but he had to develop the quality of his voice to go along with his natural gift:

◆ I was driving down, back from Montana, and my Dad was relearning the pipe-filling song. And so, when you fill the pipe, you sing a certain song for it that came so many thousands of years ago. But my Dad was handing out [the words], and they didn't hand me a paper, so I got kind of upset. So, I put the tape in my headphones, and I learned it in about an hour. And that's how I started singing, kind of just came natural to me. I can like listen to a song and go in there and sing it like a couple minutes later. Then, fifth through eleventh grade, I really didn't have much voice; I was like real low. And my friends used to make fun of me, say, "You can't sing." But you know, I kind of stuck with it 'cause I had fun anyway. And now, I'm the lead singer for my drum group because I worked on my voice by myself. And my Dad really surprised me 'cause we were sitting at Christmastime, he comes out with this big box, and he opens it up, and he had a big drum. It's about 27 inches, and it has both of our names on it. And that's the drum we've used ever since. He said we made him so proud when we sang, so he made us a drum.

Ellen (Karuk) likes music in her life. She's aware of her skills, having learned to play the piano, guitar, and, most recently, viola:

◆ I've played different things, and then I started playing the viola like a year ago. We've never had a group [before], and now it's like 13 kids, which is pretty big for this high school. We played in concerts, and this is the first year we've ever had a string group. It's just been really fun to play really good-sounding music with a bunch of kids. Whenever things are really bad, when I'm having a really bad day, the class that always cheers me up is my Orchestra class.

Interpersonal

Do you get along well with others? Do you sense how others feel and know what they want from you or others? Are you able to let others know what you want or need? When life isn't going well, are you able to think it through or talk about it and make it better? Does friendship with peers, adults, and children come easily for you? Can you read the body language or moods of others? Do you know when to take the lead and when to follow? Do you surround yourself with social activities when you have time? Do people seek you out for counsel?

We often recognize the presence of a certain skill because we enjoy doing things related to it. Martin (Mohawk) said:

- A good day is [when] we work together in groups, to discover how to do [something] together and find the right answers and how to do it properly and do more work.

Martin probably had interpersonal strengths, as did John (Ojibwe), who said:

- When people started asking questions, it got more fun. When everybody was interacting, everybody was involved with the teacher.

Relationships, especially family relationships, are very important to American Indian, First Nations, and Alaska Native people. We practice the things we value, and the things we practice often become strengths. Relationships may be very important to you; interpersonal intelligence might be something you already rely on. Many students, including North Star in chapter 2, told us that friendships were the only things that kept them in schools.

Intrapersonal

Do you understand your own strengths and weaknesses pretty well? Does your life go along pretty smoothly because you can acknowledge what is needed and plan to make things happen for yourself and others? Even when life is pretty complicated or distressing, are you able to make life be what you want it to be? Do you learn pretty easily from your own mistakes or from the mistakes of those you observe? Do you enjoy being alone so you can think about things or write about them in a journal? When things don't make sense, when you see contradictions in the world in front of you, do you try to make sense of them?

Werlth-Kerish-Nah (Hoopa) discovered he could make things work out for himself by thinking about them. He used intrapersonal skills and examined his own experiences and motives:

- I had to look within myself, inner self, figuring out that these things happen. There are things in life that you'll be dealing with, and if you let them carry you and destroy you and take you down, then that's where you're gonna dwell. But if you learn and understand them, then you will gain from them. You'll gain strength. And it's helped me out a lot, mainly when I went back to the religion, the religion of the Indian people, and started understanding the meanings again; because, for a period there, I was blind to it. I had forgotten. I think it was constantly taking the wrong path that finally made me say, "Hold on, I'm going down the wrong road. I can see that now, and I know that I have to change." And the only way that I could do it was if I examined what I was doing. It's like looking at my actions from someone else's perspective. If I do this, what is that going to do to the people around me? And that had a real impact on me. I was constantly fighting and bickering with everybody. I was more along the lines of like withering away, like a flower withering away because it doesn't have the nutrients that it needs. So I had to supply myself with what I needed to revive. It was just realizing, I guess just growing up in a sense, realizing that freedom of choice was there. It was always there, and whatever path I wanted to go down was the one that I could go down if I put my mind to it.

Growing up, in a way, is developing one's intrapersonal skills. As we reviewed the interviews, it became clearer and clearer that intrapersonal skills (examining one's own motives and experiences) are extremely valuable. The reflective students were better able to deal with life when it became tough. Some young people managed to think things through using writing; others made sense of things by talking to their peers, their relatives, or an elder. Making sense of the world helped them to have some power in it. It may be that these intrapersonal strengths are the main ingredients in the resilience described in chapter 5. Students with strong intrapersonal skills may be able to get themselves beyond breaking points more easily.

Emerging Regard for Other Intelligences

In addition to these well-accepted intelligences, scholars are investigating several other intelligences.[3] Researchers have studied naturalist, existential, and spiritual intelligence, establishing evidence to support the first two. American Indian, First Nations, and Alaska Native people have long valued the strengths connected with these "new" intelligences.

Naturalist Intelligence

Do you find yourself interested in categories of things? For instance, do you like to identify trees, plants, animals, or minerals? Do you like observing things and thinking about how they are similar to and/or different than other things? Many cultures place a value on such recognition, especially if the items are useful or dangerous. For instance, tribal cultures usually honor

---

[3] See Gardner, *Intelligence Reframed*.

those who can identify healing herbs and who know how and when to use them. Do these kinds of things interest you? You might even recognize things by smell (a sort of olfactory intelligence) or touch (a sort of tactile intelligence). Naturalists, farmers, hunters, fishers, and gardeners can all benefit from this intelligence. For those who live in the city, maybe you are adept at identifying and categorizing things like models of automobiles. You might be good at recognizing the sounds of different engines or artistic styles or musical classifications. Even poets or researchers can benefit from this type of intelligence by seeing patterns in life or in data.

Gina (Navajo) expressed interest in being an artist, although her ability to categorize things might make her a good researcher in the social sciences:

◆ It's kind of weird like I can see something that [other students] don't see, or I understand things that they don't understand. Like, I drew back from society a while and just looked at the entire school population. I'd kind of step back, and I'd just observe the entire playground and all of the little cliques and groups that were kind of scattered out, and I'd notice the similarities between them and the differences. That's where the observation part really came in. Like, sometimes when you'd be left alone or you'd be walking, you just kind of have thoughts in your head, and you just kind of stay in your head all day long. Those are really good days. Observing is a big part of it, like learning from other people's mistakes.

Sonny (Hoopa) has blended his naturalistic interests with a desire to help his community become more self-determined:

◆ I hope I can help my community change when I'm older. I plan on going to college and coming back. I'll be able to get our tribe more natural resources because, now, they're just relying on timber. There's a lot of things they could do; we have really good soil content. I always wondered why they never grew [their] own produce to sell to their own people so we [wouldn't] have to buy shipped-in produce, which might not be any good. They can do a lot of gardening, a lot of orchards; they could even grow mushrooms, a lot of old mines they could utilize. They could do preserves, such as jams. They could also have a winery. We have to get half our water back; we only get 10 percent now. We need more of our river water back; we aren't keeping our salmon [from] dying out. We could grow water; we could grow hardwood. We could sell fresh vegetables, eggs, and bottled water in the community. My uncle used to have 100 chickens to sell eggs. I would be circulating the money, and we wouldn't have to have our food shipped in.

Spiritual-Existential Intelligence

We group spiritual and existential intelligence together because the two closely interrelate. While existential intelligence has been given the researcher's stamp of approval,[4] spiritual intelligence is harder to validate because

---

[4] For more distinctions between spiritual and existential intelligence and the distinctions that Gardner makes between the two, see Gardner, *Intelligence Reframed*.

no scientifically reliable ways have been found to investigate these gifts. Answer the following questions to see whether you have or are developing these gifts.

Do you wonder about the meaning of life and death? Do you wonder about things so small they are unseeable or so big they are unfathomable? Do you wonder about the ultimate destiny of the world? Do you share your thoughts about what is meaningful and important in the world so that people come to you for guidance when distressed? Are you intrigued by and highly interested in the wisdom that elders have? Are you particularly sensitive to the meanings of your dreams? Do you seek to understand your dreams and allow those dreams to guide you? Do you take your intuitions seriously and see them working well for you?

While scholars try to understand these forms of intelligence, many Native people feel no need to question what they perceive as very real gifts. Researcher Allan Charles Ross has studied the deep history connected to dreams and D/Lakota people:

> In studying D/Lakota history, I found that we had dream societies a hundred years ago. The people used dreams to guide their lives at that time. A person would have the holy man of the dream society interpret the dream in a ceremony. Maybe the dream foretold an event. The people attending the ceremony would then share this information with friends and relatives.[5]

Ross points out that dreams come from the unconscious portion of our minds. We are rarely conscious of a dream's symbolism without serious reflection and/or guidance from someone who has the spiritual experience to help interpret. Ross concludes that few dreams have literal interpretations.[6]

As well as having intrapersonal strengths, Werlth-Kerish-Nah (Hoopa) might also have these well-honored spiritual strengths:

◆ I went back to the religion, the religion of the Indian people, and started understanding the meanings again.... I was doing the sweat house and going through the ceremonies, going through fasting, all of this looking for the answer. And in a dream, about two years into it, where I was still searching for that answer, [my uncle] had been given to me in a dream, to just talk to him. When I was talking to him in my dream, it was in nothing but [my Native] language, which I speak [only] a little bit. But he was speaking to me in [my language]. And when I went to speak to him, when I went to talk to him about it, the dream, it was like he was telling me the same exact thing that he had said in the dream, but it was in English. And I could make a lot of connections now because I've learned a lot more of [my] language.... I can still see it really very vividly in my mind, and so I can understand the connection. And I'd imagine the more of the language

---

[5] Ross, *Mitakuye Oyasin*, 12.
[6] Ibid.

that I learn, the more connection I will also understand.

Ross might say that Werlth-Kerish-Nah used his dream vision to find a new path in life. He used both his intrapersonal and spiritual strengths to guide him on his way. Many people are able to sense when good or bad is happening and know how to act. As a member of the Seventh Generation, it is time to call up your own spiritual gifts. Open your mind to search for the path and to allow in messages about the way to go.

The Interrelatedness of Your Gifts: Holistic Approaches

Notice that all these intelligences and their related skills have been separated out. Although the modern world sometimes depends on specialists (for example, lawyers, doctors, and artists), most life tasks depend on multiple intelligences, and even specialists draw upon multiple strengths to improve their work. A surgeon needs both scientific knowledge and bodily-kinesthetic skills to operate with sure hands. We wouldn't want surgeons on our case if they had only logical-mathematical intelligence. Think about several relatives of yours. How integrated are their strengths? In some middle schools and fewer high schools, interdisciplinary programs enable students to use all their skills in one class. Have you had such classes? Most high schools, unfortunately, have only the more traditional classes that develop one strength at a time, and, if you are lucky, they offer a broad range of electives that tap into your extracurricular intelligences. In chapter 2, Maria had time in her daily schedule for English, Biology, Choir, Geometry, American History, Spanish, and Pottery, and after school, she ran track. Each subject addressed an individual intelligence during a separate time period. That wasn't the way the Plains Indians developed their hunting skills in the past.

Many of the students who enjoyed learning talked about situations that allowed their intelligences to work together. Educators call this holistic learning. Bigg Dogg (Ojibwe) found that school became both fuller and fun when he was allowed to use hands-on techniques and combine new learning with what he already knew:

◆ I really don't like science, except for lab. I liked learning the periodic table 'cause I already knew most of it, and then we started doing the dot diagrams. Labs are fun, but then when the teacher just sits in front of the class and talks, it gets boring, and then you start to hate it.

Holistic and interdisciplinary learning were so popular among the students that we will tell educators more about them in chapter 9.

Cherishing Your Intelligences and Developing New Strengths

In today's world, various experiences can help develop your gifts or hinder their development. Sometimes, you can control the experiences that help cultivate your strengths, and, at other times, the world can work against that development.

Choosing a learning style doesn't have to be an either/or situation. You can continue learning in a style that works best for you while opening yourself to many new ways of learning. Likewise, you can put yourself around people who have the same gifts as you do while apprenticing with those whose skills you admire. You also can practice. Those who want to get better at basketball practice for hours.

As with the hunters of yesteryear, developing and using your gifts contribute to your happiness, your survival, and the betterment of those around you. You probably won't starve in our modern world if you don't make the most of your skills and talents, but you should be highly motivated to become self-sufficient, happy, and purposeful in life. We have given examples of nine different intelligences. Remember, you likely have strengths in several of these areas and the potential for developing other strengths.

So, What's the Connection with Learning Styles?

Quite a number of students we interviewed realized they were more adept at certain learning styles. For example, many said, "I'm a visual learner." Indeed, some students had actually been tested to determine their best learning style; however, not one student thought that learning style correlated with special intelligence. Learning styles are products of the ways in which you are intelligent.

You need to take your gifts seriously because if researchers have learned one thing, it's that feeling good about yourself can make you more confident and able in school. As Jeremy said, "I have art going for me," and that made a difference for him in school. Daisy (Yurok) felt that she had come to believe in herself too late:

◆ I look back now, and I could have done so much better. Like, I know now that I can apply myself and actually achieve the goal. And I'm not realizing it until this year, and

I just wish I would've believed in myself when I was a freshman, sophomore, and junior, applied myself, and I could have done a lot better.

So much of success is about believing in yourself and your abilities, even when your special abilities aren't the ones that schools recognize. It also is important to learn new abilities, even if you know you probably won't ever be exceptional at them. Have you been told you have a certain learning style? Does it make sense given the questions you've answered about yourself in this chapter? Are you using your gifts and believing in yourself?

Attention and Intelligences

Fred (Choctaw) reflected on a friend who dropped out of school because it didn't relate to his world:

◆ If he just could have found something in school that interested him, that would have kept him here. That was the main reason why he didn't want to go anymore. It was always learning about a society that wasn't him because he was raised up in a traditional way. He knew our history, but he was being taught the dominant society history in school, and it was of no interest to him. He couldn't find that good feeling that he got from accomplishing something, like we did in artwork [with his father]. [If he felt] the accomplishment, the gratitude that he deserved, I guess he probably would have stuck it out.

Attention is an interesting thing. Our inner attention is held when we get good feelings from doing something or when others appreciate what we do. We tend to get bored with things that are hard for us. Fred's friend hadn't found anything in school that was relevant enough to him to hold his attention.

Each person's attention span relies on his or her *short-term memory*. We can concentrate on about five things at any one time. Any more than five crowds something else out. Things that are interesting or troubling seem to have first priority; things that are uninteresting get crowded out, particularly if we are upset or if distractions are present.

What kinds of things interrupt your attention during the school day? What do teachers do to keep your attention or to let it stray? Have you found ways to bring your attention back to a topic if you've been distracted? Some students have found they have more luck paying attention if they can think hard enough about what is being taught or find ways to connect their lives to what is being taught.

Many students wanted school to keep their attention. People generally enjoy doing things they are good at, so challenging subjects take a certain control of one's attention. Having varied ways of learning seemed to help students like Casey (Ojibwe) find fun in learning:

◆ I want to go to a community college to be a mechanic, get my own shop, hopefully do good there, so I can do whatever I want to. I'd [like to] make school less painful. I'd teach hands-on. Reading, you probably couldn't throw out; but, for a lot of other classes, there's gotta be a better way to teach than the way it's going now. There's gotta be a way to make it more fun.

North Star (Abenaki) went a step further, recognizing that when education isn't fun, other things become more tempting:

◆ Let's say the teacher doesn't always have to talk about mathematics. Sometimes, he could talk about other things for 15 minutes, "What did you do today?" You gotta make it fun because nobody will ever want to [go to school]. That's when people start smoking and doing other things—too boring in school.

The students liked changes in learning activities, and no one complained about changes occurring too frequently. Some students have long attention spans, while others have shorter attention spans. What is your attention span like? What topics and subjects hold your attention? How do they relate to your strengths? How might you keep your attention when working in areas that don't come naturally to you?

You Can Develop Many Intelligences

Scientists who study the way the brain works have learned that experiences and learning can change people's mental abilities.[7] Education and other experiences can strengthen an intelligence you already have or reinforce a weakness. It's important to know your strengths, but don't cut yourself off from learning in other ways that will help your mind grow in its flexibility and promise. You can develop more ways of learning and think beyond your current strengths, thus expanding the ways you can learn about and act upon the world.

Human beings essentially do two things: take in information about the world through their senses and use this information to act upon the world through their own will, voice, physical actions, and expressions. A rock star will use words, voice, movement, and music to act upon the world, making people aware of experiences, beliefs, opinions, and feelings. A writer uses the written word to do the same. The more ways we have to take information in and act as a result of it, the more resilient we are when things aren't going well.

---

[7]See the work of Marian Diamond from the University of California at Berkeley, as cited on page xxi of Linda Campbell, Bruce Campbell, and Dee Dickinson, *Teaching and Learning through Multiple Intelligences*.

Gina (Navajo) worried about teachers who thought they could peg her as having only one learning style:

◆ They'll have you take a test that says you learn best by audio or by visual, but I never really liked that 'cause it kind of made me feel like this teacher's going to think he knows how to teach this to me. I guess I just don't really like tests that define me too much.

Why didn't Gina want to be pegged? Teachers usually mean well, but learning style tests should help you see your strengths, not define who you are or limit the ways you can learn. Likewise, some teachers are gifted in helping you learn and work in ways you aren't accustomed to. Gina described a teacher who could do this:

◆ Your own little spark, she just kind of would bring it out in you. I'd look up and see just a lump of clay. And I'd be like watching everybody else trying to make something, and they'd be, "Oh, I just can't do this!" And she'd go over there, and she'd start talking to them about what they like and things like that, and, eventually, she'd draw them to something, and they'd be like, "Oh, yeah, I can do that!" And it was so great to see her do that to like everybody!

Gina's teacher helped her students connect their interests with the skill she was hired to teach. She motivated them to try out a new skill many were not naturally gifted at. She and teachers like her go to some effort to recognize the skills, interests, strengths, and possibilities of all students while meeting the requirements of the local and state education systems. These teachers use pictures, films, stories, books, exercises, experiments, group work, research, and all sorts of different activities, depending on their students. Have you had such a teacher?

You probably have preferences in the ways you like to learn. Sometimes, it's a matter of tastes, likes, and dislikes, but your preferences may also be affected by your gifts and experiences. For instance, someone who likes to work in groups may have been given strong interpersonal intelligence, or that person may have developed interpersonal skills by working frequently in groups. Others may have a strong interest in wildlife (caring for the four-leggeds) but no particular knack for forging relationships with people. However, to fight for various causes, they might be forced to overcome a lack of interpersonal skills and forge alliances with other pro-wildlife activists. In working with such a group, a person with wildlife interests might develop interpersonal intelligence, naturalistic intelligence, linguistic-verbal intelligence, and logical-mathematical intelligence. This positive experience with learning could make group work a preference in the future.

In chapter 9, we have written about what students liked and didn't like. If you are a student, hearing about things other students like might help you recognize the ways you prefer to learn. If you are an educator, you will be interested in what your Native students think about their learning.

Believing in Yourself: A Personal Story
by Linda Miller Cleary

Early this spring, I was sitting at the kitchen table eating breakfast with my 94-year-old father, who still lives in the same house I grew up in and still prepares all the meals for himself and his 89-year-old wife, my mother.

He leaned toward me over the table to ask a question that must have been on his mind for years: "How come you were the daughter that got to be a professor? You didn't do that well in high school." I certainly hadn't earned the grades my sisters had, but they weren't bad grades either. Nevertheless, they weren't the straight A's my father considered to be evidence of keen intelligence, and he had wanted me to become a secretary.

During this particular visit home, I had been slipping upstairs to write this chapter, in between the long talks and the yard work. I was finishing the first draft of this chapter, so I could tell him with absolute confidence, "Dad, I wasn't smart in the ways that high school wanted me to be smart. All they wanted back then was for me to memorize facts and give those back to them in tests. I wasn't good at memorization. I'm still not, but I'm good at research. That's the way that universities want you to be smart now."

"Yes," he said thoughtfully, "I suppose that is right. You were always full of questions and were always trying to explain things." And, finally, I felt respected by my father for the first time.

I would have been miserable as a secretary because, besides having difficulty with memorization, I'm also terrible at dealing with details and repetitive tasks. My father might have approved, but he didn't live in my skin. Having others recognize your particular set of intelligences might not come right away; but if you have faith in yourself, you'll have the pride and confidence to get on with what you want to do. The earlier you recognize your gifts, the sooner you can contribute to your community, as hunters did long ago. Someday, you'll be appreciated for the things you do well, if you allow yourself to do them.

A Quest: How to Use Your Intelligences to Chart Your Future

It's always wise to use the gifts you've been given to their best advantage. You'll be happier and better to be around if you're engaged in activities you like to do. If you see your particular set of intelligences as a gift given to you at birth, then a way you can return that gift to the world is to use it successfully for the people you care about and for the world in general. Most schools give assessments to help students choose a career. Some students actually gain insight from the assessments, but others just get amused by them. Quoetone (Ojibwe) laughed deeply when he told me the results of his most recent career inventory:

◆ They give us those career things every year, where you plot out your career and what you would like to do. I like working in the wood shop; I like reading. [But] when I first took [the assessment], I was supposed to be working with wildlife management. I was like, "I don't think so." But I just took it again, and they said I should be more of a college office worker, working with students, a politician, or an FBI field agent.

Charting your future is a sort of internal quest, and in taking that journey, you honor your gifts and your uniqueness. If only for that purpose, it would be good to develop the introspective and reflective skills that will help you think about what you want to do in your future. A quest to find a way to give back to the world may also be a quest to find hope, purpose, and happiness in your future. It's a challenge for everyone who turns the corner from childhood to adulthood. The main character in that quest must be you, not the administrator who gives career inventories. You'll need to take time to think, considering carefully what others have to say along the way, even the career counselor and the inventory reports. You'll get to a place where you understand the meanings and teachings of dreams, visions, and educational and spiritual guides. Only you can be the interpreter of your dreams and visions, and their meanings may not come clear all at once. Your quest will eventually lead you to a path that honors your strengths.

Here are some questions that might help you begin or continue the quest for a future. You might spend some time reflecting, paying attention to related dreams, and charting the possibilities. You have a future to find.

1. What do you consider to be several of your gifts?
2. Do you have any talents that don't seem to be described by the intelligences listed in this chapter?
3. Do you have any learning preferences that could affect the way you learn skills and develop talents for the future?
4. How does school help you develop the gifts you have? How doesn't it?
5. Could you do things at school or in the community that would help you develop your gifts?
6. Who could you seek out to help you learn the things and skills you want to

know? Could anyone else help you meet a person who could help you?

7. Can you think of a future, or several futures, you might like to pursue? Are there any things you could do now to help you achieve that future? Are there decisions you could make now that could keep you from getting to that future?

8. In what ways could your gifts or talents help the world in the future? What might be the next step?

9. How can you express where you are now in your quest? Through writing? Through drawing or painting or sculpting? Through a discussion with another? Through dancing? Through a song that you write, or through the music that you put to the song? Through conversations with insightful others?

Chapter 7
Making It in School

This chapter talks about how your family might help you make it in school and how you can stay motivated without compromising your Indigenous ways of being. As you'll see, this requires support both within and outside the school. The chapter also describes ways to make it in different subject areas.

"Always keep learning" is one of the messages to the Seventh Generation from the elders. All students need to know some ways to keep learning when school isn't satisfying their needs. In a way, learning in school is all about resilience, finding ways to bend instead of break and tapping intrapersonal resources to learn in a variety of ways.

How Your Family Can Help You Make It in School

Tom

I think my parents were pleasantly surprised I actually graduated from high school, although they never told me that. They didn't complete high school themselves, and my older brothers had all dropped out, although they all later finished the GED (general education diploma). I was sort of a nerd. I was good at school. I attended classes, did my homework, and never thought about quitting. I still hung out with all the hell-raisers on the rez, got into more than my share of trouble, and watched as all my friends (with the exception of one) quit school one by one, got sent away to reform school, or were killed in car accidents. On graduation day, my parents had a big graduation party, and, although they didn't say a thing about it, I could tell they were proud of me. They had an unspoken manner that was entirely culturally appropriate (Ojibwe parents rarely praise their children openly). Yet, they couldn't mask their pride in me. It shone in their eyes and in the way they said to all my aunties and uncles, "He's going to college, you know." I can't say I did it all for them, to make them proud. There was just no way I wouldn't have finished school. I never would have shamed them or disrespected them in that way. I respected them too much.

Just as the respect I had for my parents motivated me to finish school, the students we interviewed identified key family elements that have helped them make it in school: adult family members serving as role models, mutual respect among students and parents/grandparents, family expectations, and families discussing future goals with their children.

Adult Family Members Serving as Role Models

One of the great life lessons adults can pass on to their children is the ability to stick to things and finish them, no matter what. Parents can serve as role models for their children without ever calling themselves role models. It's done by living out a system of values that children get to witness day after day. Amber, a Hoopa student, spoke of the lessons taught by her mother:

◆ My mom, she's always worked hard. She didn't get anything easy. She's a teacher, and she's got to work with kids every day. She listens, and there are days when she's like at the end of her wits, and she can't, whatever. But she's never, never hit me or any of my brothers and sisters out of anger. And I really appreciate that. She's taught us the morals and principles that I hold, and she taught us not to judge people by their looks or religion, race, by anything. She just taught us to bear with it.

Another student, Megan (Ojibwe), admired both her parents because they had survived many odds:

◆ My mom, I look up to her a lot because she's had a really tough life. She made something good out of it. She grew up in a one-room shack with five brothers and sisters, and by the time she was in fourth grade, she'd read every book in the library. And then she borrowed some money and went to nursing school when she graduated high school, and saved up her money and put herself through law school. She was the first Native American woman lawyer. My dad went through a lot too. He escaped from the [Nazi] Holocaust when he was 12, so he's had a tough life too.

Mutual Respect among Students and Parents/Grandparents

Mutual respect is very important among students and their caregivers, parents, and/or grandparents. Students need to respect adults. Adults need to respect young people. And mutual respect among young people and adults will help young people stay in school. Mary (Hoopa) noted how her parents respect and encourage her:

◆ A lot of kids need respect. I feel very fortunate for having the parents that I do, for letting me get out to experience the world in my own eyes. Last summer, I went to Iowa for three weeks to the American Indian Science and Engineering Society (AISES). That was really fun. And it was cool because a lot of people's parents are like, "No, no, it's too far away." [My parents] always just let me experience everything. A lot of parents try to hold their kids back.

Martin, a First Nations student from Montreal, recalled how his respect for the memory of his father gave him the strength to carry on, no matter what:

◆ He'd bring me up north and visit my grandparents, uncles, cousins. And we would sometimes go hunting. He passed away about a year and a half ago. I always think my father was always there for me and always helped me, so I was not afraid. Everything was alright.

Family Expectations

The expectations families have of their children are very important in determining whether a young person will finish school. Adult family members who expect good grades, insist their children graduate, and encourage them to do well often are blessed with young people who excel. Ellen (Karuk) spoke of the importance of family expectations in her schooling:

◆ My grades have been good so far, and I want to go to college. It has just always been that way. My parents went to college, and my family encourages me to do the best I can. I can't imagine not wanting to [finish school]. No one has forced me to. It's just been encouraged. I've been encouraged my whole life. It's like sort of a normal thing.

Geraldine (First Nations Mohawk) indicated that her parents expect her to do well in school, but they have been supportive when things don't go well:

◆ My family has always backed me. I've had good grades ever since kindergarten, and they've always noticed that. Now, they expect it. But if I am struggling, they would be there to get me back on my feet.

Family Goals for Children Once They Finish High School

Families can help young people by encouraging them to pursue schooling or a profession once they complete high school. Sometimes, both the parent and young person end up sharing the same dream, as was the case with Daisy (Seneca):

◆ It sounds kind of cheesy, but my dad always wanted to be an artist. And ever since I was little, I'd always love to draw, and it was kind of like a dream for him for me to go to art college. So, it rubbed off on me. I have to do good in school because I want to go to art college.

Family members can help young people make their dreams real, as indicated by Chloe Blue Eyes (Seneca):

◆ My parents influence me a lot because they tell me, "If you don't get good grades, you are not going to get into a good school." I need to go to a good school. I want to play sports in college. Actually, I'm really interested in law. Law just fascinates me. I'm going to take a criminal justice program, a two-year program.

Chapter 7

A Kaleidoscope of Student Motivators

Amy

When writing for this chapter, I was amazed at how many different ways the students had found to make school easier or more bearable. As Indigenous students, we often take responsibility for success into our own hands. We may not have a lot of friends or a strong family network to support us, so we need to maintain balance and good feelings by finding healthy things within ourselves and around us. This isn't always easy to do, but what we need to remember is that every single one of us is motivated by our interests or strengths. The following section is a collage of student voices speaking out about ways to stay motivated and focused in school.

Quoetone (Ojibwe) observed that looking inside was the first step to finding school success:

- I just kind of took over with my schooling because, well, the most motivation you have to learn is yourself. Because if you're not motivated to learn yourself, then you're not really learning.

Sports and Physical Activity

Athletics continue to be a strong motivator for many students in schools across North America, particularly on reservations. Having to maintain a certain grade-point average to remain eligible is sometimes enough to keep students on track. Some of us need that extra reason to maintain passing grades in school. I was one of those students. Sports allowed me to release stress, keep physically active, and feel like I could do something well, despite daily struggles in the classroom.

Lu (Wampanoag) talked about how sports have motivated him to maintain his schoolwork and grades:

- Well, to be on the team, you gotta like keep your grades and like meet a C average. So, that'll make sure that you do all your work and everything, keep your grades up if you want to stay on the team. [So] you keep your grades up and do the work.

Werlth-Kerish-Nah (Hoopa) spoke about how the combination of sports and friends have taught him valuable life lessons and made school much more enjoyable:

- High school has been fun. I'd say it's mainly because of the sports. I've been involved with football, wrestling, and baseball the four years that I've been here and before that, throughout elementary too. But my high school years were so much fun because I was with all my buddies. Every sport I went to, every sport I played, it seemed like it was the same guys always right there with me. And it's been fun getting to know people more. I guess you could say sports have taught me discipline. Like, there was always a specific thing that we had to do; like football, you always had to be disciplined. If you're not disciplined enough to

110

move when the ball moves, then you get offsides and your team is penalized. And it was just small discipline like that that helped me see the broader discipline that we have to learn as people—knowing our boundaries, knowing what we can and can't do, what is expected and what is forbidden.

Sports are an excellent way to help balance academics and the things that may stress you out. Keeping the body active helps keep the mind clear. Megan (Ojibwe) talked about her involvement in sports and student council:

◆ I like soccer, and I'm in student council. I've been the state champion for five years in a row for Tae Kwon Do. I've gone to Nationals for five years, and I'd rather be doing that. I'd rather be, you know, like with my family. I'd rather be learning things about my tradition, you know. And I'd rather be snowboarding or something, but I guess I just stay in school because, well, I want to make something of myself.

Celeste (Seneca) shared her experience and the role sports have played in her life:

◆ I love sports. I play softball, but I don't play winter sports like girls' hockey. . . . When I was in eighth grade, I was in practice for my softball team, and the varsity coach was watching me. And she told me that if I could pass this test—it was like you had to hold yourself up on the bar for like so many seconds; you had to run a mile or six times around the track in 15 minutes or something like that; so many sit-ups, so many dashes, and stuff like that—and she told me that if I could pass, that she wanted me on varsity. So I passed it, and I was on varsity. And I think that was like a big accomplishment for me because I was like in eighth grade.

Effort and Responsibility

There are many ways to find motivation and get through school. For some students, sports have been the impetus for maintaining good grades; others, like Diddems (Hoopa) have looked inside for incentive:

◆ Well, you could say I've got self-motivation. Some people just don't have to go to school. I could just not come to school, but I tell myself I have to if I actually want to be something. I have to go to school. Sometimes, I come to school for my friends. Sometimes, they're having hard times, and you got to help them out when they need it. You need to motivate yourself if you want to be something.

Werlth-Kerish-Nah (Hoopa) contemplated this self-reflection as he watched his cousins not take responsibility:

◆ I do have cousins that are seventh and eighth [grade], . . . I'd say that they're going down the wrong path. They no longer care about their schooling; they would rather go out and party and kick up their heels with their friends. They don't realize the bigger picture. They don't realize that they have a meaning here. . . . everybody needs to relax and kick up their heels every now and then, but not every day, not every weekend, not making that your life. And I see them slipping to where, maybe next year, they are gonna drop out.

Grades as a Motivator

For students like Jane Sam (Ojibwe), good grades alone were enough of a motivator to keep making progress in school:

◆ I am keeping it at an A, all my . . . grades. School is good. It makes me feel good. If I get anything like bad grades, I just feel rotten for a while.

Will (Lakota/Ojibwe) related his approach to school success:

◆ It's not really hard if you think about it and if you think positive about school. . . . You do your work and you get straight A's, and you're thinking like, "Geez, why couldn't I do this in tenth, ninth, eighth grade?". . . I like learning a lot about other stuff. Now, it's really fun.

Nisha (Karuk) continued this theme:

◆ Usually it's schoolwork I always put first. I mean, you have to do that because you get a grade for it, and that's kind of important. So, I just usually try to do schoolwork before I get really behind in that . . . before I do extra stuff.

Daisy (Yurok) reflected on her aspirations of receiving a good grade in a hard class and how that motivated her:

◆ I think accomplishment is achieving something in a hard class. Like an A, a good A in a hard class like Chemistry. I tried so hard in that class to get an A. And that's what I really want, is a good grade in a hard class.

Future Goals and Plans

Keeping an eye on the future helps many students get through school. Although you may not know exactly what you want to study in college or do for a career, just knowing you have goals or are committed to finding a way to give back to your community is motivation enough.

Werlth-Kerish-Nah (Hoopa) talked about his vision of sharing with young children his fluency in his language and knowledge about traditions:

◆ Five years from now, I'm still in school, still striving to accomplish what I'm setting out to do—fluency in my language, teaching the younger [kids], starting from the very young, from kindergarten and the babies, and incorporating our language and our traditional ways throughout their life so that by the time they're my age, they don't have to go searching for answers; they already have them.

Carol (Navajo) contemplated her goals and commitment to giving back to her community:

◆ I'm definitely going to go to college. I want to help; I want to stay on the reservation. Sometimes, I want to be a doctor—an obstetrician—and deliver babies and help out in Indian medical centers. And sometimes, I want to help out with like tribal government. And sometimes, I want to be a Native American lawyer and fight for Native lands.

Although Carol may not know exactly what she wants to be, she has thought about the future and what she can contribute to her community and the health and well-being of Indigenous peoples. This is admirable. For me, it took two starts and stops to get through college and secure myself in a career I truly love. If you asked me back in high school what I wanted to be after I graduated, the last thing I would have said was a teacher. Now, I can't think of anything else I would rather be. I believe the Creator has a plan for each and every one of us and leads us on to the path we are to follow. We may not find ourselves on it right away, but when we do, everything else seems to fall into place and our lives seem content and balanced. Having ideas about what you would like to do and trying those things out put you one step closer to that path.

Friends for Personal Support

It is important to find individuals who will help you set and pursue your goals, whether they are inside school (a friend, counselor, or teacher) or in the community or your family. These caring people will help you stay resilient when the going gets tough.

During our school years, our friendships can be the most important aspects of our lives. We all need and want friends. As we get older, our needs and types of friends may change, but friendships will remain an important part of maintaining a healthy, balanced life. I remember going to school some days and feeling like my friends were the only reason I was there. Gordee, whom I wrote about in chapter 4, was an important part of my school day. When he left school, I felt a sense of loss. Even though we remained friends, school just didn't seem the same without Gordee's company. Many students we interviewed shared similar friendship stories. Tiffany (Navajo) talked about how friends can make school a positive place to be:

◆ When I was in sixth grade, I was on the drill team. And like my friends and I used to always go to each other's houses and practice the dances that we'd made up during practice. Every Friday we'd go to the skating rink, just hanging out with my friends. And it always made school more enjoyable. Like going to class, I always had [my friend], and we had every single class together. We used to always go together, and it used to make me try harder at school.

Desirae (Aleut) explained the connection between friends and success in school:

◆ One of the things that makes it really easy for me is my friends. They are all there, and I know everybody in the school, and I am friends with everybody. There was a point [when I] got into trouble, and I was way down.... But when my friends are there and we hang out and stuff, I guess you feel good about yourself.

When I asked Jimi (Ojibwe) what makes him successful in school, his answer was short and to the point:

◆ My friends. Nothing would make me more successful.

When asked what a school would look like if she could create it, Lisa (Ojibwe) focused on friendships:

◆ To have everyone in the school like know each other and be friends. And you know, have culture taught and teachers that are understanding and help you learn. And everybody knows each other, and it's just like a good place to be, I guess, and you feel good when you're there.

Gina, a Navajo student spoke to the idea of having friends as role models:

◆ I have two friends who are pretty good role models for me. Well, I think they're really good role models because they have kind of that drive, that need to learn, like I do. So, it's kind of nice to surround yourself with people with . . . the same drive. . . .

School is one phase of life that requires multiple resources to keep us motivated and focused. Those resources may be a combination of internal strengths (for example, a vision for the future) and external support mechanisms (for example, friends or participation in sports). Let the sorts of supports the students spoke about in this section or others you discover on your own refuel you, so you can make progress and be successful in school.

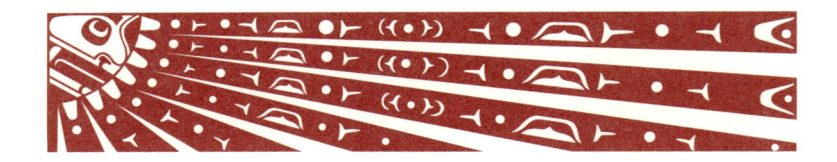

What to Do When Motivation Isn't There

Linda

For those who feel ready to give up on school, one or more suggestions from a student halfway across the continent might be enough to pull you through to graduation day, so keep reading. The 120 students we interviewed had some really good advice about how to keep learning. It is arranged here from simplest (least life altering) to most complex (most life altering).

First Step: Let Teachers Know How to Help

The large majority of the teachers Thomas Peacock and I interviewed in past research wanted very much for their Native students to be comfortable and to learn. Unfortunately, this isn't always the case. Maria, in chapter 2, described a biology teacher who didn't seem to want Maria to succeed. There will, most certainly, be a similar teacher or two in your life, but most teachers don't sign contracts for the sake of money alone.

For any kind of relationship to succeed, people must let each other know what they need. This section is written for both teachers and students. With all the different learning preferences students have, it's a wonder more teachers don't go a little crazy; but they surely can't work for the best learning of every student unless they know what each student needs. Fred (Choctaw) had a teacher who seemed to adapt her style to suit the students:

◆ Miss Poe knows when to be firm and when to be gentle. A good teacher needs to be able to decipher feeling. Watch people carefully and see what their actions are. We don't all have the same feelings every day. Some days, we might be in shock.

It would be nice if all teachers had the skill to figure out what each student needs. But sometimes, as a student, you just have to tell them; sometimes, as a teacher, you simply have to ask. The best time to do this is not in front of the whole class, which might embarrass teachers and students. Before or after class is better. It's also good to tell teachers what you need either before anger arises or after a cooling-off period. You can start by telling them why something isn't working for you or what your learning strengths are, and then ask your teacher if any adjustments are possible. Not all teachers will be open to students' input about their teaching, so if that doesn't help, try some of the other suggestions in this chapter. Jazzy (Ojibwe) offered really good advice to students and teachers:

- I really don't think that the teachers know that I'm Indian, so I am treated as a normal student. But some people don't want to raise their hands, or they don't want to do that because they feel that people will look down upon them or [think] they are dumb. I was talking to somebody who heard that Indian students don't want to [give] answers, or something like that, or raise their hand, or they don't even go up to the teacher. But you come, and you want to have an education, you want to learn, so if you don't want to raise your hand, then go up and at least talk to the teacher. Maybe it has something to do with culture, I don't really know. If I was a teacher, I would go and check 'cause I'd be curious on what's going on. Why aren't they even doing anything?

The easiest solution, of course, is to ask for help if you need it, but that may just be too difficult. What next? Many students have found that special advisors or tutors are especially helpful in this regard. Will (Lakota/Ojibwe) said:

- When my math teacher explains things, I can't really understand the way she explains it. That's why I usually go to Miss H. She'll sit down and show you how.

It would be wonderful if everyone had a Miss H in their school. Some advisors or relatives will let teachers know you need help. But it needs to start with you. Is it easy or hard for you to let someone know you need help? Who could give you advice about how to ask for help? Getting such help is an important part of finding success in school.

Getting and Giving Help: A Circle of Help from Peers

When academics and teachers become a heavy burden, seeking help from peers is another alternative. Many, many students talked about getting help from peers when teachers were unable or unwilling to provide needed extra help.

Shana (Ojibwe) provided advice for students coming from her reservation school into a public high school:

- Some students come here not knowing about the racism or not having their parents tell them that. I told them . . . how you just gotta behave. You can't fool around like you did eighth-grade year.

Fred (Choctaw) said:

- A lot of kids feel comfortable talking to someone that's their own age. Maybe that would lessen that feeling of bitterness and lessen that feeling of wanting, you know, to join a gang.

Some schools have peer advisors like Daisy (Yurok):

- I'm a precounselor. [The other students] need to talk to somebody. They just like air it off their chest if they're having problems at home or a teacher's bothering them. So, it feels good for them to be here, for them to talk to somebody.

Shana (Ojibwe) had been suspended from school, but friends and others helped her get back in. After that experience, she became an informal counselor, giving back to others, although it wasn't directly to those who had helped her. What goes around comes around and around and around:

◆ I got suspended, but my friends pretty much helped me through that. Friends do a lot for me, and my counselor helped me through it too. It took a long time. I'd have to say comforting words helped me get back into school, helped me out with classes too. [Then] I knew a girl in my International Studies class that just sat there, I mean, every day, and never did nothing. She just wanted to spend time with her baby, but if she can sit here and work, she can graduate next year. Then she'll have the rest of the semester and the rest of her life to spend with her kid. She was failing, and me and one of my friends, we just talked to her, and we told her you better do this because she's got a kid, and you don't want your kid to look at you and think, "I don't need to graduate." But her actions now are going to affect her kid later in her years. We would bring her in our group [and say] "You gotta do this," and now she's passing. We just made her think about a lot of stuff. We just like nagged on her, and now she just changed it all around. . . . So, we got a test back today, and she got A's, and she's gotten B's, and she's just happy.

Help from American Indian Education Counselors: A Tribute to Melvin and Ms. H

American Indian education counselors and tutors can help students see how to get beyond stuck places. While interviewing students in the north country of the United States, I met Melvin and a stream of students who came to his office. We've already heard about Melvin in chapter 2. He's the one Maria always fled to when she was too mad to keep going with her day at school. He's the one who cheered her on when she made State in track, and he's the one who helped her out when she found a racist marking in a text she was supposed to read. Shana (Ojibwe), another student in Maria's school, said:

◆ Melvin's always worried, and my mom talks about it all the time with Melvin. He says, "How are you doing in this class? Want to get a report and see how your grades are?" Just stuff like that. And when I get my reports back, like I just got some, I have all A's in classes, so it like brought me up a lot. Like my self-esteem just like boosted right up. He guided me along. If I had a problem, I would come to him. If I needed to switch out of class because of a [teacher, sometimes a racist student] he would manage to switch me into another class.

Those are some tributes to a fine man who helped many students get beyond the racism in Maria and Shana's school. And Ms. H's name kept coming up too. Here was Lisa's (Dakota) tribute to this fine counselor and tutor:

◆ I don't usually go to lunch 'cause I hate standing in line, so I just go in there, and I

116

get to study in [Ms. H's] room. She'll talk to the teacher about my grades, and she'll go to each of my teachers and find out my grades and help me get them up. They have an Indian Options Program, and they have a support class. I didn't take that last year, but this year I took it. And like my grades have just gone up because I have that hour just to get everything done, and I have tutors that can help me, so it's going pretty good. A lot of Indian kids in high school don't have that program to help them out like I have. I think that's why I get really good grades.

Will (Dakota) added:

◆ Ms. H's class is the American Indian Support class, and even if she doesn't know how, she'll learn how to help you learn how to do it. And sometimes, she'll show you the easier way to do it. I see how smart she is, and I want to be that smart too, know all that stuff. So, I just went to her classroom, and she showed me how to do all that stuff, and I got all my work done, and I was like, "Alright!" And my teacher said, "It's good that Ms. H is around." I was really happy 'cause I'm glad I didn't quit.

This section was a tribute to Melvin and Ms. H, and it is a tribute to all the others like them who are doing their best. Do you have such tutors or a counselor available to you? If you do, you are lucky indeed. Keep in mind that sometimes you have to be the one to ask for assistance because teachers or advisors might not see your need automatically.

Doing Assignments in a Way That Interests You

Many teachers might be open to having you demonstrate your knowledge of something by presenting it in an alternative way. Ask teachers to let you do special projects that replace other assignments, projects that combine your strengths and interests with the things they want you to learn. Quoetone (Ojibwe) was not shy about asking:

◆ By junior and senior year, [you should have] a lot more freedom to work on independent projects, have them count for something. Encourage [students] to really reach out with their studies and their thoughts instead of sticking to the same old curriculum. I think they'd really want to go out and learn stuff about different people and different things.

Nahami (Abenaki) developed a project that won him a trip to a major city:

◆ I did a project for Heritage Canada. We talked about our history. I talked about my family and what they do, and I had a genealogical dictionary, went back seven generations. There were other young people from different parts of the country, like 10 from British Columbia, 10 from Quebec.

You may remember Travis (Dakota) and his history project from chapter 4. Travis was an inner-city American Indian who wasn't shy about identifying himself that way. When projects were being divided up, everyone left the one American Indian subject to Travis. Partly out of frustration due to the lack of attention given to Native Americans in this history class, Travis delivered a detailed account of the Wounded Knee Massacre.

Although Travis's teacher included Wounded Knee on the list of projects from which students could choose, other teachers might not offer a topic selection you want to study. However, you can always ask to do a project on a particular topic and to approach it in a way that fits your interests and strengths. Some teachers may say no, but many others might just say yes. Getting to do a project that really motivates you can help the quality of your work and hold your attention through to completion. Can you think of ways to change any of your assignments now, or in the future, to make them more interesting to you? It's worth asking.

Finding Someone to Learn From

If you aren't learning what you want to learn in the way you're gifted to learn, you can always ask someone if they will be your guide. Find someone who is good at what you want to get good at, someone who knows more than you do about a subject you might have some talents to learn. You may remember from chapter 2 that North Star's brother needed such a person because he wasn't going to find that teacher in school. His brother liked working on mechanical things, especially fixing bikes. North Star thought it would make a big difference for his brother, who had trouble sitting still in class, if he could participate in a class that really interested him and allowed him to learn by doing.

North Star's brother probably hadn't thought about seeking a teacher outside of school or using his outside-of-school interests to keep him going until he could graduate. Being an apprentice is an ancient practice. Is there someone in your community who might be willing to teach you what you want to know? Such people often feel pleased when students recognize their skills and are more than happy to become teachers.

Finding Extracurricular School Activities, Cultural Programs, Clubs, and Support Groups to Keep You Going

As Amy Bergstrom wrote earlier, sports can help you become motivated and successful in school. It's a commonly known fact that athletes get better grades during the sports season, even if they don't need them to qualify for a team. Other activities can keep you going too. If people get a chance to do things they enjoy, it helps them do the things they need to graduate. Extracurricular activities may be geared more to your strengths. Many students used school or reservation cultural clubs and/or drumming and dancing groups to keep them going; other students wrote for student publications or were photographers. Still other students participated on sports teams or in activities such as orchestra, karate, skiing, visual arts, theater, auto mechanics, carpentry, drill team, arts council, band, and student council. Some students even took the initiative to start new groups when the activity they wanted to participate in wasn't available at their school. Several felt the need to push for rights, like getting school bus service to take them home after school hours. In all instances, students found ways to do the things they were passionate about, which helped keep them sane

Making It in School

in school. To get started, most sought the assistance of a teacher.

Some students felt more isolation in public schools than in reservation schools. Megan (Ojibwe) said:

◆ Sometimes, you feel like you're the only one, only one of a kind, and you don't really fit in anywhere.

Back in chapter 4, Jazzy (Ojibwe) described what happens to some youth when they feel isolated and uncared for:

◆ A gang is a group of people who come together, and they are kind of like a family. They are there for each other.... It's not positive because they do horrible things.

Gangs have spread from inner cities to reservations. In another city, Tiffany (Navajo) said:

◆ If they have more clubs to come to, instead of having so much free time on their hands where they can get into groups, get into gangs, they could have them join clubs to keep them out of trouble.

Megan, Jazzy, and Tiffany articulated the value of programs that help bring Native students together and feel a part of something important, usually something that connects them with their culture. Some schools are sensitive to the gap between the culture of the school and the culture of the Native students' homes, a gap into which students can fall. The best approach would be to make every school and classroom more culturally relevant and Indigenous friendly. Few schools attended by students interviewed for this book had risen to this challenge, but many did provide programs and support groups to help Native students get along in school. Ms. H and Melvin ran such programs; this section says more about the programs themselves.

Students talked about a great many programs, including community, school, and summer programs with a variety of names: Indian Club, Indian Upward Bound, Indian Education Club, Seeking Wisdom, Vision Quest, National Youth Leadership Camp, Success Both Worlds, Indian Education Program, American Indian Club, Minority Inclusion Program, Masters/Apprentice Language Program, Math Club, Youth, AISES, Council, Tutoring Group, Indian Center, Indian Book Group, American Indian Support Group, Indian Options Program, Future Bound, Dance Group, Drumming Club, Crafts Club, Cultural Club, American Indian Knowledge Bowl, American Indian Health Professions, Native American Resource Center, Peer Support Group.

If you are a student in a school that has such programs, they will probably help you feel more welcome. Students felt particularly grateful when educators took part in these programs. As Sonny (Hoopa) noted, some programs organize special events:

◆ I'm vice president of the Indian Club, so we had to basically take a week off school to get Indian Day together because some of the teachers would help us and some wouldn't. We did it, though. We put on a dress show, guest speakers, stick games. Basically, we got a lot of kids together to help us put it on, and we called around for a lot of donations and called a lot of businesses. Families helped us too. So, that was cool.

Werlth-Kerish-Nah (Hoopa) learned about the grim history of his people from a similar program:

◆ I went to United Indian Health, a school activity throughout [several] counties. There was a big explanation about things that were taught in books... mainly a dominant literature and literacy. There was the Gold Rush and the '49ers, and you see the pictures, and they're all happy doing what they do. But they told us about the slaughters that happened to clear the land for gold mining, and the mass destruction, like when they were using the water cannons to blow down the hills, literally flatten hills, simply for the gold.

Many school and community clubs have been started to help students learn about their cultures. Lisa (Dakota), who lived in a big city, was not aware of her culture until she and her family participated in a variety of programs. She talked about how support groups, programs, and clubs have had a profound effect on her life and family:

◆ Once we moved up here and we started learning these things, my parents don't drink no more. It made a big difference in our lives just learning our ways. And I danced, and my brother started a drum group, and just being part of that helped my family. And sometimes, I think if I didn't have my culture, I'd be like an alcoholic, wouldn't be the way I am today. Sometimes, I'll get in fights with my teachers, and I'll just go to Indian Ed and just chill out for a little bit, and they'll give me a pass back to class. It mainly means support. They're always there if you need somebody to help you with your work, or if you are having trouble with another group of kids.

Once a year we do the culture fair, and we make our booths; like last year we had this really cool booth. It was like a teepee. We had to make a food, so we made a bunch of fry bread. And we have a drum, and [Indian Ed teachers] stay on Wednesday nights and practice, and they have a drum feast for the drum group. And a lot of the girls at our school are dancers.... They [and some of the guys] did like a presentation in front of the whole school. They had different sections throughout the auditorium, and they did a whole thing about Native American culture, and they got to drum and dance, and they did like some storytelling, and all the kids put it on.

I'm in a program, Alliance with Youth, and I learned a lot from that program because I think it is kind of cool. It's really like volunteer work, and I get to work with all the little Indian kids, and they're just cute, and you get to show them how to do beadwork. The thing they need to improve on for the Indian students is attendance—need to show the Indian kids that it's important to be in school. I want my grandchildren to be really smart and be able to help future generations.

Programs, clubs, and extracurricular activities can't heal all the challenges that Native youth face, but some can be mighty fine Band-Aids. Are there such activities in your school that connect with your interests? Would it be possible to start such activities?

Finding Alternative School Settings

Alternative schools are intended for students who just can't tolerate continuing in their schools. Some students consider alternative schools wonderful places; others don't find them challenging enough. Students often are able to learn in more holistic ways in alternative schools.

Quoetone (Ojibwe) said the following about his alternative school:

◆ I think being here at the Learning Center has been for the best so far. I've had some of the best discussions here. The learning is an individual thing that everyone has to do at their own pace. I've done projects [on] my own culture, on the Jewish culture, and I did a lot in wood shop, working on cars occasionally.

Gina (Navajo) is artistically and linguistically gifted, so the Mosaics class in her alternative school appealed to her:

◆ I didn't really know anything about mosaics, but I really liked art, so anything that really had to do with art, I like. . . . We got to design a mosaic. We all worked together. We tried to get everybody's opinion and thoughts into this, and it's turning out really good. We got to break our own tile for it and make the symbols that we're putting in. And we're going to get it mounted.

Blue (Ute) was pleased she could go to an alternative school in the Southwest:

◆ A few months ago, we did this expedition type of thing, and we went to the tribal park, explored there. We got a workout! It was a hands-on experience in learning. [We went to] our ruins and stuff, and we hiked around, learned what their basic food was and stuff, where they lived, their shelters, what they had to cook with.

Instead of dropping out, a number of students were able to change to schools that accommodated their strengths. Is there such a school that would be possible for you? There are many alternative schools around, but you may need to search.

Resorting to Homeschooling

Several students found themselves in such despair that they stayed home for schooling. If your parents have the time and skills to help you with schooling, this may be a route for you. Wampanau (Wampanoag) remembered fondly the time she took away from public schools:

◆ I told Mom, "I don't want to go to school anymore; please don't make me go back there. The kids tease me." I remember I had two pencils stuck in me by a kid who had just sharpened one of them, but I didn't want to tell on her because I was so sick of constantly telling on her. It just got me depressed. So I didn't go back to school; my brother pulled out with me. . . . For Christmas I got a chemistry set. I loved chemistry. I asked my dad about grams and stuff. He would explain it to me, not realizing that I'm actually doing the math. He'd say, "Did you know that you actually did a fraction?" or "Did you know that you just multiplied two fractions together?" And I would be so shocked and so proud of myself. Then my mom said to me, "What if I started a program, an arts-and-crafts and theater program for kids?" I was totally encouraging her. I helped my mom get that together. So, she'd hire people, and we started doing plays, which really brought me into the acting world. The first play we did was *Pinnochio*. We loved it. I still had friends who lived right next to me. [One] was in school, and so I used to see her homework, and she would ask me a couple of questions, and I would be completely clueless. I realized, "Wow, I need to get back up on math." So, I started picking up a little bit. We started looking at private schools, at more flexible schools, at a teacher who thought, "When you're doing what you want, you're learning at the same time." I learned a lot of self-confidence over the two years I was homeschooled . . . and I learned how to deal with kids that teased me.

If getting away from school for awhile will help you regain your confidence or get past your anger at school, then that may be what you have to do. Recapturing an interest in learning may eventually prompt you to go back to school, as Quoetone did.

Taking Advantage of the GED

Some students who are truly miserable in school opt out and take an exam that tests whether they have the knowledge and skills required for a high school diploma. Some institutions and potential employers don't regard this degree as highly as they do a regular high school diploma, but the GED is an important opportunity. Many students take courses in the evenings after work to prepare for the exam. There are many options to try before taking the GED exam, but it may be a possibility for you. Jeremy (Aleut), who appeared in chapter 6, had just decided on this option:

◆ I'm going for my GED. It started because I wanted to get into art school right away. I was behind. A GED is quick. You can just get your GED and move on, focus on my art. I was pretty much old enough to drop out of school. What's bad is that I'm with a bunch of older people, and it seemed I was the neediest one. I got in there late, but I missed it by only 10 points. So, I'm retaking it this May. I'm mostly studying math. That seemed to be the really hard part, math and writing, and the teacher there actually got me information on one art school in New Jersey.

As you can see, many different paths exist for making it in school. Keep your options open and bright because failing to earn a high school diploma can limit your future possibilities and potential earning power.

Making It in School

How to Keep Motivated in Reading, Writing, and Standard English

Linda

When I pulled out all the files of what students said about reading and writing, the stack was five inches tall. Students had a lot to say, in part because we asked them questions about it, but also because literacy (the ability to read and write) is a huge part of what it takes to be successful in today's schools. Reading and writing come easily to some, but others struggle to become fluent. Research shows that the more you read and write, the better you get at them. Writing is easier if you have read a lot, and reading is easier if you write a lot. They play off each other. So, getting a lot of practice at both is the best way to help yourself.

Essentially, that five-inch stack reveals that students who care about what they're reading and writing find the process much easier and more interesting. Paula (Ojibwe) talked about how crucial *interest* is:

◆ They ask me to read a book! And write a book report on it! I don't know how. First of all, I don't know how to read a book. Well, I know how. I just lose so much interest in stuff that I don't know. Reading just doesn't interest me.

It is well worth the extra time for you and/or your teacher to find something you're interested in reading or writing about.

Reading

Reading is one way to learn information about the world; other ways might be asking, listening, observing, touching, or experimenting. Even if reading isn't one of your strengths, it is an important way for you to exchange information with others. For instance, the Internet, which offers a more interactive and colorful way of spreading information, is largely dependent on the written word.

There are several tricks for making reading more interesting. A good way to begin is to think of everything you already know about the topic. While reading, ask yourself a lot of questions like: "I wonder what's going to happen next?" or "I wonder how this connects with World War I?" You don't necessarily have to answer the questions, but just asking them helps you remember more of what you read. The final thing is to find ways that connect you personally with the reading, such as, "I wonder what Native people did during that war?" Students remember more if they take time to do this, and some students later look into some of these questions as separate projects or papers.

Reading aloud was problematic for many, prompting nervous emotions that disrupted their ability to think. Bigg Dogg (Ojibwe) talked about this:

- If we have to read out loud, I think I get nervous 'cause I want to show them that I can read really good. But just when I am reading in front of all these people, I see spots and stuff and get headaches 'cause I am nervous. If I'm reading my own work, like creative writing, when I read in front of the class, they laugh at my work. I really like that because I like making people laugh.

If you know you'll be nervous reading out loud, try two things: let the teacher know you're nervous and ask the teacher to let you practice what you'll need to read the night before. Bigg Dogg was confident reading his own work, something he knew well, but was so nervous reading a textbook out loud that his short-term memory couldn't focus on the task of reading. Nervousness is a physical condition. You need to make the situation better and practice. If you have a tutor, he or she may be able to work something out with the teacher, or you should.

Another problem is caused by teachers who see only one way to interpret the text. Tarilee (Ojibwe) said:

- The reading we are doing now has really nothing to do with anything in my life right now. In English (literature), nothing's really right or wrong if you think about it because it can always mean something else. The teacher doesn't teach it like that; she teaches like it can only be this one meaning. She should ask what we thought about it. She's not even getting our ideas. That means this, and that means that. It is whatever she says. Books mean different things to different people.

Tarilee is right; our experiences in life mold the meanings we get out of our reading. Open-minded teachers will listen to your interpretations, especially those well supported by the text; but you should be ready to have a few teachers who won't. If this happens, you have to, as North Star (Abenaki) said, "go with the program" and hope for a more flexible teacher next year.

Finally, if reading is difficult for you, it's really important to seek help. Steve Marcus at the University of Santa Barbara once said, "Literacy is knowing where the truth lies."[1] To act in the best interests of yourself, your family, and your community, you need to know what written words really say. If not, you'll be at a disadvantage because reading is perhaps the most important tool in finding out both truth and lies.

Writing

Students talked with some excitement about two purposes for writing: to make sense of how they fit into the world and to act on the world.

Jana (Hoopa) used writing to deal with depression and better understand the death of her uncle:

- I had an uncle that passed away about two years ago. I write about him a lot. I only feel like I need to write when I am depressed. I can tell anyone when I'm happy, and what I'm happy about. But when I'm depressed, I basically write.

---

[1] Pope and Golub, "Preparing Tomorrow's English Language Arts Teachers Today."

Students were excited to write for real purposes and audiences, particularly when their writing was a way of acting upon the world. Ellen (Karuk) said:

- We have a newspaper called the *Hot Pickle*. We had like a ton of subscribers. We'd write about all the local things and what we've done—like field trips or like a band was there, and there was a Native American dance. We write about that. And we always liked writing these made-up coyote stories.

As with reading, being interested in a topic can help you concentrate on writing. North Star (Abenaki) said:

- It's easy when you're the one who's writing about what you want to write, but what's not easy is when you've got to deal with the complements and the verbs and the adjectives, the grammar stuff.

Gary (Wampanoag) added:

- I like it best when you're able to write your own stories and use your own mind. I want to choose what I want to say.

What students said over and over is important for educators to hear.

Gina (Navajo) said:

- If it's a particular subject and I have some things to say about it, then writing's pretty easy for me. I can do it because it's been drilled into my head ever since I was in elementary, but some of the things they ask us to write about, well, how is that relevant to anything? At the high school, a lot of the things they'd ask you to write about would be nonsense, nothing really interesting, but here at this school, you write about what you're interested in. And writing helps you learn a lot more about yourself.

Rob (Wampanoag) said:

- Writing about my family's history, that was pretty fun, and going back to like my great-great-great-grandfather, what my family name means, how it's changed over the years. That was actually enjoyable. Writing an essay about the Renaissance, that was really hard.

A lot of students preferred writing poems and stories to writing essays. This is pretty logical since Indigenous people have always learned through stories. If you don't get to do that kind of writing in school and want to, it's important to continue it at home. Creative writing helps you develop fluency and is much more enjoyable for many students. Writing in an essay format may come less naturally to you, but John Nesbit, who teaches in the Southwest, related some advice he gives students. It's worth repeating here because he essentially confirms what North Star said about going with the program.

I tell my [college-bound] students, "When you go turn this in to your English professors, most likely they're going to be looking for this linear structure, saying what you want to say, the [examples/support] straight down, and do the stupid thing of repeating yourself at the end. If you don't, your teacher may thrash you for that."[2]

---

[2]Cleary and Peacock, *Collected Wisdom*, 193.

Do You Speak Rezbonics?

In the United States, people have joked for several years about *rezbonics* being a language for Native people, but there is truth to the jokes. William Leap has described what he calls "American Indian English," a variation of which probably exists on each reservation and reserve of North America.[3] Rezbonics is a complete language with a consistent grammar, but teachers may not know that. In any case, they will want you to learn standard English, the language of newscasters and professional writers. Learning and using standard English is necessary so people in academic circles will take you seriously; however, there is no reason to be apologetic about the language you speak. It probably relates in some way to your Native language, which you probably speak or wish you spoke. Still, standard English is the language of power in mainstream Canada and the United States. You can decide you don't want to learn it, but it might cut off some avenues for your future. Having to learn standard English can be frustrating because students who grow up speaking it as their home dialect have an easier time in school. Not fair, but it is a reality.

So, how can you learn standard English? The best way is to look at the corrections teachers put on your writing. They will probably show you the difference between the dialect you speak and the one you're trying to learn. Some students keep a log to remind them of the differences. Students frustrated with grammar didn't seem to realize it had anything to do with speaking a different kind of English. Every human being is capable of knowing more than one language, so if you just keep plugging away, you'll be able to learn it.

How to Keep Motivated in Other School Subjects

Students also talked about favorite subjects and subjects that motivated them enough to feel successful and stay in school. Speashal-One (Ojibwe) understood the relevance of math in her life:

♦ "I'm very good in math. If I understand how to do it, I'll do it. I'll use it."

Motivation tends to come easier when you know far enough ahead of time what direction you want to take in life. Lisa (Ojibwe), driven by a desire to be a doctor, was willing to put effort into math and science:

♦ Well, two classes that are really important, that I want to do really good in, are my Biology and my Math class 'cause I've just always

---

[3] See Leap, "American Indian English."

been bad at math and science for some reason. And this year, I'm finally getting a good grade, and I think that's because the teacher's actually sitting down with me and helping me. And I want to do good in those classes because I want to have some kind of a medical career in my future; and those classes, you have to be really good at.

Lindsay (Ojibwe) talked about her love of science:

- I like science. Science is my favorite subject. I'm in chemistry right now. I like chemistry, and it's fun working with stuff actually, rather than sitting there watching stuff on the board, hands-on materials. It's interesting to me. It's not just numbers and words. You actually get something out of it, like a result.

Speashal-One echoed Lindsay's feelings:

- "I love science. It's the study of what things are around you. I'm a curious person; I like to know how thing work."

Ellen (Karuk) talked about her involvement in music:

- I started playing the piano when I was little. I played the guitar. I played the drums freshman year. And then I started playing the viola.... So I've been playing for a year ... with a big group ... 13 kids, which is pretty big for this high school. And we set it up and we played in concerts and played different things.... This is the first year we've ever had a string group.

Technology is another subject that interested many students, such as this individual who wanted to remain anonymous:

- This computer technician, I've worked with him for 70-some-odd hours on a work-study program for the school. And he taught me most of the stuff I know about computer hardware, network, and all the stuff about computers; he taught me a lot of things.

Having a Positive Attitude and Caring about School

The mind is a powerful thing. It does not act alone. Things we *think* affect the body and emotions. Things we *do* affect the mind and spirit. Truly living in harmony and balance requires us to understand how the mind, body, spirit, and emotions connect with one another. In other words, what we do (or don't do) to one aspect of ourselves truly affects other aspects. Not using our minds, such as in school, affects our physical bodies and spirits. Faye (Ojibwe) talked about the power of positive thinking:

- I guess it's my attitude.... No matter how bad I do on something, if I worked on it ... I feel I did the best I can. Then, if I did the best I could, then I did a good job. I guess I have a better outlook on school when I don't feel like I am a failure when I come here.

Kristen (Ojibwe) discussed how she's used a positive attitude as a coping mechanism:

- For some people here, they're like, "Well, I don't care about this," or they have like a negative attitude, which you shouldn't have here.... [At this high school] you have to have a positive [attitude] at all times in order to get through here, in order to graduate. I've learned through my years how to cope with people, how to cope with people saying stuff to me.

Jana's (Hoopa) perception of her surroundings kept her thinking positively:

- I, myself, try to find the inner beauty of everything. Some people might think it's funny, but I can see something beautiful in just about everything. And I'd like to teach other people that. I think that words are very strong and powerful, and the way that you choose them is important. And I kind of get on myself; I'm not really good with words. [I try] to live every day to its fullest and to not take anything for granted. I mean every day. Every day that I ride the bus, I sit . . . so I can look out the window. And every day that I do, I notice something new, something different that wasn't there before.

Now that you've read through this chapter, what are some things that have helped you to be successful in school? Can you motivate yourself on your own or do you need something or someone to help that motivation along? To whom might you go for support in school?

Find out what works best for you to be successful in school and surround yourself with healthy support mechanisms. To be successful in anything you do, you need support. You can't win a softball game on your own; you need the help of your teammates. School success is the same way. Helpful support, either believing in yourself or having someone else believe in you, makes school easier.

Chapter 8
The Good Path

This chapter focuses on the Good Path, a set of traditional values upon which we have framed the collective voices of the students in this book. Realizing that other value systems exist, we chose the Good Path because in many ways, these values are universal to Indigenous people, indeed, to all humankind. The student voices offer Native people of all ages hope in our collective future and inspiration to make our vision a self-fulfilling prophecy. We conclude with "Sara's Song," a teaching story that puts many difficult issues of Native life into context and demonstrates how to apply the Good Path to our daily lives.

> Well, the way we look at it, it's a way of life, like a path. There's two paths, the good path and the bad path. [Grandfather] taught us all about how to take that path and how to keep that path going. He said we're going to run into forks in the road and said, "You're going to have to sit there, and you're going to have to figure it out yourself, which path to take. Whether you take the good path or the bad path, you just have to figure which one it is." He basically taught us how to be independent. He taught us how to live.
>
> —Karonhiakta (First Nations Mohawk)

Tom

I'm bothered by the way we Native people have become so judgmental toward one another about traditional values, especially when we tell our young people how to live their lives. I've done this myself many times, as a parent to my own children and as a teacher to other people's children: "You should respect your elders. You should give back to your community. You should protect who we are as Native people. You should be like _____; she is such a role model for tribal people." Now, as I stand overlooking the third hill of my life, I realize that approach was flawed.

Certainly, it's noble to have respect for elders, give back to our communities, protect our uniqueness as tribal people, and be like those who live in a good way. What bothers me is that, too many times, we tell our children what values they should have without living according to those same values ourselves.

Based on what I've learned from talking to Native young people, I propose that we return to a more Indigenous way of living our values. This will require a complex rethinking of the fundamental way we look at things, for we must ask ourselves: What if we live in a good way simply because it is good? What if we respect our elders, give back, protect our uniqueness, and travel the Good Path simply because these ways are good in themselves? Living this way, we would recognize and accept our humanness, with all its limitations. We would be less prone to judge others by our own or someone else's external values.

In such a world, we would continue to have role models to emulate, but they would not necessarily see themselves as models. Adults would serve as living examples of the Good Path. These adults might say, "If I live my life in a certain way, and if people pattern their lives after me, that is good; but I do not see myself as a model for others to become. They need to find their own paths. I live my way simply because it is good in itself. I respect elders because they have lived a long time and know things I can only hope to learn with age. I give back to my community because I am a member of the community, and it is a good thing to do. I show kindness to others because I am, by nature, a kind person, not because others are kind to me, or because someone said I should be a kind person, or because I have set *being kind* as a goal for myself. I realize there are times when I'm not always respectful to elders or when I do not give back, but I live in the best way I can, as the Creator put me on this earth and intended me to live."

Most of the students shared my hope that Native people will return to a more Indigenous way of living that flows from a strong traditional value system. Their collective voice sang loudly and boldly about living the Good Path. What seems fundamentally clear is that the solutions to many of the problems in Native communities, including education, lie within the values of our tribal cultures, or ways of being. These fundamental ways must form the basis of any solutions. Therein lie the answers. The solutions will be found in the simple truths (wisdom) of our teachings, which are really both simple and complex at the same time. Because it took the collective song of Native young people to tell me that, I believe they are *oski bimaadizeeg,* the people of the Seventh Generation.

The Good Path

Culture is like an identity. All of your life you search for an identity, who you really are. And this is who I am, and this is my identity, my culture.... These are the ways I live for because I really love these ways.
—Will (Dakota)

There is great commonality in Indigenous value systems, indeed, the shared values of all humankind. People call these ways similar things. Some Native people call these life ways the "Red Road" or the "Good Red Road." The Good Path is the set of values our ancestors lived

The Good Path

out naturally, without obligation, in a very concrete way. They simply lived the Good Path without someone telling them how they should live or what their values should be. Perfect understanding of the path to wisdom requires displaying values without preaching or judging. Moreover, this belief system asserts that all humans are born already possessing these values.

As world citizens, we need to accept all people's value systems, including their beliefs or nonbeliefs in a Creator. There are many paths to the truth, and one does not need to believe in the existence of a Creator to live in a good way. All of the students interviewed, however, talked in some way about a Good Path, which included their personal beliefs in a Creator. As an Ojibwe person, what I heard from these young people fit my ancient teachings, *minobimaadizi-win* (the Good Path). So, when we refer to the Creator, we are professing what the students said and what we, personally, as authors, believe.

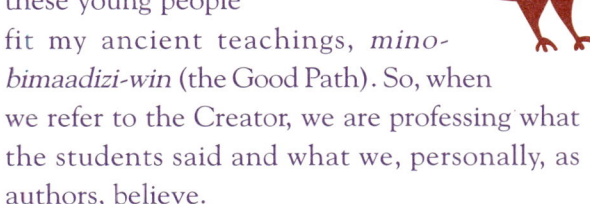

My ancestors believed that wisdom came from following the Good Path, and their Creator told them how that would be accomplished. In the Ojibwe creation story, the Creator, or the Great Mystery, created humankind and gave each and every human some of the essence of the Mystery (some of the Creator). The very essence of the Creator comprises the values of the Good Path, and the journey in search of wisdom is an inward, not an outward, journey. Individuals cannot find the Good Path by others telling them to live in a good way. They cannot find the Good Path by reading books about it or by putting a list of values on the wall as a reminder of how to live. They simply need to live these ways:

    Honor the Creator
    Honor elders
    Honor our elder brothers, the plant and animal beings
    Honor women
    Keep our promises and uphold our pledges
    Be kind to everyone, even to those with whom we disagree
    Be peaceful
    Be courageous
    Be moderate in our dreams, thoughts, words, and deeds [1]

True to the ways of our traditions, we will not tell you this is the way you should live or that you should set an external goal to live in these ways. We will simply describe these good ways to live. In doing so, we bring honor to ourselves and all whose lives we touch.

Honor the Creator

What does it mean to honor the Creator? What does that look like in a very concrete and tangible way? We each do so in our own ways. Some attend ceremonies and offer prayer or go to church. Others simply acknowledge the Creator's love. Still others recognize the Creator's presence in everything around us. For example, if we are overcome with the beauty of a place, the sparkle of sun off water, or the soft wind that comes just at sunset, we may experience these things as the very essence of the Cre-

---

[1] Basil Johnston, *Ojibway Ceremonies*, 134-136.

ator. This essence cannot be duplicated in photography or paintings. At such moments, we might whisper, "Thank you, Creator. Thank you for allowing me to be a part of all of this. Thank you for honoring me with all of this beauty."

At powwows, we might feel overcome by the love and togetherness and spirit of it all—our traditional music and elders, the dancers and busy play of children and babies, the fry bread and Indian taco stands. This feeling, too, could be understood as the very essence of the Creator. We might whisper, "Thank you, Creator. Thank you for all of the love in this place at this time. Thank you for healing us, if only for the moment."

Honoring the Creator includes acknowledging the everyday miracles that occur all around us—the rising and setting of the sun, the changing of the seasons, the hushed quiet after a heavy snow, the whisper of the grasses swaying in the wind, clouds racing across the sky, and life in all its varieties and forms. Especially in our quiet times when we are alone, we may offer tobacco or prayer or cornmeal, or we may burn sage. And during these times, it is just between the Creator and us. We might not even say anything or offer anything, but instead, we just think of how honored and humbled we are to be a part of the creation. That is another way of honoring the Creator.

The young people we interviewed showed a profound sense of respect for the Creator and found strength in prayer. Young people such as Thunder (Hoopa) live, in a very real way, the Good Path:

♦ When I go on the hills and I pray, it relieves me. 'Cause on my hill, there's this really big rock up there, and you can see the whole valley. It looks so nice; it relaxes me. Beautiful up there. Clears my head.

Tasheena (Navajo) added:

♦ I also think I rely a lot, it sounds kind of weird, but I rely a lot upon prayer to help me get through the days. Like, I'll just pray, "Please help me get through this day" or "Please help me to do this." And it always finds a way of working out. So, I think spirituality and prayer help.

Honor Elders

Recently, I took my granddaughter to a powwow, where we danced and got caught up in the overpowering collective spirit of the event. My wife and sons were there as well, my youngest son moving from drum to drum to sit with his friends and be close to the music. We were all so overcome with the spirit of one of the drums that we didn't want it to end. All of us who danced stood around the drum and danced in place. Women singers surrounded the boys who were singing, and their songs were more of a wailing, so characteristic of our female singers. All of our collective joy and pain, love and grief, hope and despair were present in that song and that dance.

All during this time, off on the other side of the dance area, sitting alone at his drum, was an elderly man—my granddaughter's great-grandfather. He didn't move from his sitting place all evening. You should've seen him smile every time she danced around the circle. Earlier that evening, I brought her over to him. He hadn't seen her in several years.

"This is your great-grandfather," I said.

He took her into his arms and gave her a

hug—ancient as bears, it was. Then, when it was time to go home, I brought her over to him again, and he said as he held her, "Your great-grandfather loves you so much. I love you. I love you so much."

He said it again and again, overcome with emotion. And his voice melded into the sights and sounds of singers chanting, dancers whirling and spinning, children running around, elders laughing and teasing one another, boys posturing, and young girls practicing being young and beautiful. An old man who loved his great-granddaughter and a great-granddaughter who was loved—together they captured the whole spirit of that place.

The young people we interviewed showed respect for elders in different ways. Jamie (Seneca) had profound respect for his elders, all of whom he had lost. Maybe he realized the importance of elders because he had lost so much:

◆ [My grandmother is] the person that has really given me strength to do what I got to do in life. I lost other people than her.... My grandfather, he taught me a lot of things in the culture. He showed me how to be strong. And my uncle, he acted like an older brother to me, but he was killed in the Marines.

Daisy (Yurok) tried to do well in school and life because of her respect for elders:

◆ The elders are always asking me, "Are you doing good? You're not doing drugs? You're going to go to college? Come back one day and help us out." So, I think mostly for the elderly people, that I want to do good for.

Margie (Hoopa) envisioned a time when she could work to bring elders into the schools as teachers of young Native children:

◆ I would try to get elders to be in the school. I'd even make a special little room for the elders, for language classes to go to.

James (Ojibwe) showed elders respect by giving some of his wild rice harvest to his grandparents:

◆ I got more than 200 pounds, gave it to my grandparents. They're old and can't go ricing anymore.

Lisa (Dakota) envisioned becoming a respected elder herself:

◆ I want [young people] to think I'm a strong Indian elder, and I want them to know that I think education is important and that it's really important to learn your culture because if the young people don't learn it, we're going to lose it. And I want them to see that I think Indian education is important because that is where we get our culture from, like our language and literature.

Honor Our Elder Brothers: The Plant and Animal Beings

Many years ago, I took a group of Native young people on a wilderness expedition. We camped on a small island on Lake Saganaga on the Minnesota-Ontario border. An early riser, I was up before first light, sitting around the hot coals of the fire. This was good thinking time. Then I looked up, and not 10 feet from me stood a deer. She was so beautiful. I nodded my head to acknowledge her presence, and she wagged her tail to acknowledge me. I sat there watching for the longest time as she went about the important business of living, eating grass, and every so often stopping to look back at me and wag her tail. Then, with the breeze that often accompanies the coming of sunlight, she was gone, like breath on a window.

Just as a deer and I honored each other one morning many years ago, the young people we interviewed showed respect for our elder brothers: the plant and animal beings. Sometimes, this value is not shared at school. Quoetone (Ojibwe) found himself defending the honor of plant and animal beings in opposition to his teacher's view:

- I went to [a Catholic school]. . . . We were having a discussion one day [in first grade], and the Sister was telling us how they used to sacrifice lambs because lambs don't have spirits. . . . It's like, "But animals do have spirits. I know they have spirits because they are living, right? Everything has a spirit inside it, some kind of will for life." She goes, "Oh no, they don't go to heaven. They don't have a spirit." I got really mad, and they had to take me down to the office.

Diddems (Hoopa) honored our elder brothers through ceremony:

- When we have . . . [the ceremony], it's a renewal. We'll go for 10 days straight, you know, through the whole valley here. And it's for the water, the fish, the berries, the acorns—everything that people take for granted. We pray because it's a gift to us. We dance the sickness, the jealousies, the evil, and push it all out. We stomp it out of the earth and push it out of the valley so people can relate to each other and communicate.

Honor Women

My colleague Amy Bergstrom told me a story about a young Dakota man who had been beating his wife. Everyone in the man's family and community knew he was doing this, and his grandfather finally told him, "How honored and humbled I feel as a Dakota elder because I came from my mother's womb. Grandson, I don't know where you come from." Without directly telling the grandson he was dishonoring himself and all of creation by beating his wife, the grandfather taught him a life lesson in the ancient indirect way of his people. The lesson had a profound effect on the man, who now works in a prevention program, where he gives talks about his life as an abuser.

How do we live in such a way so as to honor women? What does that look like in a concrete and tangible way? If we are female, we honor ourselves. All of us show respect for our mothers, our sisters, our aunties, and our grandmothers. We who are men honor our wives and treat our wives' sisters as we would treat our own sisters. We honor our daughters and granddaughters.

Young people spoke of the importance of honoring women. Margie (Hoopa) told how her people honor the transition from being a girl to becoming a young woman:

- There's a lot of things that a lot of girls could brush up on and maybe get a better understanding of. A lot of people don't know much about the flower dance, a dance for girls when they come into maturity and become a woman. They were to

The Good Path

have a flower dance for her, just to let all the men in the tribe know that she was now a woman, and she could perform the tasks [of women]. They have these songs they sing, and they have these sticks that they tap, and they sing a song, and everyone is listening as the young woman is telling everyone in the tribe she is a woman now; she can do all the things that a woman does. She knows how to cook, and she can give life. The woman was also swearing to God that she would abide by all the rules.

Just like Jamie (Seneca) honored his grandmother by trying to live a healthy lifestyle, other young people also honored women. Chloe Blue Eyes (Seneca) spoke of a profound sense of respect for her grandmother:

◆ I go to my grandma. She helps a lot. If I have problems with my parents, with school, with sports, with my little sister, if it all gets to me and I don't know how to deal with it, I just go to my grandma. I talk to my grandma. She's just a good listener. My grandma's a listener. She's cool.

Keep Our Promises and Uphold Our Pledges

I know many young Native people who have been deeply hurt by their parents' alcoholism, and I've heard many examples of the loss of trust that comes from being handed too many broken promises. I know little girls who are afraid to stay with their friends on an overnight because they fear their parents will not come to get them the next day. I've known little boys who have an inordinate fear of abandonment and have a need to call their parents continually. I've known siblings who rode along with their parents on drinking binges, sitting in the back of a car late into the night as their parents drank in the bars, because they didn't want to be left alone at home for days on end. And how all of this affects them when they become adults is part of the great circle of pain that is alcoholism. They become adults who do not trust. They do not trust enough to love another person. Even if they do love, they do not trust. They protect their hearts at all costs.

The young people we interviewed realized the almost sacredness of keeping promises. Most did not speak directly about promises but of implied promises to their elders and themselves. Jamie (Seneca) discussed a commitment to his elders:

◆ They were always there when I was young. That's why I'm kind of a good kid now—because of them. They kept me away from drugs, dropping out of school. And now that I'm here, I've done it. I stayed in school and am getting a good education. That's when I think about all the good stuff that I learned from them. They're the ones that showed me at an early age.

Jana (Hoopa) made a graduation promise to her mother:

◆ I want to give her that gift, from me. And I'd like to do the college one, give her the college diploma as well.

Margie (Yurok) promised to abstain from sexual activity as part of living her traditional ways:

◆ Some of the girls don't practice abstinence, but I do myself because I'm very traditional,

135

and in the traditional way, you have to. They say your power becomes the strongest when you are a woman and you're still a virgin; and to dance, you have to be a virgin. That's the one main rule. I am the only daughter in the family, the only granddaughter on both sides of the family, so it's sort of my job to keep up that side of the culture. And I do it very well.

Werlth-Kerish-Nah (Hoopa) spoke of a promise to himself, his mentor, and his people about learning his language and becoming a language teacher:

◆ I'd say in the last three years, my mentor has been my master because I've been teamed up in the master-apprentice program of the Yurok tribe. It's total immersion into the Yurok language so that I can learn it and gain fluency over a period of time, and then I, in turn, maybe even get credentials and teach the language to other people.

Be Kind to Everyone

There are difficult times in all of our lives, and I have not been immune to life's obstacles. During a particularly difficult period, one of my younger sisters came to my house, bringing the comfort and kindness characteristic of the old ways of our People. When I opened my door, she said, "I brought you some fish." That is all she said; no other words were needed. Everything that needed saying was in that simple, kind act of her coming to my house, acknowledging life's difficulties, and sharing part of her day with me.

Showing kindness is such a simple act, and it can also be the most difficult one. Young people like Daisy (Yurok) emphasized the importance of being kind, especially to family:

◆ I value my family highly. And moving here, respecting elders, and spending time with my family has taught me a lot and has made me aware of how important family is. I hope to be a patient and loving person.

Margie (Hoopa) aspired to be kind in her future role as a parent and elder:

◆ I want my children to see me as a very loving person, a very knowledgeable person. If they ever need any help or anything, I will be there for them. And my kids aren't going to be here for a long time, so I have lots of time to learn all of that. I want my kids to see me as a highly respected person. My grandkids? I want them to see me as an old wrinkly faced woman with a nice big house [laughs], with a big warm fireplace.

Be Peaceful

On my rez, we use the rezbonics (reservation English) word *rugged* to describe living a life full of difficulties and challenges. Growing up on a rez can be a rugged experience. I have scars all over my head to prove it. To survive, we sometimes needed to fight back. I boxed Golden Gloves, got a black belt in karate, and got in more rez fights than I care to remember. I've been shot at, stabbed, thrown out of moving cars, beaten up, and pushed down stairs. Yet, I emerged from those life experiences still somewhat coherent and humbled by the fact that I survived it all. I know that many young Native people live the same way I did because life in Indian country can still be rugged. Our traditional teachings, however, speak of the need to find peace in our lives, and now that I'm a grandfather, I have found peace. But, oh, the journey to reach this place.

Many of the young people we interviewed had likewise moved beyond earlier life troubles. All showed a particular gentleness that we, as Native people, often demonstrate to one another. Even the most troubled and angry of young people were gentle in my presence. I showed respect for them and acknowledged their words as sacred gifts. They, in turn, shared with me the peacefulness of the character. Werlth-Kerish-Nah (Hoopa) explained how he turned his life around:

◆ I think it was constantly taking the wrong path that finally made me say, "Hold on, I'm going down the wrong road." And the only way that I could do that was if I examined what I was doing. . . . I was constantly fighting and bickering with everybody. I couldn't get along with anybody, it seemed. . . . Then I realized that instead of pointing my finger at everybody else and saying, "You're the problem, you are the reason why this is happening," I had to look at myself and say, "Wait a minute. . . . If it wasn't for what I'm doing, this situation would have never occurred." And that was a real changing point.

Werlth-Kerish-Nah also spoke of the need for peacefulness and the need to work to attain it, especially in ceremony:

◆ When we do our dances, it's to make medicine for everybody in this valley and also for everybody in this world. Like, our jump dance is like a cleansing dance too. It washes all the bad things away. It keeps everything in balance, makes sure nothing goes wrong. The brush dance is to pray for everybody. If somebody is sick, [we dance] to help them get better. Everybody who might be angry at one another over the past year works together to try to get things [worked out]. The community grows from this, or balances. Like, if I had a problem with someone and we saw each other on the dance grounds, everything is forgotten because it's like a sacred place, and if you have bad thoughts there, it will come back to you.

Fred (Choctaw) felt peacefulness should be taught in Native schools:

◆ I would say that an ideal [Native] school would have more emphasis on culture, more emphasis on education, peace, and harmony, and working together. That is what I think an ideal school should be.

Be Courageous

Traditional teachers were seldom explicit in the ways they dispensed knowledge. When young men were taught hunting skills, for example, their teachers did not say, "It is important for you to know how to do this; otherwise, our people will starve." Instead, they simply taught the young men by example and practice to be skilled hunters. Similarly, when young women were trained to gather herbs, their teachers did not say, "It is important for you to know these things; otherwise, our people will become ill and have no remedies." Instead, they simply taught them how and when to gather herbs by example and practice. The teachers and pupils knew the tests of the newfound knowledge would be severe. The people would need food. The people would fall ill and need remedies. The people would need to be defended from enemies and disease. Courage would be required.

Young people like Carol (Navajo) spoke often about the ongoing severe tests and the need for courage:

◆ Our government has the right to take away Native Americans' rights. They have like ultimate control. And I think that we just need to unite with other Native American [people] and stand up for our rights and what we see fit. I think a lot of what is going to save us is just speaking out for ourselves because no one else is going to do it for us.

As Lisa (Dakota) described, it sometimes takes courage simply to have pride in who you are:

◆ One of my friends got an award at the Knowledge Bowl, and she gave a really good speech about being proud of who you are, no matter who you are. Her speech really touched me because here at [school], it can be a problem. Like, I'm half. I get a lot of racism about being of mixed heritage because I'm half White and half Indian. And her speech was totally right on the button—how you should be proud no matter what you are or who you are and where you come from.

Be Moderate

Our traditional values teach that we need to be moderate in our thoughts, words, and deeds. This can be very difficult in contemporary society, where individuals who have done special things are often put in the spotlight for accolades (awards, congratulations). Throughout Indian country, it is commonplace to have honor banquets and award festivals for Native young people who have succeeded (graduated, made merit rolls, excelled in athletics or academic endeavors). What impresses me and many other Native people are individuals who maintain their humility throughout all the accolades they receive. They do not perceive themselves as particularly special or more deserving because they did special things. They don't brag about their achievements, how many points they've scored, how many books they've published, or what famous people they've had their pictures taken with. These individuals work with one or more of their strengths or intelligences and graduate from school. They make merit rolls because they feel joy in learning. They excel in sports because they practice and have some natural ability. They write books or songs because they have something to say. Their most important pictures are those of their loved ones. In a word, they have humility.

The young people we interviewed spoke of being moderate in thoughts, words, and deeds. Margie (Hoopa) wanted to return to her community, give back, and teach a way of moderation. Her words captured a message common among the young people [we interviewed]:

◆ So many people get paid so much money they don't need, and I would change that. I always wanted to close off the valley, redo everything. Everyone goes back to being equals. Nobody gets paid more; nobody gets paid less. I would even put their job description in a framed picture and stick it on their wall, so every day they walk by, and they could read it and remember what their job is and what they have to do for their tribe.

A Teaching Story

My freshman year started out rough because my cousin died. And the last time I saw her, she told me that she was kind of going downhill, and she told me never to turn out like she did—to stay in school and always do really well, and to never let drugs or alcohol stop me. And I've had plenty of chances and plenty of temptations, and I may have been sidetracked, but I never let them stop me. I let them slow me down a bit. You have to be a pure person, and you have to respect yourself and others, and that has definitely influenced me. —Megan (Ojibwe)

Our teachings instruct us to follow the Good Path, to live in a way that honors our own lives and the lives of all those we touch. The path is difficult, with many challenges and obstacles. Some of us get lost along the way. The following story is about one such person lost to alcoholism, which steals the soul and blinds people into giving up everything. But this invented story is also about recovery and hope, and how it is necessary to assist young people as they search for their own way in life's journey.

Sara's Song

by

Thomas D. Peacock

Prologue

I've been thinking of you a lot lately, Sara. In my dreams we are both children again, walking home from that Catholic mission school, where we were reminded we were sinners and heathens who would surely go to hell if we didn't change our ways. You in a worn print dress your mother found in the boxes of free clothes in the back room of the church. Me in my bib overalls and hook boots with broken and tied-together laces. That's how I remember things, Sara. You will always be perfect to me. I don't want to remember you drunk and smelling of other men. I don't want to remember you like that. I don't even know why I am talking to you. You've been gone for years now. But I know there are times when your memory comes to sit beside me.

Now my life is filled with everyday things that sometimes jolt my memory back to other times, other chapters in my story. At no particular place or time of day, a certain movement of clouds or wind will take me back to the times we would walk into your house, where your mother sat darning socks in the kitchen. In my memory, a wind is causing yellowed lace curtains to sway and dance to her songs. I remember you had her gift of music. And while I am remembering these things, for just a moment there will be a longing. Sometimes I will be walking down the street and suddenly will become immersed in the smells of a certain perfume you would wear. I will be reminded of your warm and gentle voice, and I may smile slightly. If I am with someone, they might ask me about my smile, and I will say it is nothing special. But it will be. There are other times when I will want to see you and touch you and be with you so much I will be overcome with longing. Maybe I will be out driving alone, and a song on the radio will gently touch me on the shoulder. I may have to pull over to the side of the road, put my face in my hands, and grieve again, as if it were the first day of my grieving. At such times, it is as though your memory has come to sit beside me and hold my hand, reminding me the past and present are one and the same.

This is one of those times.

◆

Eddie's Younger Brother

When Eddie pulled his old pickup truck into his younger brother's yard, he sensed there was something wrong. Brothers and sisters sometimes intuitively know when even small things are amiss with a sibling, and they find subtle and indirect ways to provide support in those difficult times. There was a manner in his brother's movement about the yard, the way his brother would work for short bursts, then stop and look off in the distance. There was a look in his eyes that could not hide his disappointment, and a meandering tone in his voice. Eddie had recognized these things about his brother for many years.

He remembered a particular winter when they were little boys and had gone snow sledding with their cousins. Grandfather had made them a toboggan from a long piece of sheet metal, and it was recognized as the fastest sled on the rez. It was faster than the car hoods that other rez kids used as sleds and much faster than the slickest piece of cardboard. Their metal toboggan easily outdistanced the town kids' store-bought ones. So on that particular day, when they went sledding down the steepest hill in Red Cliff and made a direct hit on the only poplar tree in the way, they hit it faster and harder than anyone had ever hit it before. Five little rez kids went flying in all directions, their handmade wool mittens and charity boots filled with snow. Snow collected on the knitted scarves their grandmothers had made, and snow jammed up their tattered and dirty army surplus coats. When everything cleared and they began picking themselves up, Eddie noticed that his brother remained motionless on the ground.

"We better get him home," one of his cousins said. So four little rez kids loaded their cousin and brother up on a toboggan, which would forever wear a dent to commemorate that day, and began pulling him home. Halfway up another hill, Eddie noticed a stir in his brother and motioned for the others to stop. The injured little boy slowly opened his eyes and reached out his hand to his older brother. There was a certain look in his eyes of fear and love and pain, and Eddie said to his brother, "Are you going to be alright?"

"Uh-huh."

The love Eddie had for his little brother would show in other difficult times too. As the years passed and they found themselves grieving the passing of family members—their grandparents and mother and father and aunties and uncles and cousins—Eddie would always find ways to seek out his brother, to visit him and sit with him. At times like this, he would enter his brother's house early in the morning to make him coffee and would then take it over to him when he arose for the day. If his brother was working on his car or boat, Eddie would pick up a tool and begin helping him with the repair. Always the talking between them was just above a whisper, and occasionally there was also light laughter, but for the most part, little was said. They would glance into each other's eyes to acknowledge that each was there for the other, and the unspoken exchange would be, "Are you going to be alright?"

"Uh-huh."

So it was that day Eddie went to visit his brother. He moved in his quiet way, picking up his brother's net boxes and putting them in the shed. When the work was done, they sat on the porch and Eddie pulled out a pocketknife and began whittling away at a stick of wood.

"Did you see Ronnie last night over on Madeline?"

"Uh-huh."

"He got in trouble over there."

"That's too bad."

Enough said.

It wasn't as if this was the first time Eddie had heard of his nephew's bad behavior. He remembered that just this past winter Ronnie had beat the hell out of some White kid for some stupid nothing reason. It had happened just after Eddie had spoken to Ronnie's class about how, as people, we need to live a certain way, a gentle way, and how we need to be respectful. These ways of living and being meant so much to Eddie that whenever he spoke to groups about these things, his voice would crack with emotion.

"Listen to me," he would say, speaking from the heart.

Eddie remembered Ronnie sitting in that classroom, respectful and looking proud of his uncle, even occasionally nodding his head in acknowledgment and agreement. Later, he heard that after the talk, his nephew seemed to forget everything that had been said.

Now this time, Ronnie got caught drinking, just after hearing his uncle speak to him and the other young people about the importance of knowing their history and living a certain way. Eddie remembered being so proud last night when Ronnie handed him some tobacco, feeling it was another sign that his nephew knew the importance of giving back, of thanking and acknowledging elders and people who know traditional ways.

And Eddie was thinking, why is it we are so weak? We try to be good, so many of us. But our shadow sometimes calls us to dark places. Always we need to work on living the gentle way.

The fact that his only nephew was misusing alcohol brought a sense of foreboding to Eddie for too many reasons. Alcoholism had played at center stage in his own life for too many years. He knew firsthand how it could steal a person's soul and make them give up everything good and right. Eddie had buried too many uncles and cousins and friends who had driven through trees or been kicked to death in drunken brawls, or who had died in drunken stupors after swallowing their tongues or throwing up and choking on their own vomit. He had seen too many elders lose their dignity when drunk, peeing in their pants or passing out in cars and yards and even on the sides of roads. He had seen how alcohol made people laugh too loudly and too easily. And Sara. All of Sara came flooding back to him that day.

Eddie looked at his brother, stood up, and walked into the house, his hand lightly brushing him on the shoulder as he went by. Just for an instant their eyes met and their looks said, "Are you going to be alright?" The response: "Uh-huh," with a slight smile.

◆

The Girl in the Faded Print Dress

Edward Bainbridge had been in love with Sara Ann Bear a thousand years before they met as little children the first day of ricing (wild rice) season at a canoe landing. Theirs was a love that is sometimes born and passed down through generations, only to find its way to where it belongs. Their families had been ricing a small lake just south of Ashland, where every day, early in the morning, the parking area and boat landing would begin filling with old Model T Indian cars and pickup trucks full of parents and their children. The adults, for the most part, knew each other. They were neighbors or relatives or had met at summer powwows or at other ricing lakes. They greeted and conversed with each other in familiar ways, ancient ways.

"Aneen ezhi a yah yan (Hello, how are you)?"

"Nimino, aya (I'm fine)."

Quiet laughter. Old time Indians always laughed that way. There was the thumping and clunking of canoes unloading, car doors closing, and older children being given instructions on caring for their siblings. There were the late summer smells of mud and reeds and fish, and leaves just beginning to think of fall.

"Now you watch your sisters and brothers. Don't let them go in the water. Make them stay at the landing. Make them share lunch," a mother would say, the last part with special emphasis toward the one child everyone has who doesn't know how to share.

"And no fighting either," a mother would say, looking over at the younger children. "And you listen," she would say to the child who would inevitably both fight and not listen before the day was out.

Eddie and his little brother would be cared for by their Auntie Marilyn, who was nine years old. She was a good babysitter because she let them do anything they wanted.

"I made you kids some potato sandwiches (sliced potatoes and pepper on homemade bread) and cake (chocolate, no frosting, just a large chunk wrapped in wax paper) and tea (a half-gallon jug). And Eddie, you leave your brother alone too."

Eddie glanced to the side, plotting.

Then, before anyone had a chance to think about being alone without adults for the day, his

The Good Path

father and mother were off in their canoe along with the other ricers, and about 20 children were left on the banks of the lake for the day.

Always on the first day of ricing, the kids tended to stay near their cars until they became familiar with their surroundings. As soon as their parents left, many of them went back to the cars to get some more sleep. The more outgoing boys began bartering with each other over lunches, slingshot rubbers, marbles, agates, and other trade goods that lived in their pants pockets.

"I'll trade you this potato sandwich for one of your jam ones."

"I have cookies. Oatmeal (oatmeal cookies had a higher trading value than, say, sugar cookies). Trade for some of that?" Lips would purse and point to a piece of cake, a muffin, lugalate (a pan bread), fry bread, or some other treat. Even the young people pointed the old time Ojibwe way—with their lips.

There was no trading for NBA basketball cards or handheld video games. In those days, everyone was poor, but no one knew it because it was before the war on poverty. Hand-me-downs in the form of tattered jeans, yellowed T-shirts, faded print dresses, and shoes without laces were the fashions of the day. All the kids smelled like kerosene oil or wood smoke, or both. Slingshots and mud pies ruled.

Eddie and his little brother sat in the backseat of their father's car, drinking tea and sucking on crackers while their auntie slept in the front seat. It wasn't until Eddie left for his second pee break of the day and was returning to the car that he saw her. Rounding the rear bumper of his father's old Chevy, he saw, for the first time, the girl who would become the woman he would forever be in love with. She was sitting in the backseat of her father's car, all hazel-eyed and faded blue flower print dressed. All four years old of her. When his small dark eyes met hers and he gave her a slight smile, she gave him one of those, "you smell bad" looks, and he knew. Even though he was only six years old at the time, he knew.

They didn't say a word to each other that day, or in the days that followed, but Eddie would find ways to observe the little girl as she played with her friends. If she noticed him, and he would make sure of that in some way, he would give her his slight smile. Through days of playing cowboys and Indians, shooting slingshot rocks out into the lake, playing hide-and-go-seek, trading marbles, and picking on his younger brother, Eddie would always find the time to go running past the little girl, or he would say something purposely loud enough for her to hear, just so she would notice him. Eventually, one day, she noticed that he was noticing, and on the second to the last day of ricing on that lake, she returned his smile, this little girl who, even at the age of four, made good mud pies. On the last day, he worked up the courage to say to her in a laughing way, "I'll trade you half of my potato sandwich for one of your mud pies."

To which she replied, "I don't like potato sandwiches."

But there were other lakes to rice and other boat landings where the kids would play while their parents worked, and eventually, Eddie and Sara Ann became friends.

Except for the times when they saw each other at the ricing landings each year, the two rarely played together. When Sara was old enough for school, she rode the rez bus to St. Mary's Catholic School along with Eddie. She was, however, two years younger and, therefore, in a different peer group. Eddie was a Red Cliff village kid and Sara lived far out of town, and with the exception of school and ricing, she rarely ventured from home. So it wasn't until they were older, 14 and 16, that they began really noticing each other in hormonal ways.

It turned out that Sara lived in Frog Bay—an isolated part of Red Cliff, which itself was a remote community in northern Wisconsin. She, along with nine brothers and sisters, lived in a small, white, frame house near the end of a long dirt road that wound its way out of Red Cliff some five miles and ended at the shores of Lake Superior. Sara's mother was a quiet, dependent, and enabling housewife, a White woman who could trace her French ancestry back to the sprawling vineyards near Bordeaux. Her father was also quiet, a brooding alcoholic whose binges would transform him into an abusive and neglectful man. He was one of those half-breeds, she told Eddie, who could pass for White and, therefore, was allowed in town bars that were still illegal for Indians to enter. He served as the drunken caretaker for several summer residents whose retreats far surpassed in size and splendor anything the rez residents could ever imagine themselves living in.

There was being poor and there was being dirt poor, and Sara's family was the latter. Deer meat soup and pancakes were diet mainstays in her household. When they were older, Sara would tell Eddie that her younger and mildly retarded brother would often come running into the house after a wild day out playing in the woods, would dash into the kitchen, pull the cover off the kettle, and proclaim with genuine glee, "Oh boy! Pancakes!"

And that was after a month of pancakes.

She also told him of the times her father would use her as part of an excuse to go on one of his binges. He would tell her mother that he needed to go into town to get his hair cut and would take Sara along as a decoy, thinking that if he took one of the kids along, he would stay sober and actually do what he said he was going to do. More often than not, though, Sara would end up sitting in her father's old car outside some bar for nights on end, occasionally going inside to beg her father to take her home or to get her a bottle of orange phosphate, a nut goody, or a pickled egg.

Her first boy crush, she once told Eddie, was another young person who was sitting in a car next to her father's, also waiting while his father sat drunk in the bar. She remembered that once her father took her to a three-day party out near Makwah, where she played for days and late into the evenings with strange children, all the while surrounded by adults who constantly asked her name as they breathed their wine breath on her and laughed grotesquely until they passed out in chairs and on floors. And although she never told Eddie, she remembered another time when one of her father's drunken friends touched her in places that made her feel confused and dirty and shameful, making her sit on his lap while he bounced her up and down. When she was an adult and thought back to that incident, she would question how some of her own people could have moved so far away from their traditional ways that they would do

The Good Path

these things to children. "What happened to them?" she would ask herself. What has happened to us?

When these drunken binges ended, Sara would later tell Eddie, it was she who would often drive home.

"I was just a little girl," she would say. "I was only seven or eight years old when I had to learn to drive. I couldn't hardly even see over the dash, and always my father would pass out, and there I would be, driving home in the dark with those dim old car lights blinking through the trees."

When they made it home, Sara would say, she would sneak into the house and make her way to the bedroom, where she would find a place to cuddle in the warm sprawl of her sleeping brothers and sisters. She found comfort there. She knew the father who had taken her out on one of his binges, who had fed her pickled eggs and nut goodies from a bar, who had made her drive home, would eventually become an enraged drunk before the night was out. Invariably, her father would awaken and start the car, only to find he was too drunk to drive. Sometimes he would roar up and down their long driveway, going forwards and in reverse and in and out of the ditch. Once he hit the house, shaking everyone out of bed. Other times, he would sit in the car with the headlights on, roaring the motor and honking the horn, as if to proclaim to the world he was home; the lord and king of the domain was home, wanting the attention afforded to those who ruled over domains. And always there would be a special dread when he entered the house, so much so that her stomach muscles cramped up from her fear of him. The quiet man who was her father when he was sober would transform into an abusive ogre when he was drunk.

There he would sit at the kitchen table, tapping his foot on the floor and singing some song he had heard at the bar.

"Get me something to eat," he would proclaim to a house that was filled with his frightened and silent children, as well as a frightened wife.

"Why don't you just go to bed?" their mother would ask. But he would call her something demeaning.

"You're nothing but a w_____," he would yell. "Get out here and get me something to eat."

So, while his children lay frightened in bed, their mother, the woman who bore his children, would arise and enter the kitchen, carrying the household's only kerosene lamp with her. Sara later told Eddie how she was embarrassed for her mother at times like that, for the degradation she had to endure. Once, Sara could no longer bear to hear any more abuse and went into the kitchen to confront her drunken father.

"You leave her alone! You leave my mother alone!" she screamed.

"You get out of here, you little s___," he yelled, coming after her. She remembered running from the house and seeing her father hitting her mother as she stepped in to intervene. She remembered her little brothers and sisters, sobbing and sleepy and frightened, running out with her into the cold and dark night. They ran out to the dark cleave of the field and hid behind trees, while their father stood at the door with his gun, proclaiming he was going to "kill all you little bastards." And she remembered her mother sitting in the tall, wet grass with the two smallest children, sobbing.

She told Eddie about the time her father was on a bender and sold their icebox to a couple of town men who came into their home one afternoon and sheepishly told her mother that they had bought it from her husband. Sara would never quite get over her mother putting what little was in the icebox onto the floor. And how later she came upon her mother crying softly in a corner of the one bedroom they all shared, sitting in her old rocker, fingers touching her lips, eyes filled with tears from too many years of disappointment, unfulfilled dreams, and broken promises. She would never forget, she once told Eddie, how her father mourned so greatly when her mother died that he seemed to forget all the awful things he had made his wife endure, this woman who had given up all her promise to a man who so selfishly took all her pride, all her dreams.

Unlike Sara's family, Eddie was raised in a functional home by parents who didn't abuse alcohol and who believed that children were precious gifts given to them and entrusted to their care. While he was a good listener to Sara's stories and could empathize with her, his life had not taken him down that path. How was it these childhood friends would become lovers? How was it that friends who sat next to each other on the school bus each day, friends who shared a potato sandwich at summer catechism or during ricing season, friends who passed and acknowledged each other during the long walking circles at summer powwows, would one day notice each other in the way of lovers? What was it about fate and luck and timing and circumstance that took people to certain places and put certain events before them that forever changed their life paths? Eddie tried to pinpoint it down to a day, a moment.

Always at powwows there are eagles, and once, as Eddie and Sara stood leaning against the rail that separated the dance area from the rest of the powwow grounds, she said, "I'm from eagle clan. My dad's dad, my grandpa, was a White man. So I have to be." Maybe it was then that they both realized it was appropriate in the eyes of the community for them to begin to see each other as lovers. For to see each other in that way and to be from the same clan would have prompted a talk from one of Sara's Ojibwe aunties or from one of Eddie's paternal uncles. Eddie knew his father was bear clan because the home he grew up in was filled with bear memorabilia: pictures of bears, a bear wall hanging, a bear claw necklace hanging from a family photograph. His father had told him they were part bear.

"What part of me?" Eddie remembered asking.

"Those beady little eyes," his father had said, laughing. But Eddie also had a way of extending his lower lip when he pointed to things, the ways bears do. "I think my lips are part bear too" he thought.

That is also where timing came in, because if they had been born just a generation earlier, neither their courtship nor eventual marriage would have been allowed. Sara's parents would have arranged for her marriage, and she may not have found out about who was to be her life partner until the day of her marriage. In those times, there was no refusing or questioning the decisions of parents. That was not the way. But times had changed. The culture had changed.

The Good Path

Sara Ann Bear was 17 years old when she married Edward James Bainbridge in the tiny Catholic church in the village of Red Cliff. It was the same church where, as babies, they had been baptized; where they had attended their first and second communions under the stern tutelage of nuns who didn't want to be teaching reservation children; and where they had been officially confirmed by a now long-dead bishop. Neither was a practicing Catholic. Sara lived too far from town to attend mass. Eddie was Catholic by default. One of his grandmothers shamed his mother into it. In many ways, his family still followed their traditional ways, and he attended ceremonies the church would certainly have banned if they knew of them.

Like so many rural village churches, this was both a place of great joy and of great sadness, and even when the church pews were filled for such a joyous occasion, there were the remembrances of times of loss and grieving. Among the people of Red Cliff gathered that day for the wedding, there was a collective recognition that the circle of life is a dance of light and shadow, a dance of summer's extended sunlight and winter's unending nights. Just a year earlier, Sara had attended the funeral of her sister there in the same church. A carload of drunks had slid off an icy road, and one of her brothers had rushed into the house to tell an already unhappy home of a horrible accident. Sara and her mother and brothers and sisters had rushed to the accident scene. There, her younger sister lay trapped in a car that had careened into a power pole while being taken on a drunken joy ride. What would haunt Sara most, though, was the memory of having to hold her mother back as the fire and rescue crew tried to free the girl from the car, her mother standing knee deep in snow in the dead of winter without boots or a coat, crying, "Oh, my God! My little baby!" Her mother screamed over and over again, long after the priest came to them in the emergency room at Washburn Hospital and told the family a daughter and sister had died.

Even as she was walking down the aisle of the church on her wedding day, with her half-drunken father holding her arm, Sara thought of her sister, of the smatter of blood and broken glass, of her sister laying in a coffin wrapped in the hand-sewn quilt their mother had so lovingly made.

She thought these things even as she looked Eddie in the eyes and told him she would love him forever, in sickness and in health, until death. She thought them even when he whispered in her ear, "Weedjeewaugun (my companion in the path of life)." She felt great joy and great sadness at the same time. That was her path, her way.

After the wedding, they took a long boat ride out into the blue of the lake in Eddie's family's fish trawler. They were in love, and this woman who wore the burden of joy and sadness sang to her husband what would forever become their song, "La vie en rose."

Quand il me prend dans ses bras
When he takes me in his arms
Il me parle tout bas,
He speaks quietly to me,
Je vois la vie en rose.
(And) I see life through rose-colored glasses.

They moved into a small house Eddie had built with green lumber, which stood in a clearing of clover and sumac up in the hills that overlooked Lake Superior. He worked long hours fishing commercially with his father. She was a housewife, and her days were filled with making quilts and canning and tending a garden and scrubbing floors down on her hands and knees. They dreamed of children. Her marriage to Eddie seemed to be an escape from her childhood. Although she missed her mother, as well as the fields and woods of Frog Bay, she was quietly happy living with a man whose life didn't revolve around the episodes inherent to drinking binges. In the early years of their marriage, Eddie never drank anything stronger than coffee.

Sara desperately tried to give Eddie sons and daughters. She knew his fondness for children; she saw it in the way he cared for her younger brothers and sisters, his cousins' children, and, later, Eddie's younger brother's son, Ronnie. At first, she just thought her inability to bear children was simply bad timing or bad luck. Later, they would go to doctors in Washburn, and then to Duluth, where they would be told, sitting in a waiting room with Eddie holding Sara's hand, that they would never have a child. Her body had betrayed her. And she looked in desperation into her husband's eyes, pleading for his forgiveness. He, in his gentle way, with his kind eyes and soft voice, his thin breath in her ear, his tears, said, "K'zaug-in (I love you)."

Sometimes there is a shame that cannot be swept aside and forgotten, that cannot be neatly folded and put away in cedar chests, that cannot be given away in the confessionals at church. Sara would wear her shame through the remaining days of her life, its damp and cold embrace cloaked around her like a dark shawl. A vision unfulfilled.

As the years passed and she sat alone in that small house while her husband worked out on the lake, she found herself moving into darker corners. At first just a drink of whiskey to take away the pain and allow her to face the day, but soon Eddie would come home to her wild horse eyes.

"You've been drinking again," he would say quietly, as he made his own dinner and cleaned up the messes she had long given up on. "Why are you doing this?" His voice would trail off. He would say nothing else to her.

"Chrissakes, I only had one," she would say, looking right through him, angry and defiant, still vulnerable.

What would be one day a month would become one day a week, and one day a week would become every day. Sometimes her drinking would keep Eddie away long into the evening. He didn't want to see his wife that way. And sometimes when he could no longer keep working on his boat or visiting relatives or working outside, he would go home to drink with her, and for a time, the loneliness and anger and pain would leave him too.

He remembered one time he came home and found her sober. They sat and reminisced of happier days and life events, and of things that would never be. He could not stop looking at her that day, touching her, overwhelmed with the love he felt. Just for a moment, it seemed, life returned to her eyes. Just for a moment, that little girl he had met long ago at a wild rice boat landing was there in that room with him. But the next day when he came home, she was drunk and sitting in a chair listening to the radio. And when he said something to her, she called him a son of a bitch and slapped him. She slapped him again and again until he walked

The Good Path

outside to get away. He sat on the steps as she locked the door, then waited while she drank until she passed out. He had to bust in the door of his own house so he could go to sleep with his drunken and unconscious wife.

One Thanksgiving she spent sitting drunk in a dark corner of their house, and Eddie went to his younger brother's for dinner, where an especially nosey cousin asked why he was there without Sara.

"She's not feeling well," he lied. But there was that look in his eyes, and a recognition on his brother's part, a look long recognized by the two brothers.

There were other times he would return home from the lake to find her gone, and at those times he would sit long into the night waiting for her to return from the bars. Eventually, a car would sneak its way down the driveway at some odd hour of the night, and she would emerge, drunk and laughing. He would climb into their bed and pretend he was asleep, but sleep would rarely come on those nights. There would be other times when she would not return until the next day, or the day after. He would not be able to go to work and would become frantic, thinking what might have happened to her. He would wait for the sheriff's car that he imagined pulling into his drive to tell him they had found his wife dead in a ditch somewhere or twisted around a light pole or beaten to death outside a bar. Mostly, though, he would wonder who she was sleeping with.

Even though most adults in Red Cliff knew of Sara, for the most part, they did not judge her. That was the way of many Indian people, an acknowledgment that each of us carries a unique burden, our own pain. Eddie was well respected in the community. He had a way about him, an ancient way, a gentle way. There was a depth in his words. People listened to him and respected him.

Because of the esteem in which he was held, he was often asked to speak to groups. There was a particular time he spoke at an honor luncheon for the high school graduates from the village of Red Cliff. He told them about living their lives in a certain way, of the importance of giving back, of being humble and respectful, and about not allowing themselves to be controlled by anger or by alcohol. But when he returned home from his speech, he found his wife passed out drunk in a lawn chair in the yard. He walked past her into the house, sat on the couch, put his hands to his face, and wept for all the anger and humiliation and despair of his life.

"Why are you doing this to me?" he pleaded with his Creator. "Why are you doing this to me?"

But all of the challenges the Creator had put before him did not compare to the great burden that came to him on an early winter morning. His younger brother's hesitant tapping on the door shook him from a ragged dream with a start, and he opened the door to find his brother standing before him with that look in his eyes, a recognition. That day, his brother had to tell him of the police finding Sara frozen to death in the backseat of someone's car. And just for an instant, upon hearing the words in that forever horrible moment, a flood of memory rushed before him, the memory of a little hazel-eyed girl in a faded blue flower-print dress.

Although Sara was given a Catholic burial service, Eddie grieved for her in the old way. He offered food to her spirit and built a mourning fire near the cleave of woods by the cemetery that he tended for four days, until Sara's spirit reached the land of souls. He would no longer live in the house he had built for them because everywhere were the reminders of Sara. Some people so define a place that without them these places lose their spirit, their meaning. One night, in the depths of his grief, he poured gasoline on what had been their home and burned it. He drank hard and laughed too loudly and too easily.

The pain was so bad his laughter could be heard for miles.

------♦------

The Nephew

Several days after Ronnie had been expelled from summer school, Eddie came into his brother's house and found the boy sitting in front of the television set, glued to it and so hypnotized by it that his hand would sometimes altogether miss the bag of Cheetos he was feasting on. Eddie's brother and sister-in-law were sitting at the kitchen table, drinking coffee and separating grocery coupons. Eddie went to the counter and helped himself to a cup of coffee. He poured in too much sugar and cream and stirred it with a butter knife.

They talked, all of them realizing how precious such talks are in the course of their lives. And the adults recognized that Eddie had a purpose for being there that day. There were reasons for each word, each inflection of voice, each gesture. His stories had deeper meaning.

"You remember when I was a drunk?" he said to his younger brother. "I was drunk for a couple of years and didn't work and didn't bathe and didn't give a sh___ and . . . ."

"Chrissakes, for a while you lived in that old shed out there," his brother said, pointing outside with his lips to a sagging shed that was slowly sinking into the swamp that surrounded their yard.

Ronnie sat in the other room, his eyes glued to the television set, munching on Cheetos.

"I've been sober now for 10 years," Eddie said, showing the adults his sobriety pin.

"Thanks to me," his brother said.

"Me too," his sister-in-law added. They all laughed.

They told all the drunk stories that day. This went on for a long time. Their conversations were a litany of car accidents and long dead cousins, bar fights, ugly girlfriends, near misses from beer bottles and knives and bullets, glancing blows, and fate and timing and luck and circumstance. They talked just loud enough for their words to echo into the living room, just loud enough for Ronnie to hear. They talked this way until Ronnie's parents stood up and excused themselves.

"We need to go grocery shopping," they fibbed.

Once they left, Eddie went into the living room and sat on the couch opposite his nephew.

"How you doing, nephew?"

"Uhhhhmm." Chewing. Staring at the television set. MTV.

"Did you hear us telling our drunk stories? I'm glad I don't do that anymore."

No response.

"I heard about what happened over at Madeline."

Ronnie's eyes looked down to the floor. He set down his Cheetos and turned down the television set. He listened to his uncle.

"Look at me," his uncle's voice was shaking with emotion.

The Good Path

And that day an uncle told his nephew about how we should live our lives and give honor to life by the way we live. He told about honoring others and about being kind and humble. He told of living the gentle way.

"There is a path we all need to try to follow," Eddie said. "It is hard. I know. I have been there. I have failed many times. I know. My uncles used to tell me this. There is a certain way to live."

The story went on for the longest time.

And then it was over.

"What kind of music are you listening to?" an uncle said to his nephew.

"Hip hop. You like it?"

"It's okay, I guess. You ever hear what we used to listen to when we were young?"

"No."

"I'll go get some." Eddie got up and went outside to his old truck, returning with a cassette tape.

"How do you work this thing?" Eddie was on his hands and knees with his butt way up in the air, as he tried to load the tape into the tape deck and adjust the controls.

"This is something I can teach you, uncle," replied a boy, laughing.

The music began. "La vie en rose."

C'est lui pour moi. Moi pour lui
It's he for me. Me for him
Dans la vie,
In this life,
Il me l'a dit, l'a juré pour la vie.
He has told me so, he has sworn it for life.

An uncle and his nephew sat in the living room of an old house built with rough lumber and rummage sale windows, and filled with mismatched furniture. The music consumed them and flowed out into the late summer air and around the odd collection of yard junk and into the blue of sky, and a flood of memory came to an old man. Of a little girl he had met so many years ago, all hazel-eyed and faded blue flower-print dressed. All four years old of her. For just that moment, she came and sat beside him and held his hand.

"K'zaug-in (I love you)." A tear.

He didn't even realize he had said it aloud.

His nephew gave him that look, a recognition, and they spoke to each other in a way that had been passed down for many thousands of years among the People. In silence.

"Are you going to be alright?"

"Uh-huh."

"Sara's Song" Discussion Questions for Youth

1. Uncle Eddie, Sara, and Ronnie had obstacles and issues to deal with in their lives. For all of them, staying on the Good Path was difficult. What obstacles and challenges did they face, and how did they deal with them? What obstacles or challenges have been put before you, and how have you dealt with them?

2. How might you live the Good Path right now? What would that look like in a very real way?

3. How might we teach our own children and grandchildren about the Good Path?

4. In what ways might the strengths of our traditional Native value system be used to address many of the issues, including education, in our communities?

Chapter Discussion Questions for Teachers and Educators

1. What are the moral teachings of your tribal nation or the tribes in your area? In what ways might these teachings be integrated into the education of students in your community?

2. What are the roles of families, schools, tribes, and communities in guiding young people toward living in a good way?

3. Identify individuals in your community who follow the Good Path. In what ways might you use them as examples of living in a good way without sounding preachy or without telling young people how they should live?

4. If you were to think about redesigning the existing educational paradigm to reflect the Good Path, what might that look like? How might you make it real? What would it look like in a tangible, concrete way?

Full Circle

"The answers lie within us."
—1999 World Indigenous People's Conference on Education

Maria's (Ojibwe) comments from chapter 1 demonstrate that a lot of young Native people want to live the Good Path but just need someone to show them the way:

◆ Most [Native] kids don't know any other way to prove who they are, but I go to powwows and dance and stuff. Like, at my age, there is me and maybe two other girls. A lot of my culture is lost; nobody is doing anything to bring it back. Now, there's a drum group in the grade school again. It's not cool [for Native students] to learn about [their] culture, [so] they learn about other things like gang activity. Maybe by the time they reach eighth grade, [Native students should] know where they are coming from. I think it would help a lot. I think a lot of us are just lost, searching for something to belong to. I used to spend summers up here with my grandma. It made me feel special. Like, every weekend we were at a powwow. A lot of these girls, they've hardly ever left the reservation. My grandma is part of the Midewiwin Lodge, and I really, really want to become part of that. I guess in Canada, they've got some really good ones up there. So, I'm trying to get her to go up there so then she'll know, and then she can bring me along after awhile. I'm trying to learn this stuff. When I go off, Grandma says, "You're off your road," and Grandma pulls me back. I'd like to see more of the Native American ways taught in school, all the way through schools. Then, [those ways] would start all over again.

This chapter began with the lament that, as Native people, we have sometimes become judgmental when telling our young people how they should live their lives. We have put our traditional values in front of them as the way to live without considering how we ourselves live. We have told them to do as we say, not as we do: "You should respect your elders. You should give back to your community. You should protect who we are as Native people. You should be like _____ ; she is such a role model for tribal people."

Our ancestors, however, practiced an inherently more effective, subtle, and indirect way of teaching these things. They showed their children how to live by living the example themselves, by honoring the Creator and all of creation, by valuing the important role of elders in traditional society, by performing acts of kindness, by honoring women as well as the elder brothers (plants and animals), by acting with courage, by upholding promises, and by living a life of peace and moderation. Perhaps more importantly, they recognized their weaknesses and limitations—in essence, their humanness. Like us, they did not inhabit a perfect world with perfect people. What separates them from us is that they recognized and accepted our collective humanity, with all its beauty, wonder, and flaws. And there is a lesson in that.

Our lives have become so complex, we sometimes react differently depending upon the situation or circumstance. We know, however, there is no place along the Good Path for situational ethics. For example, it is inappropriate to be kind only to those we care for and unkind to others because we don't know them or like what they do. We were not born with natural inclinations to show dishonor; be unkind; do cowardly acts; break promises; or create an atmosphere of distrust, hostility, or excess. If we believe, as our ancestors believed, that we were all born with some of the essence of the Mystery (the Creator), our individual and collective journeys along the Good Path must begin by searching within our own hearts. Therein lie the truths. And the voices of the young people we interviewed indicate that our future holds much promise.

Mash-ka-wi-sin (Be strong). Mi-i-iw (That is all).

Chapter 9
Lessons for Educators:
Teaching, Curriculum, and Research

We wrote this chapter primarily for adults, though we certainly welcome student readers (we had to put the boring research literature somewhere—just kidding). We begin by discussing the growing body of literature on Native resilience. Each study adds to our base of knowledge about what it takes to make it when everything stands in the way. The students once again offer good advice to teachers and school administrators for making schools learner and Native centered. We propose the development of truly Native education systems, all the while realizing the extreme difficulty in reforming systems that have been subjugated to external funding sources. Finally, we provide a rationale and description for the research process we used, the results of which we wanted to make accessible to those interviewed: Native youth.

Literature on Native Resilience

We have chosen to focus on the perspectives of several Native people who have written about resilience in Native youth: Iris HeavyRunner, Martin Brokenleg, Joann Sebastian Morris, and Maria Yellow Horse Brave Heart. We also look at the findings of the National Longitudinal Study of Adolescent Health on how connections to family and school affect young people.

Our ancestors survived near annihilation resulting from European colonialism. Disease, war, and genocide reduced the numbers of our ancestors from an estimated 10 million (some say much higher) to a million.[1] Our grandparents and parents survived boarding schools, the era of termination (when the government tried to take away our special status as Native people), and grinding poverty, not to mention all the social ills that accompany it. Through it all, we have survived as distinctly tribal people, with much of our culture intact and a growing sense of our collective strength. The very fact we are still here and so strong in our ways stands as a testament to our resilience.

The toll on Native people, however, has been extraordinarily high. Collectively and as individuals, many of us still suffer greatly from what some call "soul wound" and others refer to as historical trauma response (HTR). The symptoms of HTR include "elevated suicide rates, depression, self-destructive behavior, substance abuse, identification with the pain ancestors endured, fixation to trauma, somatic symptoms that don't have a 'medical reason,' anxiety, guilt, and chronic grief."[2] Significantly, HTR is passed down through generations.

Dr. Maria Yellow Horse Brave Heart suggests that reconnecting with one's spirituality can be a pathway toward healing, both individually and collectively as a people. One of her recommendations involves a Lakota prevention curriculum called Wakanheja (the children). The Wakanheja curriculum uses the Lakota belief in the sacredness of children in conjunction with the Woope Sakowin, The Seven Sacred Laws. The curriculum philosophy is for Native people to move away from identifying themselves as victims and reconnect with traditional parenting and spiritual ways.

As noted by Iris HeavyRunner (Blackfeet) and Joann Sebastian Morris (Saulte Ste. Marie Chippewa), a primary reason for our continued survival, in spite of HTR, has been that fostering resilience in young people is not a new concept:

> We have long recognized how important it is for children to have people in their lives who nurture their spirit, stand by them, encourage and support them. This traditional process is what contemporary researchers, educators, and social service providers are now calling fostering resilience. Thus, resilience is not new to our people; it is a concept that has been taught for centuries. The word is new; the meaning is old.[3]

HeavyRunner and Morris feel that the strength in our traditional ways should form the basis of any effort at fostering resilience in Native youth. These traditional ways, common to many tribal cultures, are often portrayed as a circle, a medicine wheel with four essential, interrelated parts:

1. spirituality (maintaining a belief in the interrelatedness of all things)
2. mental well-being (having clear thoughts)
3. emotional well-being (balancing all our emotions)
4. physical well-being (attending to our physical selves—our bodies)

When a young person has personal difficulties, one or more of these areas need to be addressed.

---

[1] See Zinn, *A People's History of the United States*.
[2] In Yellow Horse Brave Heart, "Oyate Ptayela" as cited in "Historic Trauma Response," 8.
[3] In HeavyRunner and Morris, "Traditional Native Culture and Resilience," 8.

Difficulty in one part affects the others. Likewise, strength in one part can help heal other parts in jeopardy. These strengths have enabled our ancestors to survive all the horrific events they have dealt with since colonization.

Psychologist Martin Brokenleg (Rosebud Lakota) has spent much of his life working for the betterment of Native young people. Brokenleg, along with Larry Brendtro and Steven Van Bockern, wrote the book *Reclaiming Youth at Risk* about working with young people who engage in risky behavior. They describe four things that can cause young people to reach their breaking points, when it is not possible to maintain harmony and balance among their spiritual, mental, emotional, and physical parts:

1. *Destructive relationships.* Young people who feel rejected or unclaimed are hungry for love but unable to trust, and expect to be hurt again.

2. *Climates of futility.* Young people who are insecure feel inadequate and have a fear of failure.

3. *Learned irresponsibility.* Young people may mask a sense of powerlessness by indifference or defiant, rebellious behavior.

4. *Loss of purpose.* In a generation of self-absorbed youth, many are seeking meaning in a world of contradictions (conflicts in the values they are told are important and the reality of what they see in the behavior of adults or in the community).[4]

Brokenleg feels that fostering self-esteem can counter these destructive characteristics and that traditional Native ways of building self-esteem will work with today's young people. Traditional cultures held four bases of self-esteem:

1. *The spirit of belonging.* From the time they were born, children were cared for by caring adults. Learning to treat others as related, what the Lakota people call *Mitakuye Oyasin* (we are all related), children developed a sense of respect, concern for others, a minimum of friction, and good will.

2. *The spirit of mastery.* One of the purposes of traditional education was to foster spiritual, mental, emotional, and physical wellness, or an overall sense of balance. This was done using stories that provided lessons on appropriate behavior and ways of seeing the world. Games and play that modeled adult responsibility were also encouraged.

3. *The spirit of independence.* Many traditional Native cultures placed a high value on individual freedom, and young people were trained in self-management. Young people were never offered rewards for doing well. Practicing appropriate self-management was seen as the reward in itself.

4. *The spirit of generosity.* Giving to others and giving back to the community are fundamental values in many Native cultures. In traditional cultures, adults stressed generosity and unselfishness to young people.[5]

Native people who have written about resilience all place great importance on using our traditional values to foster resilience in Native youth. Each has described these belief systems and values as interrelated parts that form a circle. The circle represents a powerful symbol in many Native cultures. Black Elk, an Oglala holy man, reminds us that our natural resilience is always

---

[4]Brendtro, Brokenleg, and Van Bockern, *Reclaiming Youth At Risk,* 46-59.
[5]Ibid.

present and represented in the circle of strength:

> You will notice that everything an Indian does is in a circle, and that is because the Power of the World always works in circles, and everything tries to be round. In the old days when we were a strong and happy people, all our power came to us from the sacred hoop of the nation, and so long as the hoop was unbroken, the people flourished. The flowering tree was the living center of the hoop, and the circle of the four quarters nourished it. The east gave peace and light, the south gave warmth, the west gave rain, and the north with its mighty cold gave strength and endurance. This knowledge came to us from the outer world with our religion. Everything the power of the world does is done in a circle. The sky is round, and I have heard that the earth is round like a ball, and so are all the stars. The wind, in its greatest power, whirls. Birds make their nests in circles, for theirs is the same religion as ours. The sun comes forth and goes down again in a circle. The moon does the same, and both are round. Even the seasons form a great circle in their changing and always come back to where they were. The life of a man is a circle from childhood to childhood, and so it is in everything where power moves.[6]

Connections That Foster Resilience

Unfortunately, negative labels have been attached to many youth, particularly American Indian, Alaska Native, and First Nations students. A common misconception about young people who engage in risky behavior is that race, ethnicity, family structure, and economic status inevitably have a major impact on success or failure in school and, ultimately, in life. However, the most important factor is how young people connect with their parents, families, and schools. As you read the following sections, think of examples where Native youth in your community may feel connected, or disconnected, from their parents, family, or school.

The Importance of Family

What kinds of family connections foster resilience in young people and help protect them from risky behaviors (often called at-risk behaviors, which include using alcohol or other illegal substances, engaging in sexual activity, skipping school, and getting involved in gangs)? The National Longitudinal Study of Adolescent Health researched more than 90,000 young people from many cultures/races and determined that the following family characteristics help foster resilience:

1. *Parent and family connectedness.* Whether they had a resident or nonresident mother

---

[6]In HeavyRunner and Morris, "Traditional Native Culture and Resilience," 32-33.

or father, youth felt understood, loved, wanted, and attended to by family members.
2. *Parent/adolescent activities.* They engaged in a number of different activities with resident and/or nonresident parents.
3. *Lack of access to guns at home.* They did not have access to guns at home.
4. *Lack of access to substances at home.* They did not have easy access to cigarettes, alcohol, or illegal drugs at home.
5. *Lack of family suicides or attempts.* They did not have any suicide attempts or completions by any family member in the past year.
6. *Parents' disapproval of sex.* They had parents who disapproved of youth having intercourse at an early age.
7. *Parents' disapproval of contraception.* They had parents who disapproved of youth using contraception at an early age.
8. *Parental school expectations.* They had mothers or fathers who had high expectations for high school and college completion.[7]

School Connections

The study also found a number of important conditions associated with school. Students who went to schools with the following features were less at risk:
1. *School connectedness.* Teachers treated their students fairly, and the students felt close to people at school and got along with teachers and other students.
2. *Lack of student prejudice.* Fellow students were not prejudiced.
3. *High attendance.* Schools had high daily attendance.
4. *High parent-teacher organization participation.* A high number of parents were involved with a parent-teacher organization.
5. *Low drop-out rates.* Schools had low drop-out rates.
6. *School types.* The schools were comprehensive public, magnet, or parochial schools.
7. *Teacher education.* A high percentage of the teachers had master's-level degrees or higher.
8. *College.* A high percentage of students were college bound.[8]

Individual Factors

The study also found that the following personal beliefs and behaviors positively affect resilience:
1. *Self-esteem.* Youth felt they had good qualities, they liked themselves, and they felt loved and wanted.
2. *Religious identity.* They affiliated with a religion, and they prayed.
3. *Sexual orientation.* They were heterosexuals.[9]
4. *Perceived risk of untimely death.* They felt their chances were low of dying before age 35.
5. *Work.* They worked for pay for less than 20-plus hours per week.
6. *Physical appearance.* Their appearance fit with the norm; i.e., they appeared neither younger nor older than their peers.
7. *Repeated a grade.* They never had to repeat a grade level.

---

[7] Adapted from Blum and Rinehart, *Reducing the Risk,* 16.
[8] Adapted from Blum and Rinehart, *Reducing the Risk,* 21.
[9] Probably because of the way this society treats homosexuality, youth who have same-sex attraction engage in more risky behaviors.

8. *Grade point average.* They kept their grades up in English, math, history/social studies and science.[10]

Because this study asked young people themselves, its findings have important implications for families, schools, and communities. Across all of the health outcomes examined, the results point to the importance of family and the home environment for protecting adolescents from harm. What emerges most consistently as protective is the teenager's feeling of connectedness with parents and family. Feeling loved and cared for by parents matters in a big way. When parents are physically in the home at key times, youth are less likely to use cigarettes, alcohol, and marijuana, and less likely to be emotionally distressed.

What matters is the students' sense of connection to the school they attend: If students feel they are a part of the school, are treated fairly by teachers, and feel close to people at school, they have better emotional health and lower levels of involvement in risky behavior. Feeling that other students are not prejudiced is also protective for students in some cases.

Finally, the adolescent's own attitudes, beliefs, and experiences have an important influence. When self-esteem is high, emotional distress is low. When adolescents feel religion and prayer are important in their lives, they are less likely than others to smoke cigarettes, drink alcohol, or use marijuana, and more likely to delay sexual activity.[11]

While these findings pertained to a number of ethnic and racial groups, many Native students were included in the study.

Good Teachers, Teaching, and Curriculum

The Native students we interviewed had plenty to say about the characteristics of good teachers and teaching, including the need for more Native teachers. Those who work with Native youth—teachers, administrators, faculties in schools of education, staff of funding agencies, or oversight bodies—might consider the next two sections required reading.

What students had to say can be roughly divided into two sections: teaching characteristics and personal characteristics of the teacher, although we know these are sometimes indistinguishable and often involve other learning and curricular considerations. Positive teaching characteristics include having cultural knowledge, using encouragement, using explanation, using examples and analogies, having high expectations, being fair and demanding respect for all learners, being flexible, being helpful, being interested in students, listening and trying to

---
[10] Adapted from Blum and Rinehart, *Reducing the Risk,* 26.
[11] Blum and Rinehart, *Reducing the Risk,* 31.

understand, and using multiple approaches. Personal characteristics of the teacher include being caring, being friendly, being fun, being mellow, being open-minded, having patience, respecting students, and *staying* (as opposed to leaving the school or community). Students also commented about what sorts of learning events worked for them. These comments might help teachers and other educators build success into the school day.

Characteristics of Good Teaching

The research on effective teaching practices is mandatory knowledge in teacher training programs. Putting the science of teaching to practice, however, is much more difficult. Teacher candidates who write splendid papers about teaching and learning theory are not always the best teachers. Teacher candidates who have mastered their content areas do not necessarily master the art of teaching. Some measure of knowledge, skill, personal attributes, and art all combine to make for effective teaching. What makes teaching even more challenging is that what works with one group of students, or with an individual student, may not work with another group of students, or another individual student; likewise, what works on some days may not be as effective on other days. Those are the intangibles of teaching, the things that cannot be easily measured. As teachers, however, we know when we are right on target; we know when we are connecting with students and when our magic is working. What makes otherwise average teachers good teachers and turns good teachers into great teachers is their ability to connect with students effectively and often. This is accomplished by displaying many of the characteristics students we interviewed talked about. Everything these Native students said concurred with the research-based effective teaching practices touted in education literature.

Does that mean that if teachers adopt these practices, we will somehow magically transform Native education? The answer to this question is a big *gaween* (no). The issues are far too complex. Adopting these practices will, however, help teachers connect more effectively with Native students. In the long run, adopting these practices will pay off in a big way for our students and our schools.

Having Cultural Knowledge

The teacher education program at our university is one of the few in the United States that requires a course in teaching American Indian students.[12] Attention to diversity, particularly with American Indians, is a central theme in our learner-sensitive teacher education model. That doesn't mean we crank out the best teachers of Native students. They do leave here, however, possessing some fundamental cultural

---

[12]The authors teach at the University of Minnesota at Duluth.

knowledge of local Ojibwe and Dakota people.

Native students think teachers should know something about the tribal people they teach. As Carol (Navajo) observed, when teachers do know something of Native culture, students enjoy the class much more:

◆ Last year, I had one teacher, Mr. S_____. He was a history teacher, and I like usually don't like my history teachers 'cause they never teach anything about Native Americans. I walked into the room, and all I saw on his walls were pictures of Native American people. And I think, "Okay, I'm going to like this guy." And then, when we got to Native American subjects, I think he spent about four weeks.... I liked that guy, he was pretty nice. And the weird thing about it was, he'd always ask me after he said something if that was right.

Using Encouragement

Many of us have fond memories of our favorite teacher. Mine always encouraged me, the young Thomas Peacock, and he would do so in little ways, sometimes with a slight wink as I was leaving the room, or a whisper of, "Stick with it, man." He knew how tough it was for Native kids in our school, how so many didn't finish. As reflected by the comments of Doc C (First Nations Mohawk), teacher encouragement plays an extremely important role:

◆ Whenever I [was] feeling a bit discouraged, for instance, the teacher would quote somebody, or they would say something that would empower me, that just by using words would pick me up by the bootstraps, make me keep going, not be discouraged, see me through. It works.

Using Explanation

Good teachers explain things so students understand the concepts. They don't necessarily try to cram heads with a lot of knowledge just for the sake of knowing it. They facilitate in-depth knowledge of the subject. Fred (Choctaw) said:

◆ One teacher I would say that impacted my life was Laura _____. She was one of those who was gentle when she needed to be but firm when she needed to be. And the way that she taught the class was really great because she just didn't teach you something and give you a grade for it and then forget about it. She'd teach over and over. And a lot of teachers don't do that in school. They teach something and then they move on to something else, and we never really go back to it. But she was one of those teachers who kept reaffirming, bringing it back up. So, she really impacted my life at that time.

The students we talked with appreciated teachers who would tap their prior knowledge and help them connect it with new knowledge. The best teachers would encourage or require them to practice what they had learned by thinking, writing, or speaking about it.

Using Examples and Analogies

Using examples and analogies is one way to help students connect what they already know with what they need to know. Lisa (Dakota) said:

◆ One time, [the teacher] was trying to explain chromosomes, that you had to have like a certain pair. And she used like her car keys, and she was showing me that you know this one key can only fit into this one and this into this one, and I understood it. . . . And she said, "That's the same way with genetics," and I was like, "Oh, okay, I get it now!"

Having High Expectations

Professional education literature acknowledges that most students want teachers to set high standards; yet, teachers must still maintain a sense of humanity and caring, i.e., the tough-love approach. Thunder, a First Nations Mohawk student, echoed this appreciation of high expectations:

◆ Ms. K_____ . . . [is] hard, but yet she's not. I don't know. She explains things. She's easy to understand, probably [has] a bigger vocabulary. I just like the way she has us write. Like, some days she will have us write about ourselves, you know. Like, she made us write about us, where we stand in the world, who we are. It pretty much started out like, "I am L_____," you know, "quick, fast, strong," just telling about our personalities.

We learned that students, until they became disheartened, really wanted to learn. They didn't like going to classes that they felt would not give them what they might need in life.

Many students got the most excited about courses that challenged them. Chloe Blue Eyes (Seneca) spoke about a particular teacher who didn't set the bar high enough:

◆ I don't like how he teaches. It's a real free class, not a Regents class, so that's why it's kinda set up the way he's got it. He jumps around in the book, so if we were to get off on a topic, we'll just talk about that topic. I think that they need to set high standards so that you reach for them, and sometimes, I don't feel that teachers really put enough there. I like giving my opinion on books that I've read, doing oral presentations. I think teachers need to have students just write a lot.

Students like Ellen (Karuk) felt bad when teachers gave up on them:

◆ "[Students] just kind of give up on themselves, and the teachers just kind of give up on [the students]. There's no way to get them out of that rut."

Being Fair and Insisting upon Respect

We've all had teachers we considered unfair. We didn't like them as teachers, we had trouble learning from them, and our blood pressure still goes up whenever we think about them. Daisy (Yurok) reflected on a bad experience with a teacher:

◆ There's this one teacher. If you're not a softball player, he doesn't like you. And if you're not from _____, he really doesn't like you. He's racist in about like seven different ways. If you're an Indian, you have to be like a big name, you know, because, around here, there are about five big names. And if you are a big name, he thinks you're great. If you're from _____, which is like the White district, he thinks you're great. I don't like teachers who play favorites. And he doesn't grade you on your work. He grades you on whether you talk to him or not.

If Daisy's teacher had been fair, learning might have come more easily to her, but teachers also need to demand fairness from their students and respect, both for other students and for themselves. The students we interviewed admitted that it is fun to get away with things for awhile, but Dee (Ojibwe) said what many said:

- Biology everyday was almost like a day of chaos, students were arguing or talking, and [the teacher] had a tendency to just let it go. Once a teacher shows that weakness, it's going to be hard for them to control the class; but if you catch it, reprimand them, and be stern and be firm, they'll learn to respect. The students kind of felt bad because of that.

Being Flexible

In *Collected Wisdom*, we quoted a school administrator who said, "I need rubber band teachers."[13] In other words, teachers need to be flexible. The teacher described by Amelie, a Native student from the Wampanoag community, certainly knew how to be flexible:

- My science teacher was the *awesomest* science teacher in the entire world. She's this short, quite old, little round woman, and she is incredibly full of excitement and joy and energy. And it was so fun to watch her in class. She has an accent. And it was so fun to listen to her. She says "shedule" instead of "schedule." She speaks very proper English. I remember one day, she was giving such a simple question, a really simple question, something about the earth going around the sun. It was early in the morning, and we were all just like, "Oh, my gosh, we can't do this. Don't make us think." And she asked us the question again, and we all just put our heads [down], and some of us sighed, and we were completely dead. She was like, "Oh, come on! Come on!" She got so frustrated, so finally, she was like, "All right, this class has ended." We all kind of looked up, and she's like, "Everyone get up." And she was very serious. So we all get up, and we're all taller than her, and we have this little lady there standing in the middle of the room, and she says, "Alright, everyone. Put your arms in the air." So we all put our arms in the air, and we're all thinking, "What the heck is she doing?" And she says, "Now jump up and down!" So we all start jumping up and down, and she says, "Do jumping jacks! One, two, three!" So she's doing them with us, and we all start laughing so hard because she just wanted to get our brains working. She was like, "I understand you guys are tired, but you need to work." And she started getting us singing and trying to get to work. And she had us move our mouths, a warm-up for our brains, and do quick math questions, like one plus one, two plus two. It was so funny. I mean, that was great.

Students really appreciated it when teachers were imaginative in getting them beyond stuck places. They were also appreciative when teachers were a little flexible about how to get the work done. Many students had heavy family responsibilities, so teachers who were flexible in how they would receive work were more apt to get it.

Being Helpful

Teachers don't have to be the most well-liked people to be good teachers, as illustrated by Desirae (Aleut):

- There was a math teacher that we had before. Everyone was like, "He's so mean." He'd get complaints all the time, and yet, I

---
[13] Cleary and Peacock, *Collected Wisdom*, 51.

did learn when I was with him. He might have been a horrible teacher, but I did learn. After he left, I realized how much good he did do because I was getting A's on everything, and I was getting all my work in, and I was getting the help that I needed. If I wanted to come in after school, no matter if I were behind, he would be happy to help me.

Many students wanted help without having to ask for it. Karonhiakta (First Nations Mohawk) liked one teacher who was so willing to help that Karonhiakta didn't feel badly asking him: "The teacher was just like hands-on. He'd just roll up his sleeves and jump right in and help you with your work, and just sit down and talk to you if you needed to talk."

Many students spoke about wanting help during their learning, and many of those who didn't feel comfortable seeking it out were very grateful when it was offered.

Being Careful Not to Single Students Out

Though students found teachers' help to be wonderful, they didn't like to be singled out in the process. Some learned to tell the teacher they didn't want to be singled out.

A young man who wanted to be called Hard Core (Seneca) was self-conscious when learning was not going well. Hard Core wanted teachers to keep his learning problems private:

◆ When school gets too tough, man, that's the time to drop out. Like me, man, I'm just a slow learner. I won't be able to catch what they say. And they use hundred-dollar words, like what they say. Most times, I shouldn't even be here. And like, when you tell a teacher about a problem, it's like the whole class knows, "Oh man, he can't do the math," so they start talking about you, and then it goes around the whole school.

North Star (chapter 2) shared similar feelings. He would hold back questions so others wouldn't know he didn't understand. Many students, even the ones who did well in school, were very self-conscious about how they learned. Praise in front of the class was very uncomfortable for some; indeed, some schools have found that successful students prefer private gatherings for honor society awards. Finally, students talked about not wanting to be the resident Indian expert in public high schools. Although they appreciated their culture being recognized in the school, most wanted teachers to check with them first before calling on them for cultural knowledge or before assuming they would have or want to share this information.

Being Interested in Students

Teachers who show real interest in students' success without being phony tend to fair well with Native students. Quoetone (Ojibwe) spoke about a teacher who showed genuine interest in him:

◆ One of my favorite teachers . . . [is] over at the [Area Learning Center] right now. He's just a really neat guy. He's working on his doctorate in education. He's somebody you can talk to just about anything. He's like also the librarian over there. [We] talk about books, philosophy, issues, anything, pretty much. His first wife was Lakota, so he has a little bit of understanding. That's kind of cool.

Listening and Understanding

It's pretty obvious that good teachers are good listeners. Here's what Valerie (Seneca) had to say about a teacher who took the time to truly understand her students:

◆ I get along with my English teacher very well. She understands where we are coming from. She gives a lot of support and guidance to us. She spends a lot of time with us, you know, explains things that I don't understand. She's very understanding about when we have our ceremonies and stuff like that. Usually, some of them are for five days, you know, for like a whole week. She'll give me time to make up my work, so she's understanding about things.

Using Multiple Approaches

Students thrived when teachers used multiple approaches. For instance, although two students actually liked to learn from listening—the lecture approach—the vast majority said things like, "Good teachers don't sit there and talk all the time." Jazzy (Ojibwe) said:

◆ Sometimes, I wish that the teachers would teach differently instead of being in the classroom and lecturing. I wish there were more activities. I think if you do something, you'd learn a lot more than just sitting down and absorbing what the teacher is saying. Actions speak louder than words. That's the kind of learning I like. I like to visualize things, like when a teacher says something, but I like hands-on more because I learn better from it. I wish education would be more like stuff that you would really be doing out in the real world. Then, I think students would care more about coming to school.

If students like lectures, then lectures provide an excellent way of learning. If they don't, the amount of information they can learn from a lecture will be limited. Likewise, students didn't like to get all their learning from books. Zel (Ute) said:

◆ The old book routine did not really catch my attention, but [when I was first in school] that wasn't a choice for me. Here, they do a good job of not just giving us a book routine. We go out and do water samples, we do science, and we do science projects here in our class. We discuss what makes a reaction. We discuss a lot of stuff here, not like the teacher talks to one student. All the students come in, sit down, and talk about whatever we learned today and write it down in a log.

Students really liked it when learning integrated many activities and approaches. This theme resonates from chapter 6 as well. Holistic learning captured most students. Students who were excited about learning often described experiences that included multiple approaches. Perhaps Sonny (Hoopa) said it in the simplest way: "I like to hear it and see it at the same time." Students who have several strong intelligences probably thrive most with holistic learning, but it is logical that such an approach allows everyone to connect in some way. Blue (Ute) said:

◆ We get on the computers. We have to draw a diagram. I got the digestive system. I'm almost done. It's really fun. I'm on colons, the transverse colon and the ascending and descending colon. They took us on an all-day field trip back in the mountains in sixth grade. They wanted you to write a story about the wild, and you had to work with compasses and learn how to read compasses. There's a whole big area, and there's a whole bunch of trees, and you had to use your compass to go to each place. . . . When you reached that place, you got a stamp. So they were hidden, you had to use your compass. It was pretty much . . . science, math, writing; it was all of them really mixed together.

Using Collaborative Approaches

The large majority of students appreciated learning in collaboration with other students. Until students do something independently, they are in a zone between what they can do alone and what they can do with the help of others—what Lev Vygotsky called the *zone of proximal development*.[14] Students who are more proficient than their peers can model skills that other students are in the process of acquiring. When multiple approaches to learning are used simultaneously with collaborative learning, students with different strengths can help pull their peers ahead toward a final goal. Students who live in relatively tight-knit communities, as many Native students do, learn to work together at an early age, and most of the students we interviewed preferred to learn together. "School would be better," said Watski (mixed blood), "if you could work with each other and learn stuff from different students, instead of just sitting there by yourself trying to figure it out." Quoetone (Ojibwe) was particularly pleased with one teacher who offered group problem-solving experiences:

◆ Julie was a great teacher. Instead of being boring about things, she chose a couple of movies and put us into little groups every day and gave us a daily activity. Like, if someone had blue eyes with a recessive gene and another person had black eyes with a recessive gene, then find out what color [eyes] their baby would have. What are the chances that their baby would have blue eyes? Things like that.

Nevertheless, several students liked the option of working on their own. Speashal-One (Ojibwe) said:

◆ I like working alone. That way, I don't have to depend on other people, and people don't have to depend on me. I have asthma really bad, so it's hard for me to come to school day after day. I'm very good at making up work.

Will (Lakota/Ojibwe) had his own reasons for wanting to work alone:

◆ I usually want to work by myself because I do it faster, and I don't have to wait for anybody.

Although these students have understandable reasons for working independently, group projects are still important for building interpersonal skills.

---

[14] See Vygotsky, *Mind in Society*.

Personal Characteristics of Teachers

We have spent many years in-servicing teachers about integrating soft skills (human relations) into their teaching. Invariably, there will be a cynic who lectures me about being a content specialist only: "I was hired here to teach math. And teaching math is hard work. I can't be these kids' friend." But, these kids need friends—all the good, supportive friends they can get. And they need good math teachers too.

Being Caring

We reminded teachers in *Collected Wisdom* that caring was not enough.[15] Teachers need to move beyond just caring to make positive changes. Caring does, however, go a long way in establishing a positive relationship with students, and it is an important first step. Phil (Abenaki) described a very special, caring teacher:

◆ She was like really short, and she had like straight black hair, and she was just always fun to be with because she always wanted me to be like my other relatives. I was attached to her. If I was late for school, she would always make sure I'd get there. She was always looking out the door. Like, if I missed the bus, she would drive me home. Or like we could go out for lunch together during lunch or after school. We'd like go for a movie. She was more a friend than a teacher. I could always talk to her. She was like the best teacher I've ever had. If I ever had any problems, I could always talk to her. Like, I told her some of my most deep secrets. It was like when she left, I cried. She had kind of tears in her eyes. It was like we knew it was going to be the last lunch. It was hard.

Many of the students, like Zel (Ute), recalled one teacher in particular who stood out because of his caring and friendly attitude:

◆ My teacher is a really good teacher. He can teach you something really good, not only education wise, but also about life itself, and drugs. I'd say that he's a counselor, a friend, someone that you can talk to about anything. We have students that have short tempers here, that want it their way or the highway, but he does not let them run him over. He's really good to them; he doesn't give up on them. He doesn't want to see them going down a bad path, and that, I think, is his goal in life—to see that he got at least one of his students to go down a good path. I think it's all of his students that he wants to succeed.

Being Fun

We all remember the good teachers who completely enjoyed what they taught. We could tell they enjoyed it because they would become

---

[15] See Cleary and Peacock, *Collected Wisdom*.

animated, their eyes would sparkle, and they couldn't mask their own excitement over the subject matter. They made learning fun. Even math can be fun, as attested to by Jazzy (Ojibwe):

◆ I had an algebra teacher last year, and he made math really fun. He talked a lot about life and how to use it in our everyday [life]. And he was just fun. But other teachers . . . [should] make school fun. I mean, not all the time, but if you sit down and do [just] book work, then people aren't going to learn, and they are not going to like it.

Being Mellow

There is something good about individuals who, to use popular slang, "know how to chill." They don't get overly excited about things. They maintain their cool when everyone else is freaking out. Students enjoy and respect these mellow teachers. Jeremy (Aleut) talked about one such teacher:

◆ I'd have to say my math teacher . . . was pretty cool. He was pretty mellow with everybody. He taught me about . . . the important things we need to do in life. If we didn't do anything, he would just say, "Sit there until I can get to you." When I first got into his class, I was sitting in the normal desks, and I moved to the back, the very back wall, and just sat there. He let me keep that as my desk. So, I just pretty much stayed there. He didn't keep me out of conversations. He made sure that people would talk to me and stuff.

Being Open-Minded

We asked Carol (Navajo) to dream about the ideal teacher, and this is what she said:

◆ If I could create a teacher, I think it would be a teacher that was really open-minded to a lot of new ideas, and someone who doesn't like seem like they're so much above you—like, more like a friend, and someone who really thought of you as a person, kind of someone that felt like they could speak with you on your level. And you would feel really comfortable.

Having Patience

Many of the students we interviewed were not verbally articulate. They had a difficult time with the process. As researchers, this makes the reporting of information difficult because we strive to capture specific stories and a deep understanding of the world as Native students understand it. Occasionally, however, just one word would capture the whole essence of meaning. Chloe Blue Eyes (Seneca) was not one of the quiet students we interviewed, but she did say something short and sweet (and useful) when I asked her if she could give her reading and writing teacher some advice.

◆ "Patience," she said.

Respecting Students

Quoetone (Ojibwe) is a true intellectual. Given the right breaks, he should become a brilliant scholar and join the growing legions of Native intellectuals. He had something to say about r-e-s-p-e-c-t:

◆ I got this 12-page paper to write on the Women's Rights movement, and I was just wracking my brains trying to think about what to write about. So we talked a little bit about it. Then we talked about postmodernism yesterday. That was a pretty interesting discussion. And then we went up on a field trip a couple of days ago, a men's retreat. And we had a big discussion with 20 guys, pretty much all of different backgrounds. And you really see postmodernism in effect. That was kind of cool. [The teacher] respects my intelligence for the most part, not speaking down to me. That helps because you have teachers that speak down to you, when they are the idiots. And that's something I can't stand. That's the quickest way to get me out of the classroom.

Staying

Several lives ago, I did BIA (Bureau of Indian Affairs) school monitoring visits, where a team of education specialists would visit selected Native schools. At one BIA boarding school in the Southwest, the school administrator arranged for me to tour the campus with one of his prize eighth graders, who asked, "So, when are you going to leave?" That question spoke volumes because imbedded in it were all kinds of other questions like, "Are you going to leave here like everyone else does?" and "Do I dare become your friend?"

I was heartbroken by what he said. On the average, teachers stay at these schools just over a year, and, as a tribal school administrator, I saw teachers come and go at our small reservation school like nervous herd animals at a watering hole. Most stayed only until they got that dream job in the suburbs or in a "regular" (i.e., White) school. Almost all of them lived far from the reservation and only knew the "rezers" (rezbonics for reservation Indians) from 8:00 a.m. to 4:00 p.m. Yet, these young people are Native 24/7, and being Native can be a rugged experience. They need teachers who won't ditch out on them at the drop of a hat. Thus, the teachers who stick with them earn these students' respect. Desirae (Aleut) noted:

◆ I think you respect the teacher more if he or she is there longer. Like, during my high school, I could just see like every year, we get a new teacher or something, and it seems like totally disrespectful because they have a lot of students. And then I go to the next class where the teacher has been there for a while, and the kids are just like whole different people. They are like, "OK, I got to listen to this one."

Though Native students are less inclined to tell teachers directly what they want and need to do well in school, their strong voices are articulated in this book to let you, as educators, know.

The Need for Native Teachers

With so many different attributes and skills that Native students want/need from their teachers, it is no wonder that teachers have trouble getting it right. Native teachers have an easier time figuring out what is needed than teachers who are culturally different from the students they teach. Non-Native teachers who have gotten it right deserve the respect they inevitably get. The students, however, crave more Native teachers.

All over Indian country, we are trying to lure Native people into the teaching profession. In the United States, the federal government recently launched a massive grant program to train more Native teachers. Our university applied with one of the local tribal colleges, and we now have an exciting and long-overdue Native teacher training program.[16] I have to say it's one of the most wonderful things I have ever been involved in. Training effective Native teachers is critical to undoing all the past harm education has done to us. What Native teachers have over non-Native teachers is experience with many of the same issues Native youth now confront on a daily basis. They have "been there, done that." Lisa (Dakota) spoke for many of the students:

◆ The best teacher I have right now would probably be [Ms. H], my Ojibwe language teacher. I don't usually go to lunch 'cause I hate standing in line, so I just go in there, and I get to study in [Ms. H's] room. Any kind of class I need help in, she'll always sit down with me and help me out if I'm stuck on something. She'll talk to the teacher about my grades, and she'll go to each of my teachers and find out my grades and help me get them up. She cares, and most teachers don't worry about your other classes. She does.

Toward An Indigenous Model of Education

Tom

Several years ago, I attended an Indian education research conference at which I soon felt like Rick Nelson, the late pop singer who, in a song, lamented about attending a garden party with fellow musicians. In "Garden Party," everyone wanted to hear the old songs, and nobody wanted to hear anything new. Finally a brave young Diné (Navajo) woman stood up and said what some of us were thinking. It went something like this: "We didn't come here to be spoken to. We are hearing the same

---

[16] This program is a collaboration between the University of Minnesota at Duluth and the Fond du Lac Tribal and Community College in Cloquet, Minnesota, with funding from the U.S. Department of Education's Office of Indian Education.

things we have heard for years now, time and time again."

Hail to hearing something new. Read on if you think the only way to change Native education for the better is to turn what we are currently doing upside down and inside out or scatter it to the wind altogether.

What if we turned the existing education paradigm inside out, so to speak? The essence of the new paradigm would be that all American Indian education planning begins from an Indigenous perspective. All aspects of education systems—vision, philosophy, mission, objectives, assessment, curriculum, content, instructional methodology, activities, research, and evaluation—would be rooted in traditional Native values. This approach would be radically different from most current Native education efforts, which integrate Native content into primarily mainstream education models.

We, as authors, are far from the first people to propose such a radical departure from the status quo. Gregory Cajete's *Look to the Mountain* proposes an Indigenous way of reshaping Indian education. A book by Karen Swisher and John Tippeconnic III, *Next Steps,* gives us some strong direction in reshaping education practice and research.[17] Based on all the interviews with teachers and students we conducted in Indian country these past eight years, we have concluded that if Native people are truly to offer their children and grandchildren acceptable alternatives to the existing education systems (and at the same time exercise true self-determination), we must break free from the existing education paradigm and develop our own. That is easier said than done, given our dependence upon external funding for education, with all the attendant rules and regulations. We, however, need to begin moving that way in earnest.

For those who still need to be convinced about the need for change, we provide a sample of what several other articulate voices in Indian country had to say about this very issue, beginning with Wayne Newell, a Passamaquaddy language teacher:

> In the 70s, my heart was in the right place, and I was going to make schools just the way the white man wanted me to. "Teachers have to get these kids ready for the outside world." I'm sure you've heard that a thousand times. BIA didn't invent that; it was a missionary philosophy. And it only took one generation, and then what we did was to perpetuate it ourselves. We, the victims, have been the victimizers also. We have been trying to solve our community problems from the white value system that caused them. We never thought that maybe the solution is [solving] them according to the strong values within ourselves, and then the next generation will take over. Right now . . . for me to succeed in today's world, I have to forget who I am? What people didn't understand is that those boarding school terrorists thought that it [culture] could disappear in a generation, and they would have white thinking children. But they couldn't erase it, and thereby lies the hope. Right there. I might see it in my lifetime. And when that spirit is reawakened, it is more powerful than anything that I have ever met in my whole life.[18]

---

[17]See Cajete, *Look to the Mountain,* and Swisher and Tippeconnic, *Next Steps.*
[18]Cleary and Peacock, *Collected Wisdom,* 55.

Lessons for Educators: Teaching, Curriculum, and Research

Wayne Newell's wisdom is simple and complex at the same time: simple in the sense that he acknowledges that the solutions to many of the problems in Native communities, including education, lie within our traditional Native value systems; complex in the sense that implementing new education paradigms will be extremely difficult, with both non-Native and Native educators fighting against change all the way. However, to continue educating our children and grandchildren in schools that relegate our histories, cultures, and languages to an occasional sideshow (under the guise of "diversity") and that ignore the presence of institutional, overt, and covert racism is to doom another generation of Native young people to educational failure. Ultimately, the status quo will perpetuate the very colonialism our ancestors were forced to endure, a colonialism we Native educators resolved ourselves to change years ago. Vine Deloria observes:

> A continuous treadmill of western culture, philosophy, science, and social thought is the utmost in cultural imperialism. It is imperialism because it assumes that the Native tradition has nothing to contribute in either process or content and that the student need not pause in the struggle to get an education to reflect on the progress to date. Without the opportunity to evaluate the reasonableness of what is occurring, the student is simply placed within a prolonged fiery furnace and expected to burn off the dross of his or her cultural heritage and replace it with newly acquired as yet uncriticized non-Indian heritage. . . . We should reject the present educational programs and theories as absolutely as did our ancestors years ago at the Treaty of Lancaster for present education does not enable us to become socially adjusted to either white or Indian society; it does not provide us with philosophical understanding which would enable us to use the technical knowledge we receive constructively; and it ultimately demeans us. . . .[19]

Deloria's troubling message about Native education speaks eloquently and strongly about the need to implement Indigenous models. But why do many Native education programs mimic mainstream models? One reason, as noted by Larry D. Foreman, may be that we have not considered an Indigenous perspective:

> Dropout rates, grades, attendance and discouragement by Indian students present a very real dilemma for educators, schools, and the communities served by them. Proposed solutions very often take the form of reworking the same ideas that have been tried time and time again with only minor changes and disappointing results. A void seems to exist in areas that examine ways by which American Indian values and world-views might be incorporated into educational designs appropriate for the age of self-determination.[20]

Foreman goes on to offer a disturbing message about the direction of our education efforts, suggesting that Native people themselves may be impediments to change, given both the nature of our own training (as mainstream-educated Native people, we are successful products of a system we now propose to change) and the

---

[19] Deloria, "Education and Imperialism," 62-63.
[20] Foreman, "Curricular Choice in the Age of Self-Determination," 2.

way in which oppression is internalized. In this scenario, mainstream education systems typically resist change and endeavor to change persons more than the other way around. According to Foreman, true self-determination and truly Indigenous models of education may be difficult to implement because we have internalized the colonizer's models. Finally, Foreman cuts right to the heart of many Native education efforts, indicating they are, at best, superficial:

> Many current educational programs which claim to address cultural needs of American Indian students do little more than string a few beads or draw pictures of horses and buffalo. Curricular change as superficial as this, however well meant, surely cannot represent the extent to which self-determination will change American Indian education.[21]

What Might an Indigenous Education Model Look Like?

Assuming we can move beyond our own inability or unwillingness to implement truly Indigenous models, we will be confronted with perhaps the most formidable challenge in making real change in Native education. We are hopelessly dependent upon outside funding, be it state, provincial, federal, or private resources. Each time we accept outside funds, we compromise our educational freedom. Rules, regulations, standards, decrees, and proclamations come with every influx of outside funding. Monitoring visits, progress reports, accreditation, test scores, and continuation grant applications are just a few of the ways we are kept in line. But let us just dream for a moment that we have the courage to really change.

Given the great diversity of Indigenous philosophies, we cannot assert one model that all Native people should follow. Tribal nations will have to develop their own models, using their own philosophies or modeling themselves on others. Such models are beginning to develop, and the impetus for change can already be seen in some tribal institutions. Several wonderful models exist in Indigenous communities in Hawaii and New Zealand, where Hawaiian and Maori language immersion schools have brought Native languages back from near extinction. These schools operate with an Indigenous focus, having language maintenance and renewal as the central goals upon which other parts of the curriculum (e.g., mathematics, writing, or science) are built. These schools may serve as examples for First Nations, American Indian, and Alaska Native communities truly interested in language preservation.

Another model is the *Gekinoo'imaagejig* (American Indian Teacher Corps) at Fond du Lac Tribal and Community College (FDLTCC), a joint program with the University of Minnesota at Duluth Teacher Education Program. Sixteen students, 14 of them Native, are completing their undergraduate teaching degrees in a program based on Anishinaabe philosophy. All aspects of the program—vision, philosophy, mission, objectives, assessment, curriculum, content, instructional methodology, activities, research, and evaluation—have traditional Native values at their core. What makes the model so

---

[21]Ibid., 5.

remarkable is that it meets all state and national mainstream accreditation and licensing requirements. This was done by first ensuring an Indigenous perspective and then integrating mainstream theory and standards. Following are the program's vision and mission statements:

Vision Statement

Our people will follow mino-bimaadizi-win, the good path of the Anishinaabeg. They will live in ways which both honors themselves and all lives they touch. Individuals, families, communities, and tribal nations will be spiritually, emotionally, and physically healthy and whole again. Through this education program students, staff, and faculty will walk this path together.

Mission Statement

All students who complete the FDLTCC American Indian Teacher Corps Program will be actively working for the betterment of Indigenous peoples. Upon completion of the program students will have received an education that has embedded in it the core values, mino-bimaadizi-win (the good path), of the Anishinaabeg:

- Honor Gitchie Manitou
- Honor Elders
- Honor plants and animals
- Honor women
- Keep our promises and uphold our pledges
- Kindness should be shown to everyone, even those with whom we disagree
- Be peaceful in body and spirit
- Be courageous
- Be moderate in our thoughts, works, and deeds

The mission of the program is first and foremost guided by these values. The knowledge, skills, abilities and attitudes students acquire will be based on validated research and presented through an Indigenous epistemology.[22]

What does this look like in a real way? The curriculum includes, and shows teachers how they can teach with, respect for all living things. Ceremony and spirituality play a central, daily role in the program. Elders serve as teachers. When individual students are stressed, the group works to assist and offers insights to balance. Euro-western education

---

[22]Gekinoo'imaagejig, "Vision & Mission."

theory is studied, but only if it does not conflict with Anishinaabe philosophy. Education theory such as constructivism, cooperative learning, active learning, and relational psychology (being a part of all living things, we can't disassociate ourselves from others and from their life experiences) are taught. Assertive discipline, language phonics (isolated skill and drill), and stage theories of development (as opposed to a holistic view of human development) are not taught because they conflict with Anishinaabe philosophy.

Towards an Indigenous Model of Research and Its Dissemination[23]

When students tell you their stories, when you begin to realize some things from their stories, com-bined with your own reading and experiences, it is a natural instinct to want to get that information out, to herald it immediately to all those who are affected by and interested in Indigenous education. We made certain decisions about how this research would be re-ported based on our own epistemological philosophies and on the immediacy of the need in the field. This section describes our research, the methodology and its underlying epistem-ological philosophies, and our rationale for the mode of dissemination we have chosen.

The three of us—Amy Bergstrom, Linda Miller Cleary, and Thomas Peacock—entered into this research because we knew that Indigenous communities were at a critical point. In the United States, The Indian Nations At Risk Task Force study (1991) suggested that despite several decades of programs and efforts at both the federal and state level, and the efforts of tribes and American Indian organizations, overall dropout and achievement data for American Indians had not markedly improved. Their conclusions found the rates of educational failure uncomfortably similar to an earlier study, the Kennedy Report on Indian Education of 1969. Nationally, 40 percent of American Indian students drop out, and at the secondary level, many of them lag two or more years behind their non-Indian peers on standardized achievement measures.[24]

In a state like Minnesota, 57 percent of the 14,000 Indian students failed to complete the requirements for high school graduation in 1997.[25] Many obstacles must be overcome, both in and out of school, to improve these dismal

---

[23]This section is adapted from an article by Cleary and Peacock titled "Disseminating American Indian Educational Research through Stories," which was first published in the *Journal of American Indian Education*. It is used here with permission.

[24]See Indian Nations At Risk Task Force, *Indian Nations At Risk*; Senate Special Subcommittee on Indian Education, *Indian Education* (also known as the Kennedy Report); and Quality Education for Minorities, *Education That Works*.

[25]See Minnesota Department of Children, Families and Learning, "American Indian Data."

numbers: low teacher expectations, tracking, inadequate financing of schools and education programs, few minority and American Indian teachers, testing issues, poorly trained teachers, and a disregard for diversity in both education standards and content.[26] Donna Deyhle and Karen Swisher's review of literature on American Indian education cited these problems: (1) economic, social, and health issues confounding students and the schools that purport to educate them; (2) inadequate funding of facilities and programs; and (3) schools that do little for the academic, social, cultural, and spiritual well-being of American Indian students.[27] Out of school, many of these children face grinding poverty and all its side effects, including racism, negative peer pressure, and hopelessness. Children also mistrust education systems, and this is compounded by the absence of a positive educational legacy from many of their parents and other significant adults.[28]

The Indian Nations At Risk Task Force pointed to schools as essential to the social, cultural, and intellectual health of communities, and to literacy as essential to the well-being of American Indian people. Other international congresses of Indigenous people have come to similar conclusions.

A serious concern is that the emerging research on American Indian, First Nations, and Alaska Native students may not find its way into classrooms in time to save languages and cultures and keep students in school. Some years ago, a study found a 50-year gap between the time most research was first reported and when results were first used in the classroom.[29] In many schools serving Indigenous children, this gap has persisted. In this section, we describe our methodology because we want you to know our process in putting these students' voices before you. We are particularly interested, however, in your reading the subsequent section in which we provide the rationale for the mode of dissemination we have used in *The Seventh Generation*. One of the main goals of this book is to close the gap between research and its application—for educators and, most importantly, for the students themselves.

Methodology

The data generated for *The Seventh Generation* come from in-depth phenomenological interviewing based on a method developed for the study of community colleges by Irving Seidman and Patrick Sullivan and later described by Seidman in *Interviewing As Qualitative Research*. The theoretical underpinnings of this method stemmed from the research of phenomenologists in general and Alfred Schutz in particular. This model emphasizes the experience of the participant (e.g., Indigenous students) with regard to the subject being studied (e.g., education). This interviewing structure strives to maximize the participants' rendering of that experience.[30]

In our research, a series of three interviews provided enough time, privacy, and trust so the participant could relate his or her experience, reflect on that experience, and, to some extent,

---

[26] See Quality Education for Minorities, *Education That Works*.
[27] See Deyhle and Swisher, "Research in American Indian and Alaska Native Education."
[28] See Cleary and Peacock, *Collected Wisdom*.
[29] Lehmann and Mehrens, *Educational Research*, 10.
[30] See Seidman, *Interviewing As Qualitative Research*, and Schutz, *Phenomenology of the Social World*.

make sense of it. We conducted open-ended interviews of 120 American Indian, First Nations, and Alaska Native high school students representing reserve, reservation, village, and urban communities, and private, tribal, and public schools. We identified schools in the Northeast, Southeast, Midwest, Southwest, and Northwest parts of the United States and in western, midwestern, and eastern Canada. Participants were selected using purposive (type of community, type of school, grade-point average, and gender) sampling. We asked the designated contact (administrator or guidance counselor) to select students who were doing very well, doing average work, and struggling in school, in equal numbers. Students participated only if they were willing to participate and sign a written consent form.

The study explored students' perceptions of how schools, people, circumstances, and curricula assisted or hindered their success. Students discussed effective teaching and teacher-student interactions and made suggestions about conditions that would create success. The first interview explored their past experiences in education. The second interview focused on present instructional and noninstructional issues that students perceived as helping or hindering their education. The final interview explored the meanings students made of their experiences and their suggestions for improving classroom practices for themselves, their children, and their grandchildren. Follow-up questions gave students the opportunity to explore their experiences further.

The research design was qualitative and used grounded theory to study the circumstances that helped and hindered the education of Indigenous students. Grounded theory relies on the constant comparative method, the joint coding and analysis of data using analytic induction, and the premise that theory evolves from the body of data and is illustrated by examples from it.[31]

Because theory evolved from emerging data in this research, there was no hypothesis at the inception of the research. Interview data were sorted into emerging themes and based on the juxtaposition of what the different students said. Category codes based on themes were developed and were 260 in number. The three open-ended, tape-recorded interviews with each participant were approximately one hour each in length. Because students were absent on some occasions, all three interviews were not completed with each of the students. Tapes of the completed interviews were transcribed as interviews were completed. The interview data were sorted and analyzed with the assistance of Ethnograph, a qualitative research software program.

The Rationale and Mode of Reporting the Research

As researchers, we have consciously and conscientiously disobeyed the dominant conventions for reporting our research because we believe research must be of use to those researched and make its way into the hands of practitioners as quickly as possible. We chose not to publish this study in a topic-appropriate scholarly journal. Further, most of our book relates stories culled from our own experiences, representative stories from more than 120 students, and fictional case studies based on fact. Stories allow

---

[31] See Glaser and Straus, *Discovery of Grounded Theory*; Bogdan and Biklen, *Qualitative Research for Education*; and Ely, *Doing Qualitative Research*.

readers to assess our report on the basis of their own untold stories and experiences. As American Indian male, American Indian female, and non-Indian female researchers, stories are a natural way for us to report this research.

The Limitations of the Discourse of the Dominant Research Community

Academic discourse, primarily in scholarly journals and college textbooks, is the mainstream method of reporting research findings. One way to look at the reporting language of academia is as male-versus-female rhetoric. Based on studies by Tom Farrell, Jean Sanborn, and Donald Rubin and Kathryn Greene, one might characterize male rhetoric as that which begins with final conclusions, adds argumentation and facts as support (with little room for interesting lines of thought or questioning of results), and repeats the conclusions at the end.[32] In contrast, female rhetoric has been described as an additive style, contextualizing points with narrative and deferring conclusions. This nonlinear form of discourse entertains the legitimacy of opposing viewpoints.

Perhaps unconsciously, researchers have written for practitioners in a way they would write for their peer researchers, using words and discourse structures less familiar to many practitioners and assuming knowledge that practitioners, who are very involved in their work, might not have had time to acquire. In no way do we mean to imply by this that teachers are not able to make sense of academic discourse; they just need time and impetus to enter the researcher's discourse community.

We believe research should be accessible to those researched. Unfortunately, academic research often is reported in a manner too convoluted to be understood by the students being studied. The cultural differences (real and often unrecognized) of Native students can render the research even less accessible.

Another way to view discourse differences is to consider the lens from which the researcher views and interprets the world. Viewing and reporting research findings from an Ojibwe standpoint epistemology, which is rich in stories and metaphor, runs counter to the linear reporting of data, facts, and findings.

As male and female American Indian and non-Indian researchers, we consciously chose to report our findings by combining elements of narrative rhetoric and Ojibwe standpoint epistemology, lenses with which we each view the world. We avoided, whenever possible, extensive use of literature reviews commonly used in academic discourse because they incorporate language and style uncommon (and often not useful) to many practitioners. We included some of that material in this chapter. When we did refer to the existing research base, it was to confirm and emphasize the findings from the students in our study. Moreover, we consciously avoided a rigorous review of literature until after we had collected and analyzed raw interview data from the students, so it would not influence our own findings.

As researchers and disseminators of our research, we wanted to take the moral high ground. We did not write exclusively for an audience of researchers who had been steeped in the language and discourse of academia. For

---

[32] See Farrell, "The Female and Male Modes of Rhetoric"; Sanborn, "The Academic Essay"; and Rubin and Greene, "Gender-Typical Style in Written Language."

years, qualitative researchers have fought for recognition of research that moves inductively from real contexts to results, further questions, and emerging themes. It is our stance that this research should be presented, both initially and immediately, in a way that can best reach those most closely involved with the education of North American Indigenous students.

Collected Stories

Many Native people learn their ways in life through stories. So, to be consonant with our topic, much of our material was introduced with stories. This style reflects Ojibwe epistemology and differs from what many academic readers are used to.

James Clifford said, "Any story has a propensity to generate another story in the mind of the reader (or hearer), to repeat and displace some prior story."[33] As Clifford suggests, "convincing" or "rich" stories can be almost metaphoric. They can lead readers to patterns or associations with their own experiences and generate their own unique meanings.

Students related most of the stories in this book, and, as authors, we added case-study narratives, posed questions and problems, and told our own stories so readers might better understand their own educational issues. Thus, although Indigenous students-as-soloists were featured in profiles, and the rest of the 120 students came in with a chorus of quotes, all of us—students, readers, and authors—took part in composing meaning from the material. And through this composing, we all constructed a new knowledge base from which to act.

Using Students' Voices

In our research we were scrupulous in moving from the wisdom we collected from students via analytic induction to our results. After reading what all the students related about their experiences, we present the commonalities and raise questions about divergent data, all through the stories of students and authors. In a way, we allow readers to be researchers and challenge them to compare their own experiences in school settings with that of the students. We hold this more inductive presentation to be particularly important in reporting research to Native students and to teachers, prospective teachers, administrators, and concerned citizens from two cultures.

Putting together stories, ideas, data, and snapshots inductively may be the most ethical way to report research to people who come to understandings and who think abstractly. Those who are researched have a right to direct access to the findings. For this reason, we have chosen a student audience as the primary audience for the text, with added sections that might lack interest for that audience.

Using Case Studies

Case studies (fiction based on fact) are integrated throughout the book. They allow readers to view each chapter's concepts and theory in context. Cases studies are, in actuality, stories, the traditional way in which knowledge and, ultimately, wisdom is passed down in Indigenous communities. Nineteenth-century author and Ojibwe chief George Copway (Kah-ge-ga-gah-bowh) wrote:

---

[33]Clifford, "On Ethnographic Allegory," 100.

The Ojibways have a great number of legends, stories and historical tales, the relating and hearing of which form a vast fund of winter evening instruction and amusement. There is not a lake or mountain that has not connected with it some story of delight or wonder, and nearly every beast and bird is the subject of the story-teller, being said to have transformed itself at some prior time into some mysterious formation—of men going to live in the stars, and of imaginary beings in the air, whose rushing passage roars in the distant whirlwinds. These legends have an important bearing on the character of the children of our nation. The fire-blaze is endeared to them in after years by a thousand happy recollections.[34]

An example of how this knowledge was given in story form is shown below in an excerpt from "The Storyteller" by Thomas Peacock, a case study in which a young boy's uncle comes into a classroom to tell traditional Ojibwe stories:

He then told the students about some of the different plants and how the Ojibwe used them as food, medicine and in ceremonies. He told them the story of when rabbit ate all the roses, and how that affected the balance of things and how all the animals that depended on roses were harmed. And in telling the story he explained how the rabbit and the rose came to be as they are today.[35]

Using Researchers' Voices

We added our own voices to those of the students presented in the book. We believe that research is shaped by the researchers and that researchers owe it to their readers to declare their connections to the topics being studied. For this reason, we included our own experiences, clearly indicating when we have spoken from our own opinions rather than from the data in the study. Finally, we didn't mask the intense emotional connections we have to the topic. We hope that the results of our research will have immediate positive effects on the education of our own grandchildren, and on their children, so we put our hearts and souls into the book. To quote Horace Axtell and Margo Aragon:

When you talk to a person, you tell them. Instruct them. You want them to know you talk with your heart. When you talk from your heart it goes up out of your eyes, into the other's eyes, and comes back down into their heart. That's the way these stories and instructions were told to me.

It goes from one heart to another heart and it keeps going around like that. That's the way our old people did it and that's the way I think about all the things that I do now. The old ones passed it from heart to heart. That's the way I was told. They'd say, "Look at me. I want to talk to you."

So you sit there and you don't say anything back. You just keep quiet. When they get to a certain point and they want to make you understand, their voice changes

---

[34]Copway, "Traditional History and Characteristic Sketches of the Ojibway Nation," 72-73.
[35]Cleary and Peacock, *Collected Wisdom*, 118.

and becomes like, ready to cry, it gets so intense. That's when you know they are very sincere. Their voice gets shaky.

"Listen."

You listen. Then you can feel the tears come out of your eyes and you know the feelings that they've given you. They stay there. It's so intense.[36]

The problems of Native education need resolution sooner, not later. There are things to be accomplished; there are disappearing languages and oral histories and stories to be protected, rights to be protected, and purposeful and hopeful futures for students to find. The youth of the Seventh Generation deserve it, and their collected wisdom demands it.

Full Circle

"In the time of the Seventh Fire a new people will emerge to retrace their steps to find what was left by the trail."

—Edward Benton-Benai

Some time ago at a dinner party, my wife was telling a colleague about a new Ojibwe history book that I wrote, which was due to be released.

"So how many books does that make now?" the colleague asked. "Three, four? You really are committed to the publishing part of academia, aren't you?" Academic types like me have to publish or perish for tenure and promotion in university settings.

"I'd be afraid to put my writing out there because [a well-known Native writer] would probably rip it to shreds," she continued.

There is always a risk in putting research and writing out there for others to critique. Native people can be overly critical of one another to the point of being mutually destructive. It bothers me a lot when this happens because it is a sign we have internalized our oppression in that way. Then I think of my granddaughter and little nieces and nephews, whose tribal history and language goes untaught in the mainstream schools they attend, whose story goes untold in the popular media, and who must endure racism in all its forms despite efforts to eradicate it. I think about how they have no voice in the miseducation they receive.

I think Native educators need to quit giving out awards to one another at conferences, quit writing and passing conference resolutions that go unimplemented, and get to the serious job of turning our education systems upside down and inside out to meet young people's

---

[36]Axtell and Aragon, *A Little Bit of Wisdom*, 204-205.

needs. And we need to step forward and say that.

So, I am one who doesn't really care that much about what _____ (insert your favorite national Native writer or educator) thinks about my research and writing. I write because I am part of a growing legion of Native people who demand real change in our schools and tribes and communities. We love children too much to expect any less.

Recently, I attended one of the summer powwows in my reservation community. By powwow standards, it was relatively small. There were, according to my brother Pnuts (one of the organizers), "28 drums and nearly 400 dancers." The powwow was held at a primary treatment center for Native people, a place where many of my friends and relatives have gone to heal from the ongoing tragedy of alcoholism. I remember as a young boy that the land was occupied by one- and two-room tar paper shacks and that my father would sometimes take me there on his drinking binges. Times have changed. For the better.

By nature, I am an avid listener, and I spent much of the time at the powwow sitting in the stands watching and listening to the music. Members of the Seventh Generation were all around me. Young people were engaged in the ancient rituals of being young. Little ones, one and two years old, were out in the dance arena, some of them barely able to walk, trying to dance. A young fancy dancer, probably not yet 10, proudly danced by, his bells in perfect harmony with the music. A gifted fancy shawl dancer held the audience's rapt attention as she floated gracefully around the arena, all of her in perfect synch to the drumming. Most of the drums were peopled by young men as well. Their voices were so clear and full of hope and joy and pride and honor that, at times, I had difficulty maintaining my composure. I was so overcome with my pride in them. And the long walking circle around the arena was filled with young people. Teenagers, some wearing "Native Pride" shirts. Still others wearing gang paraphernalia. Teenagers with babies. Too young to be having babies, I was thinking. Nephews and nieces were working at various concession stands. One of my younger brothers was helping his partner make fry bread at a food stand. Another was a drummer. My youngest brother was herding his children to their favorite sitting spot. A sister was sitting in the stands with her grown children and her young grandchild. Other adults, the formerly young, were there as well, many of them people I had grown up with, raised hell with, and now am growing old with. We are a complicated and evolving and prideful people, with a whole series of unresolved issues and problems, but with so much more promise and purposeful vision. And that is part of the circle of things.

Everything that I witnessed at the powwow that day stands as a testament to where we are as people. As tribal people, we have come to a place along the Good Path, where we are retracing the footsteps of our ancestors, where our language is being more frequently and joyfully spoken, where our ancient songs are sung again, and where we are collectively renewing our strength and hope as the Indigenous people of this continent. Our young people are so much stronger—emotionally, culturally, and spiritually—than my generation was at their age. The cultural and spiritual renaissance of Native people that began when I was a young child now places us firmly on the threshold of greatness.

We are rushing headlong into the past, and all of that is good.

Appendix

Interview Questions

Appendix

Interview Questions

Background Information

1. Name?
2. What is your birth date?
3. What grade are you in?
4. Who lives with you?
5. How long have you lived there?
6. If you have lived in other places, how long did you live there?
7. What are some of your favorite hobbies or interests?
8. If we use a quote from you in our book, instead of your real name, what made-up name would you like us to use?
9. Will you please give us the name and telephone number of someone outside of school who can always reach you?
10. What is your caregiver's educational background?
11. What kinds of work have your caregivers done?
12. Do you speak languages other than English?
13. If so, what are they?
14. On a scale of 1-10, with 1 being light, 5 being medium, and 10 being dark, how do you rate your skin color?
15. What can you do with a computer? For example, can you write a paper on one?

Interview One

1. Tell me the whole story about what school was like for you when you were younger. In elementary school? In middle school? In high school? Who was important to you then? Why? Are they still in your life?
2. Tell me about the communities you grew up in. Tell me about the community you live in now.
3. Tell me about a really great school experience or experiences you've had. Who was there, what sorts of things were you doing? What about another really good school experience? (Will) Can you tell me about another one?
4. What about a time when school wasn't so great? (Who was there with you? What types of things were you doing at this time in your life? Were you in your home community or was it a different community?) How about another time when things weren't so great?
5. If you had to describe one person you really looked up to or wanted to be like, who would it be? (Tell me about this person and your relationship with them. What kinds of things do you do with this person? Are they still a part of your life?)

6. When school/home has been tough, extra heavy (feels like a ton of bricks on your back), what have you done to carry the load? Who have you looked to, to help lighten the load?
7. Thinking about school, how has culture been a part of your schooling experience in the past? If school was a huge puzzle with a bunch of pieces, would culture have been a part of that puzzle or would it have been a separate puzzle altogether? Why/why not? (What role has culture played in your life?)

Interview Two

1. Right now, what is it like being American Indian and going to school?
2. What feels important/unimportant about school right now?
3. Tell me about a good day you've had at school. Tell me about a bad school day.
4. What teacher is the best teacher for you now? Tell me about a time when that teacher was a good teacher for you.
5. What teacher is not a good teacher for you right now? Tell me about a time when the teacher wasn't the best for you.
6. What would the ideal teacher be like in school for you right now?
7. Tell me a story about the reading/writing experience that has been the most/least enjoyable for you this year. When you are asked to read or write, do you ever think you go about it differently than others or than the teacher expects you to?
8. What are some things that keep you in school when things are tough? What kinds of things help you manage the load?
9. What are the kinds of things that get in the way of school for you?
10. What are some things that make you enjoy some of your classes; or regret being in some?
11. Can you tell me about a time this year when things were really bad and when there was something in school that made it better?
12. Sometimes some people in school have more things than others have. Can you tell a story about a time when you had less/wanted more? (Cup half full—how do you fill it?)
13. Tell me how programs/people/activities inside and outside of school influence your learning.
14. Are you or any of your friends thinking about leaving (or have they already left) school? Why?
15. Tell me about racism (or the lack thereof) in your school.
16. You are probably encouraged to be involved in cultural "stuff." What is that like for you?
17. Tell me about gangs. Why do kids join gangs (Indian kids in particular)? What do schools do about gangs? What can be done to keep kids out of them?

Interview Three

1. How have things in the past affected the way things are in school for you now? (What sense do you make of your past schooling?)
2. What are some things that will keep you in school? (If it is important that you graduate, why? Why are you and some of your peers making it and others aren't—e.g., motivators, resilience?)
3. As a parent, what will you say to your children about their education?
4. What would the ideal school for American Indians be like? (What will have to change in order for this to happen? Who is responsible to make this happen—future focus, altruism?)

5. Where do you see the place of "culture" in the future? (Should culture be a part of schooling?)
6. What kinds of changes are needed in your community to ensure a better future for tomorrow's children? (What roles do schools, governments, individuals, agencies play in making these changes happen? What is your personal role, if any, in this?)
7. What do you see for yourself in the future—5 years from now? 10? What are the greatest barriers to achieving your dreams (perceived impediments to goals)?
8. Tell me a time when you went after something you wanted but haven't yet been able to get it.
9. If you could give your reading and writing teachers some advice, what might it be? (What might help you be a better reader or writer?)
10. How would you like education to change for your children? For your grandchildren? What kind of person would you like your children (grandchildren) to see when they look at you (role modeling, mentoring, social status)?

References

Alexie, Sherman. *The Business of Fancy Dancing: Stories and Poems.* Brooklyn: Hanging Loose, 1992.

Axtell, Horace P., and Margo Aragon. *A Little Bit of Wisdom: Conversations with a Nez Perce Elder.* Lewiston, ID: Confluence, 1997.

Benton-Banai, Edward. *The Mishomis Book: The Voice of the Ojibway.* Hayward, WI: Indian Country Communications, 1988.

Blum, Robert W., and Peggy Mann Rinehart. *Reducing the Risk: Connections That Make a Difference in the Lives of Youth.* Bethesda, MD: Add Health, 1997. ERIC Document Reproduction Service No. ED412459.

Bogdan, Robert C., and Sari Knopp Biklen. *Qualitative Research for Education: An Introduction to Theory and Methods.* Boston: Allyn and Bacon, 1982.

Brendtro, Larry K., Martin Brokenleg, and Steven Van Bockern. *Reclaiming Youth At Risk: Our Hope for the Future.* Bloomington, IN: National Educational Service, 1990.

Bruchac, Joseph. *Roots of Survival: Native American Storytelling and the Sacred.* Golden, CO: Fulcrum, 1996.

Burns, Diane. "Sure You Can Ask Me a Personal Question." In *New Worlds of Literature,* edited by Jerome Beaty and J. Paul Hunter. New York: Norton, 1989.

Cajete, Gregory. *Look to the Mountain: An Ecology of Indigenous Education.* Durango, CO: Kivaki, 1994.

Campbell, Linda, Bruce Campbell, and Dee Dickinson. *Teaching & Learning through Multiple Intelligences.* Needham Heights, MA: Allyn and Bacon, Simon and Schuster Education Group, 1996.

Cleary, Linda Miller. *From the Other Side of the Desk: Students Speak Out about Writing.* Portsmouth, NH: Boynton/Cook, 1991.

———. "'I Think I Know What My Teachers Want Now': Gender and Writing Motivation." *The English Journal* 85 (January 1996): 50-57.

Cleary, Linda Miller, and Thomas Peacock. *Collected Wisdom: American Indian Education.* Needham Heights, MA: Allyn and Bacon, 1998.

———. "Disseminating American Indian Educational Research through Stories: A Case against Academic Discourse." *Journal of American Indian Education* 37 (fall 1997): 7-15.

Clifford, James. "On Ethnographic Allegory." In *Writing Culture: The Poetics and Politics of Ethnography: A School of American Research Advanced Seminar,* edited by James Clifford and George E. Marcus. Berkeley: University of California Press, 1986.

Copway, George. "The Traditional History and Characteristic Sketches of the Ojibway Nation." In *Touchwood: A Collection of Ojibway Prose,* edited by Gerald Vizenor. St. Paul: New Rivers, 1987.

Deloria, Vine. "Education and Imperialism." *Integrateducation* 19 (1981): 58-63.

Deyhle, Donna, and Karen Swisher. "Research in American Indian and Alaska Native Education: From Assimilation to Self-Determination." In *Review of Research in Education,* vol. 22, edited by Michael W. Apple. Washington, DC: American Educational Research Association, 1997.

Ely, Margot. *Doing Qualitative Research: Circles within Circles.* London: Falmer, 1991.

Farrell, Thomas J. "The Female and Male Modes of Rhetoric." *College English* 40 (April 1979): 909-21.

Finley, Mary. *Cultivating Resilience: An Overview for Rural Educators and Parents.* ERIC Digest. Charleston, WV: ERIC Clearinghouse on Rural Education and Small Schools, 1994. ERIC Document Reproduction Service No. ED372904.

Foreman, Larry D. "Curricular Choice in the Age of Self-Determination." *Journal of American Indian Education* 26 (January 1987): 1-6.

Gardner, Howard. "Are There Additional Intelligences? The Case for Naturalist, Spiritual, and Existential Intelligences." In *Education, Information, and Transformation: Essays on Learning and Thinking,* edited by Jeffrey Kane. Upper Saddle River, NJ: Merrill, 1999.

———. *Frames of Mind: The Theory of Multiple Intelligences.* New York: Basic, 1983.

———. *Intelligence Reframed: Multiple Intelligences for the 21st Century.* New York: Basic, 1999.

Gekinoo'imaagejig. "Vision & Mission." http://www.fdl.cc.mn.us/web/tc/VisionMission.htm (30 October 2002).

Glaser, Barney G., and Anselm L. Strauss. *The Discovery of Grounded Theory: Strategies for Qualitative Research.* Chicago: Aldine, 1967.

Grinde, Donald A., Jr., and Bruce E. Johansen. *Exemplar of Liberty: Native America and the Exolution of Democracy.* Native American Politics Series, no. 3. Los Angeles: American Indian Studies Center, UCLA: 1991. ERIC Document Reproduction Service No. ED373941.

Grover, Linda LeGarde. "The Class of 1968." In *Ojibwe Waasa Inaabidaa: We Look in All Directions,* edited by Thomas Peacock and Marlene Wisuri. Afton, MN: Afton Historical Society Press, 2001.

HeavyRunner, Iris, and Joann Sebastian Morris. "Traditional Native Culture and Resilience." *Research/Practice* 5, no. 1 (1997). http://www.coled.umn.edu/carei/Reports/Rpractice/Spring97/traditional.htm (13 June 2002).

Indian Nations At Risk Task Force. *Indian Nations At Risk: An Educational Strategy for Action: Final Report of the Indian Nations At Risk Task Force.* Washington, DC: U.S. Department of Education, 1991. ERIC Document Reproduction Service No. ED343753.

Johnston, Basil. *Ojibway Ceremonies.* Toronto: McClelland and Stewart, 1982.

Leap, William L. "American Indian English and Its Implications for Bilingual Education." In *Linguistics for Teachers,* edited by Linda Miller Cleary and Michael D. Linn. New York: McGraw-Hill, 1993.

Lehmann, Irvin, and William Mehrens. *Educational Research: Readings in Focus.* New York: Holt, Rinehart, and Winston, 1979.

Man, Humbatz. "Reconsecrating the Earth." In *Profiles in Wisdom: Native Elders Speak about the Earth,* edited by Steven McFadden. Santa Fe: Bear, 1991.

Minnesota Department of Children, Families and Learning. "American Indian Data." 1995.

Minnesota Humanities Commission and Minnesota Council of Teachers of English. *Braided Lives: An Anthology of Multicultural American Writing.* St. Paul: Minnesota Humanities Commission, Minnesota Council of Teachers of English, 1991.

Nelson, Annabelle. *The Learning Wheel: Ideas and Activities for Multicultural and Holistic Lesson Planning.* Tucson: Zephyr, 1994. ERIC Document Reproduction Service No. ED387302.

Pewewardy, Cornel. "The Holistic Medicine Wheel: An Indigenous Model of Teaching and Learning." *Winds of Change* 14 (autumn 1999): 28-31.

Pope, Carol A., and Jeffrey N. Golub. "Preparing Tomorrow's English Language Arts Teachers Today: Principles and Practices for Infusing Technology." *Contemporary Issues in Technology and Teacher Education* 1, no. 1 (2000).

Quality Education for Minorities. *Education That Works: An Action Plan for the Education of Minorities.* Washington, DC: Quality Education for Minorities Project, 1990. ERIC Document Reproduction Service No. ED316627.

Rogers, Mary Beth. *Cold Anger: A Story of Faith and Power Politics.* Denton, TX: University of North Texas Press, 1990.

Ross, Allan Charles. *Mitakuye Oyasin: "We Are All Related."* Fort Yates, ND: Bear, 1989.

Rubin, Donald L., and Kathryn Greene. "Gender-Typical Style in Written Language." *Research in the Teaching of English* 26 (February 1992): 7-40.

Sanborn, J. "The Academic Essay: A Feminist View on Student Voices." In *Gender Issues in the Teaching of English,* edited by Nancy Mellin McCracken and Bruce C. Appleby. Portsmouth, NH: Boynton/Cook, 1992.

Schutz, Alfred. *The Phenomenology of the Social World.* Translated by George Walsh and Frederick Lehnert. Evanston, IL: Northwestern University Press, 1967.

Seidman, Irving E. *Interviewing As Qualitative Research: A Guide for Researchers in Education and the Social Sciences.* 2d ed. New York: Teachers College Press, 1998.

Senate Special Subcommittee on Indian Education. *Indian Education: A National Tragedy—A National Challenge,* 91st Cong., 1st sess., S. Rept. 91-501, 1969. (Also known as the Kennedy Report.)

Swisher, Karen Gayton, and John W. Tippeconnic III, eds. *Next Steps: Research and Practice to Advance American Indian Education.* Charleston, WV: ERIC Clearinghouse on Rural Education and Small Schools, 1999.

Vygotsky, Lev S. *Mind in Society: The Development of Higher Psychological Processes.* Edited by Michael Cole and others. Cambridge, MA: Harvard University Press, 1978.

Willetto, Frank Chee. "An Invitation to Elders." Albuquerque: National Indian Council on Aging, 2000. http://www.nicoa.org/message.html (13 June 2002).

Wilson, Alex. "How We Find Ourselves: Identity Development and Two-Spirit People." *Harvard Educational Review* 66 (summer 1996): 303-17.

Yellow Horse Brave Heart, Maria. "Oyate Ptayela." In "Historic Trauma Response," by Rosemary WhiteShield. The Circle 21 (2001):8-9.

Zinn, Howard. *A People's History of the United States.* New York: Harper & Row, 1980.

Zukav, Gary. *The Seat of the Soul.* New York: Simon and Schuster, 1989.

Index

Abenaki, 23; stories of, 13–15, 20–22
Abenaki interviews: about connections, 36–37; about drugs, 54; about education, 102, 117, 125; about racism, 30, 46; about teachers, 168
Aboriginals: stories of, 20–22
absenteeism, 66–67
abuse, 48
"A Coat of Armor," 27–28
adoption, 51
alcoholism, 48, 68–69, 135; story about, 139–51
Aleut interviews: about coping, 53; about education, 89–90, 122; about friendship, 113; about teachers, 164–65, 169, 170
Alexie, Sherman, 30
alternative schools, 18–19, 121
American Indian education counselors, 116–17
American Indian English, 126
American Indian Teaching Corps, 174–75
anger, 67
Anishinaabe, 1, 27, 28, 34, 37–38, 47; Indigenous education model and, 174–76; stories of, 40–42. See also Ojibwe
Aragon, Margo, 181–82
assignments, 117–18
attendance policies, 66
attention, 101–2
attention spans, 102
Axtell, Horace, 181–82

"The Beads of the Eagle: A Teaching Story," 55–62
"Believing in Yourself: A Personal Story," 104
Benton-Benai, Edward, 182
Bergstrom, Amy, 3, 25–38, 39–47, 110–14, 126–28, 134
blood quantum, 29, 30, 37
boarding schools, 49, 156
Brendtro, Larry, 157
Brokenleg, Martin, 155, 157
Bruchac, Joseph, 36, 37
Burns, Diane, 25

Cajete, Gregory, 172
Canada, 36–37
career inventories, 105
case studies, 180–81
Choctaw interviews: about anger, 67; about communities and oppression, 49–50; about education, 101, 137; about emotions, 53; about peers, 115; about teachers, 114, 162

"The Class of 1968," 63–64
Cleary, Linda Miller, 1–4, 5–24, 39, 52–62, 87–106, 114–26, 176–82
Clifford, James, 180
collaborative learning, 167
Collected Wisdom, 3
colonialism, 156, 173
colonization, 29, 39, 48
community problems, 49–50
connections, 36–37; cultural, 34–35, 70–71; resilience and, 158–60; school, 159
contradictions, 48–49
coping, 52–55; story about, 55–62
Copway, George, 180–81
courage, 137–38
Creator, 131–32
cultural knowledge: of teachers, 161–62
culture: as identity, 130; loss of, 50
curriculum, 44–45, 171–76

Dakota interviews: about absenteeism, 66–67; about alcoholism, 68; about American Indian education counselors, 116–17; about cultural identity, 130; about cultural learning, 120; about education, 45; about elders, 133; about family dysfunction, 51; about musical intelligence, 94; about pride, 138; about racism, 44, 46; about skin color, 31; about teachers, 162–63, 171
dancing, 93, 137
decision making, 84; story about, 72–84
Deloria, Vine, 173
democracy, 48
Deyhle, Donna, 177
discipline practices, 45–46
discourse, 179–80
discrimination, 39
D/Lakota, 98
dreams, 33, 98
dropouts, 66–69; story about, 40–42
drugs, 13–15, 48, 54, 68–69
dysfunction, 49, 51–52

education: Indigenous model of, 171–76; problems in, 176–77. See also teachers
educators: lessons for, 155–83; questions for, 84–85
elder brothers, 133–34
elders, 132–33
expectations, 69, 70, 71, 109, 159, 163
extracurricular activities, 118–20

193

families, 95, 107–9; dysfunction in, 51–52; resilience and, 158–59
Farrell, Tom, 179
Fond du Lac Tribal and Community College (FDLTCC), 174–75
forced assimilation, 48
Foreman, Larry D., 173–74
French Canadians, 20–22
friendships, 95, 113–14
funding: educational, 174

gangs, 5–9, 18, 52, 67, 119
Gardner, Howard, 88–89
GED, 122
genocide, 48
gifts: use of individual's, 87–106
goals, 112–13
Good Path, 1, 34, 47, 129–54
Good Red Road, 130
"Gordee's Story," 40–42
grades, 112
Great Law of Peace, 48
Greene, Kathryn, 179
grounded theory, 178
Grover, Linda LeGarde, 49, 64, 85

HeavyRunner, Iris, 155, 156
historical trauma response (HTR), 156
holistic learning, 99, 166
homeschooling, 121–22
Hoopa interviews: about connections, 36; about cultural learning, 71; about education, 47; about elders, 37, 133; about extracurricular activities, 119–20; about goals, 112; about intrapersonal intelligence, 95–96; about moderation, 138; about motivation, 111; about naturalist intelligence, 97; about peacefulness, 137; about positive thinking, 128; about pride, 35; about promises, 136; about role models, 108; about spiritual intelligence, 98–99; about spirituality, 32–33, 132; about sports, 110–11; about women, 134–35; about writing, 124
HTR (historical trauma response), 156
hunting, 87–89, 99

identity, 25–38, 32, 35, 37–38, 130; definition of, 26–27; story about, 27–28
identity development, 26–27, 30; culture and, 35
Indian magnet schools, 17–18
Indian Nations At Risk Task Force, 176, 177
Innu, 21

intelligence, 88–89; bodily-kinesthetic, 92–93; interpersonal, 95; intrapersonal, 95–96; linguistic-verbal, 91–92; logical-mathematical, 91, 92; musical, 94–95; naturalist, 96–97; spiritual-existential, 97–99; visual-spatial, 93–94
interdisciplinary learning, 99
Interviewing As Qualitative Research, 177
interviews, 177–78. See also specific names, e.g., Abenaki interviews
Iroquois, 48

Karuk interviews: about education, 112; about family expectations, 109; about musical intelligence, 94–95, 127; about teachers, 163; about writing, 125
Kennedy Report on Indian Education, 176
kindness, 136
Kiowa: stories of, 16–19

Lakota: 156
Lakota interviews: about cultural identity, 35
Leap, William, 126
learning styles, 40, 100–101, 103
literacy, 177
Look to the Mountain, 172

Maine, 23
Man, Humbatz, 2
Marcus, Steve, 124
Mayans, 2
memory, 101
Midewiwin, 1
Minnesota, 176
moderation, 138
Mohawk interviews: about family dysfunction, 51; about family expectations, 109; about the Good Path, 129; about interpersonal intelligence, 95; about pride, 70–71; about teachers, 162, 163
Morris, Joann Sebastian, 155, 156
motivation, 110–28

National Longitudinal Study of Adolescent Health, 155, 158–59
Native languages, 174
Navajo interviews: about alternative schools, 121; about communities, 50–51; about courage, 138; about culture, 50; about education, 44; about expectations, 69; about extracurricular activities, 119; about friendships, 113; about goals, 112; about learning styles, 103; about naturalist intelligence, 97; about sexism, 69; about spirituality, 53, 132; about teachers, 162, 169; about visual intelligence, 93; about writing, 125

Index

Nesbit, John, 125
Newell, Wayne, 172–73
Next Steps, 172
Nunavut, 21

Ojibwe, 1, 72, 107, 131, 181; epistemology, 179, 180; stories of, 5–10, 16–19. See also Anishinaabe
Ojibwe interviews: about absenteeism, 67; about alternative schools, 121; about career inventories, 105; about coping, 52, 53, 54; about cultural identity, 35; about discrimination, 45–46; about education, 101–2, 117; about elder brothers, 134; about elders, 133; about family dysfunction, 51; about friendships, 113; about the Good Path, 153; about holistic learning, 99; about interpersonal intelligence, 95; about linguistic intelligence, 91–92; about motivation, 110, 111, 112, 126–27; about peers, 116; about public schools, 119; about racism, 29–30; about reading, 123–24; about resilience, 71; about respect, 139, 163–64, 169–70; about role models, 108; about skin color, 31; about spirituality, 34; about teachers, 115, 165, 166, 167, 169–70; about teen pregnancy, 68; about visual intelligence, 94
oppression, 29, 45, 47–48; internalized, 48, 55

peacefulness, 136–37
Peacock, Thomas D., 3, 39, 47–52, 64–85, 107–9, 129–54, 155–76, 171–76, 181, 182–83
peer harassment, 46–47
peer pressure, 68–69, 177
peers, 115–16
plant and animal beings, 133–34
poverty, 48, 156, 177
prejudice, 20
pride, 35–36
public schools, 5–9, 27–28, 40–42, 115, 119

Quebec, 20–22

racism, 26, 28, 29–31, 39, 45, 46, 48, 69, 173, 177; interviews about, 5–9, 19, 42, 115; in required reading, 44
reading, 123–24
Reclaiming Youth at Risk, 157
Red Road, 34, 130
research: Indigenous model of, 176–82
research methodology, 177–82
resilience, 63, 64–66, 70–71, 84, 96; connections that foster, 158–60; literature on, 155–58
respect, 108–9
rezbonics, 126
rhetoric, 179

role models, 108, 113–14, 130
Ross, Allan Charles, 98, 99
Rubin, Donald, 179

Sanborn, Jean, 179
"Sara's Song," 139–51
Schutz, Alfred, 177
"Season Spirits," 72–84
The Seat of the Soul, 55
Seidman, Irving, 177
self-determination, 172, 173, 174
self-esteem, 157, 159, 160
Seneca, 65
Seneca interviews: about communities, 50, 51; about coping, 53; about curriculum, 44; about elders, 133, 135; about goals, 109; about resilience, 65–66, 71; about spirituality, 33–34; about sports, 93, 111; about stereotypes, 45; about teachers, 163, 165, 166
sense of self, 29–31
sexism, 69
skin color, 30–31, 37
special education, 90
spirituality, 26, 27, 32–34, 36, 53, 156, 175
sports, 92, 93, 110–11
stereotypes, 25, 45, 46
stories, 180
"The Storyteller," 181
"Strengthening the Sacred Circle: 2000 and Beyond," 24
substance abuse, 54. See also alcoholism; drugs
suicide, 48
Sullivan, Patrick, 177
Swisher, Karen, 172, 177

tardiness, 66–67
teacher education, 161, 171, 174–76
teachers, 114–15; characteristics of, 160–70; native, 171. See also education
teaching practices, 44–45
teen pregnancy, 10–13, 51, 67–68
termination, 156
"13/16," 30
Tippeconnic, John, 172
tribal enrollment, 30

University of Minnesota, Duluth, 171n, 174
Ute: stories of, 10–13
Ute interviews: about alternative schools, 121; about holistic learning, 166–67; about peer pressure, 68–69; about teachers, 168; about teen pregnancy, 67–68

values, 129–30, 131, 153; education and, 172–75
Van Bockern, Steven, 157
Vygotsky, Lev, 167

Wakanheja curriculum, 156
Wampanoag interviews: about communities, 50; about coping, 53; about drugs, 68; about homeschooling, 121–22; about sports, 110; about teachers, 164; about visual intelligence, 94; about writing, 125
Web sites, 21
Willetto, Frank Chee, 24
Wilson, Alex, 27

women, 134–35
Woope Sakowin (Seven Sacred Laws), 156
writing, 124–25

Yellow Horse Brave Heart, Maria, 155, 156
Yurok interviews: about cultural connections, 34–35; about elders, 133; about kindness, 136; about motivation, 112; about peers, 115–16; about promises, 135–36; about success, 100–101; about teachers, 163

Zukav, Gary, 55